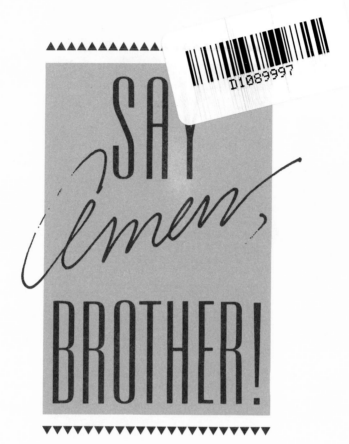

African American Life Series

*A complete listing of the books in this series
can be found at the back of this volume.*

General Editors

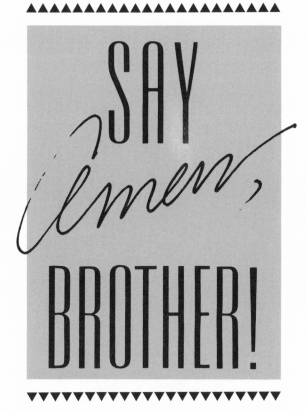

OLD-TIME NEGRO PREACHING:
A STUDY IN
AMERICAN FRUSTRATION

WILLIAM H. PIPES

Introduction by
Cornel West

 Wayne State University Press Detroit

Originally published in 1951 by The William-Frederick Press, New York.
Reprinted 1992 by Wayne State University Press, Detroit, Michigan 48202.
Copyright © 1951 by Anna R. Pipes. Copyright renewed 1979.
Copyright © 1992 by Wayne State University Press.
Manufactured in the United States of America.
99 98 97 96 95 94 93 92   5 4 3 2 1

Library of Congress Cataloging-in-Publication Data

Pipes, William H. (William Harrison), 1912-
Say Amen, brother! : old-time Negro preaching, a study in American
frustration / by William H. Pipes : introduction by Cornel West.
p. cm.—(African American life)
Reprint. Originally published: New York : William-Frederick Press, 1951.
Includes bibliographical references and index.
ISBN 0-8143-2383-9 (alk. paper).—ISBN 0-8143-2384-7 (pbk. : alk. paper)
1. Afro-Americans—Religion.   2. Preaching—United States—History.
3. Afro-American preaching.   I. Title.   II. Series.
BR563.N4P53   1992
251'.0089'96073—dc20   91-19572

Designer: Mary Krzewinski

Cover art: Mary Krzewinski

For and with
my wife
Ann

"Ye shall know the Truth,
and the Truth shall make you free"

Contents

Charts

Introduction

William H. Pipes' book is a neglected classic in an overlooked field of American cultural studies. It is ironic that in this moment of intense interest and inquiry in popular culture—past and present—scholars ignore one of the most rich and lively traditions in our midst: black preaching. With rare exceptions like the literary critic Hortense Spillers, the cultural critic Jon Michael Spencer, and the theologian Henry Mitchell, the complex artistic practice of black preaching has failed to attract the kind of subtle analysis it deserves. The availability of William H. Pipes' *Say Amen, Brother!* to a broad public will help correct this situation.

But why this ignorance of such a crucial dimension of black artistic and cultural life? And given the vast interest in black music, how do we account for the paucity of substantive scholarship about black preaching? In what specific ways will Pipes' text help rectify this situation? First, it is important to note that American preaching per se has not received the kind of academic examination it deserves. This is so primarily because such examination carries little weight in an academy that puts a premium on the written rather than the spoken text. There is an even greater ignorance of black sermonic practices, primarily owing to prevailing stereotypes of black religion as mere emotionalism and cathartic release. Yet on sheer aesthetic grounds preachers such as Black Harry and John Jasper in the past or Manuel Scott and Gardner Taylor in our day deserve the kind of attention given to a Ma Rainey and Bessie Smith or Nat King Cole and Dinah Washington. Furthermore, on social and political grounds, black preaching—in its diverse styles and functions—must be understood if we are to grasp how and why many black communities survived or thrived. So the relative ignorance of the complexity of black sermonic practices—on behalf of black and white scholars of American culture—is rooted in a refusal to take seriously the lived experience of black religious persons as church parishioners, as well as a reluctance to discover how many black people have sustained their sanity in this country.

The study and appreciation of black music is far more developed than that of black preaching for three basic reasons. First, black music is the most original art form created in the U.S. Hence its centrality cannot be overlooked in any serious understanding of American culture. Second, black music is more commodifiable than black preaching. It can be marketed more easily outside of a ritual context, transcending personal beliefs and convictions. This holds even for black religious music, spirituals, and gospels, for example, owing to the universality of rhythms, harmonies, and melodies. Third, black preaching is tied to a certain theological content, namely, its message of the Christian gospel. So it tends to ward off easy reception to those who may be uninterested or even offended by its religious substance.

Yet I do believe that black preaching will become more of an object of serious investigation in the future. The turn toward the study of rhetoric in American cultural studies cannot but mean that research will begin to focus on one of the major sources of public rhetoric in the past few decades, as exemplified by Adam Clayton Powell, Jr., Martin Luther King, Jr., and Jesse Louis Jackson. This is especially so in a period in which so few public officials can speak with passion, skill, and insight. The ascendancy of rap music in popular music forces critics to tease out the black sermonic sources of rhythmic rhetoric among young rap artists. This definite but distant link between hip-hop culture and black preaching is fertile soil for any scholar of American culture and art. Lastly, the uncovering of past scholarly works about black preaching will contribute immensely to a focus on its form, content, role, and function. William H. Pipes' text is one such work—indeed one of the pioneering works of this sort.

Pipes' scholarship is a breakthrough study in three basic ways. First, it situates and locates black preaching within social, political, and cultural contexts in the past and present. His particular focus is on "old-fashioned" black preaching in Macon County, Georgia—"that part of the 'black belt' which has clung most closely to the conditions of the old days" (p.4). This focus permits not only a detailed study of a select group (7 in this case) of actual *recorded* sermons but also a comparative study of black preaching over time and space. Pipes' intriguing subtitle, *Old-Time Negro Preaching: A Study in American Frustration*, is significant precisely because it views black sermonic practices as integral to black cultural, social, and political quests for empowerment and emancipation. Similar in theme to James Melvin Washington's brilliant, seminal, and pioneering study of black Baptists, entitled *Frustrated Fellowship: The Black Baptist Quest for Social Power* (1986), Pipes' study is concerned with how black preaching did or did not serve as a vehicle for black progress toward "first-class citizenship," (pp. 8, 89, 107, 132, 142, 155, 158-61). Like Leroi Jones' *Blues People*, which is a social history of black music in light of a human quest for freedom, Pipes' *Say Amen, Brother!* is a cultural history in light of an American quest for black democratic citizenship.

Second, Pipes' historical concerns and political convictions do not lead him to put forward reductionist readings of the sermons he examines. Instead, he gives us subtle interpretations of the forms and styles that go far beyond a crude reportage of their contents. His fascinating examination—aided by the works of Stanislavsky, Freud, and James Weldon Johnson—of the structural intonations, rhythmic syntax, metrical units, and bodily (drum-like) motions of black preaching combines a formal analysis within a particular ritual context and socioeconomic situation. I know of no other study of black sermonic practices written at the time Pipes published his text that operates simultaneously on these different levels of inquiry.

Third, Pipes' work is an exemplary critical history of black cultural practices in that he explicitly assesses a usable past for the present black struggle for democratic citizenship. This usable past enables and equips black people to more effectively and efficaciously acquire first-class citizenship. In fact, his immediate concern with black preaching—alongside his scholarly interest—has to do with the profound crisis of black leadership after the Second World War. Since a disproportionate number of black leaders were preachers, members of the most important institution in black civil society, Pipes' study of their homiletics includes a crucial critique of their impact on black progress. This critique is both candid and harsh. He concludes that the forces of secularization in America—the lures of scientific authority, social mobility, and cultural cosmopolitanism—will more than likely decrease the authority and legitimacy of old-time black preachers. Pipes acknowledges the rise of modern black preachers—those, for example, who were influenced by the towering tutelage of Benjamin Mays and Howard Thurman—and sketches the dilemma of highly educated and socially-conscious black clergy leading less educated and more other-worldly oriented parishioners. He does not discount the contributions the black clergy can make, yet he also refuses to overlook the trials and tribulations they must undergo. For Pipes, one of the obstacles of black progress—besides the racist practices of the larger society—is the fact that (in 1951) old-time black preachers comprise the majority of black leaders. He reminds the small black educated class of writers, educators, and ministers not to "delude themselves into thinking that they are the true Negro leaders" (p. 160). Since Pipes' basic concern is "improving the Negro masses" (p. 160) he calls for a more visionary, sophisticated, and connected black leadership.

The most astonishing moment in this erudite and exciting work is Pipes' rejection of black leaders who are either "economically dependent on the goodwill of prejudiced white persons (which eliminates many college presidents and teachers) or who are economically dependent upon the masses of Negroes (which seems to minimize the effectiveness of the leadership of the average Negro minister, who is dependent upon Negroes for his income)" (p. 160). This claim is astonishing not only for its insight but also for its courage: it is written by a former professor and president of a black college with a Ph.D. from the University of Michigan! Pipes is dispelling two major myths rampant in black America then and now: the myth of the autonomy of black colleges and the myth of the freedom of the black church preacher. The latter is more deeply rooted and widely held than the former. Pipes does not dismiss the importance of black colleges. He simply is candid about the degree to which black educators and administrators in black colleges are severely circumscribed by relatively limited and tainted white financial resources. These resources may not always have strings attached, but decisions made by black college presidents are always affected by considerations of when and from where more monies will come. Even the most visionary and progressive presidents, like Dr. Johnetta Cole of Spelman College in our day, must wrestle with this dilemma.

Similarly, Pipes calls into question the notion that black preachers are the freest leaders in black America. He suggests some may be, but most must cater to the parochial prejudices of their parishioners—as in our day, to sexist and homophobic prejudices—that render most preachers captive and thereby prohibit prophetic leaders to emerge. Pipes forces us to wonder whether Martin Luther King, Jr., could have remained pastor of a black church given his bold and defiant stands against American racism, capitalism, and imperialism, or whether his co-pastorate status and presidency of a group of mainly black prophetic preachers (the Southern Christian Leadership Conference) actually freed him to be a more prophetic leader. Pipes' book leads one to raise these kinds of rarely asked questions.

Yet Pipes' response to the query about where the new leadership principally will come from is vague, a cry of genuine and heartfelt desperation. He writes, "government workers (postal clerks, etc.), housewives, and retired persons seem to offer the best examples of the most effective type of Negro leaders: they are not always economically dependent on the masses of Negroes or upon prejudiced white people and they have some time to devote to the improvement of their people" (pp. 160-61). Pipes' turn toward the public sphere is salutary, yet he wrote before there was a strong black presence in trade unions of public workers and before there were powerful black public officials. His openness to the leadership of black women is prophetic—the development of such a leadership is still very much in process. And his mention of older black people may be prescient given the demographic balance tipped toward elderly citizens in the next decade or so.

In short, Pipes' challenging text raises some of the most basic questions confronting contemporary cultural critics and freedom fighters in this country—questions of form and content in popular culture, religion, and secularism in cultural struggle, the crisis of leadership in progressive politics, and the future of social hope for poor and working peoples in our century and beyond. Yet this is what neglected classic works do: open doors that even four decades later we have yet to walk through.

Cornel West
Professor of Religion
and Director, Afro-American
Studies Program,
Princeton University

Preface to First Edition

THE PREACHER tells of days long ago and of a people whose sufferings were like ours. He preaches of the Hebrew children and the fiery furnace, of Daniel, of Moses, of Solomon and of Christ. What we have not dared feel in the presence of the Lords of the Land, we now feel in church. Our hearts and bodies reciprocally acting upon each other, swing out into the meaning of the story the preacher is unfolding. Our eyes become absorbed in a vision. . . . The preacher's voice is sweet to us, caressing and lashing, conveying to us a heightening of consciousness that the Lords of the Land would rather keep from us, filling us with a sense of hope that is treasonable to the rule of Queen Cotton. As the sermon progresses, the preacher's voice increases in emotional intensity, and we, in tune and sympathy with his sweeping story, sway in our seats until we have lost all notion of time and have begun to float on a tide of passion. The preacher begins to punctuate his words with sharp rhythms, and we are lifted far beyond the boundaries of our daily lives, and upward and outward, until drunk with our enchanted vision, our senses lifted to the burning skies, we do not know who we are, what we are, or where we are. . . .

We go home pleasantly tired and sleep easily, for we know that we hold somewhere within our hearts a possibility of inexhaustible happiness; we know that if we could but get our feet planted firmly upon this earth, we could laugh and live and build. We take this feeling with us each day and it drains the gall out of our years, sucks the sting from the rush of time, purges the pain from our memory of the past, and banishes the fear of loneliness and death. When the soil grows poorer, we cling to this feeling; when clanking tractors uproot and hurl us from the land, we cling to it; when our eyes behold a black body swinging from a tree in the wind, we cling to it.

Some say that, because we possess this faculty of keeping alive this spark of happiness under adversity, we are children. No, it is courage and faith in simple living that enables us to maintain this reservoir of human feeling, for we know that there will come a day when we shall pour out our hearts over this land.[a]

RICHARD WRIGHT

---

[a] 12 *Million Black Voices* (Viking Press, New York, N. Y., 1941), pp. 68, 73.

I. He's Got the Whole World in His Hands

OLD-TIME NEGRO PREACHING—"You May Have All Dis World, But Give Me Jesus." That is the title of the Spiritual which strikes at the heart of the church for a great many of American Negroes, and among Negroes[1] "the church has been the largest and probably the most influential organization. . . ."[2] Old-fashioned preaching[3] is still the vital factor in the church.[4]

It is not a difficult matter to explain this popularity of the church among Negroes when one realizes that "the Negro church is the one institution where the colored people of the community are in full control. It is their own."[5] Also, in addition to the profoundly important religious urge, Negroes cling to the church because it serves a social purpose by being a center where friends meet. Whether a Christian or a sinner, the Negro attends church because it is often a substitute for the clubhouse, the amusement park, and the theatre. Negroes, "whether they derive any particular joy therefrom or not . . . must go to church, to see their friends, as they are barred from social centers open to whites. They must attend church, moreover, to find out what is going on."[6] Many young Negroes, Christian or not, go to church partly to meet their sweethearts, to impress them, and to woo them in marriage. Many farmers go to church partly to learn of developments in the outside world.

The church *is* of vital importance to the Negro in the United States, and its role in the life of the black man has excited not only the interest of sociologists, but also the general public. Radio programs, such as "Wings Over Jordan," feature aspects of Negro religious services. A prominent daily newspaper, even while a world was at war, carried a feature story on services held in a small, old-fashioned Negro church:[7]

> "It was a hot Sunday morning, crinkling with the comfortable sounds of hammering, cars being parked, shouted greetings and laughter. Inside the Creek Colored Church, near Shelbyville, children were singing. There was no melody to their song; only a thumping rhythm as steady as the beat of a tomtom.

[1]

Get right with God
And do it now.
Get right with God,
He'll show you how.

"The Rev. . . . stood on the steps of the church watching people coming into the churchyard. 'Mighty fine crowd we've got this year,' he said, waving one hand toward the line of parked cars. . . .

"The Rev. Mr. . . . fluttered the leaves of his hymnal for attention. 'The organist,' he announced, 'will now play 'Blest Be the Tie That Binds.' Let us all sing to praise the Lord.'

"After lunch there would be two afternoon sermons, by different preachers. The women fixing lunch hummed, as they bustled around. 'He's Got the Whole World in His Hands.'

"One woman unwrapped [*her food*] and dropped the newspaper on the ground. 'Bombs Fall on London,' said the juice-stained headline. It looked strangely unimportant."[8]

Such a religion does arouse interest—sufficient interest in the institution to warrant this study of its most vital constituent, its preaching.

The reader might well wonder if preaching like that mentioned above and the sermons which have been recorded in this book[9] are indeed preaching. Phillips Brooks defined preaching as the "communication of truth by man to men."[10] The Oxford dictionary comes closer to a tangible definition, referring to preaching as the delivery of a sermon or public religious discourse. This work assumes no obligation to prove that Negro preaching is genuine preaching; however, the treatment of the Macon County sermons will show that the Negro minister, unknowingly, observes many of the traditions of sacred rhetoric. His preaching, to be sure, is unique; he must interest his hearers, but he must not mention their most vital problem: white supremacy in the South. Therefore, the Negro minister appeals mainly to the emotions of his audience and leads his hearers to think primarily of things of the world which is to come after death,[11] "for God's Got the World in His Hands."

This study is concerned with the *preaching* of the Negro church, furthermore, because this phase of the creations of the American Negro has not been studied extensively. As Dr. Johnson points out, "A good deal has been written on the folk creations of the American Negro: his music, sacred and secular; his plantation tales, and his dances; but that there are folk sermons, as well, is a fact that has passed unnoticed."[12] Since Johnson made this statement, some interest has been shown in old-fashioned preaching. The moving picture industry, the newspapers and the radio have given attention to the subject. However, in almost every instance, the Negro's religion is used for entertainment; it is not considered seriously. But, students of sociology[13] are finding Negro preaching virgin soil for serious thought. Dr. Charles S. Johnson has recorded nine Negro sermons for the Files of the Department of Social Sciences at Fisk University, and Alice Jones has written a master's thesis on the subject: "The Negro Folk Sermon: A Study in the Sociology of Folk Culture" (Fisk University, 1942). For two years the Julius Rosenwald Fund sponsored a study by John Henry Faulk,[14] who recorded Negro sermons in Louisiana. The Negro preacher has received some attention in the field of English.[15] Dr. Harry V. Richardson recently completed a study on the Rural Negro Church (*Dark Glory*, Friendship Press, New York, N. Y., 1947). But as public address, the field into which Negro preaching most certainly falls, old-time Negro preaching has not been studied extensively.

The fact that Negro preaching has not been studied thoroughly in this field might not justify this investigation if it were not also true that, within the Negro's most important institution (the church), the preacher (and his preaching, of course) is most important. "The Negro ministry is still the largest factor in the life of this [*the Negro*] race."[16] Dr. W. E. B. DuBois, the eminent sociologist, evaluates the Negro minister in these terms: "The preacher is the most unique personality developed by the Negro on American soil. A leader, a politician, an orator, a 'boss', an intriguer, an idealist — all these he is, and ever, too, the center of a group of men, now twenty, now a thousand in number."[17]

It should be stressed here that the old-fashioned (old-time)[18] Negro is the unique personality referred to, for the more educated, unemotional Negro ministers preach much the same as ministers of other races. But the "old-time Negro preacher has not yet been given the niche in which he properly belongs. He has been portrayed only as a semi-comic figure. He had, it is true, his comic aspects, but on the whole he was an important figure, and at bottom a vital factor. . . . It was also he who instilled into the Negro the narcotic doctrine epitomized in the Spiritual, 'You May Have All Dis World, But Give Me Jesus.' This power of the old-time preacher, somewhat lessened and changed in his successors, is still a vital force; in fact, *it is still the greatest single influence among the colored people of the United States.* The Negro today is, perhaps, the most priest-governed group in the country."[19]

STATEMENT OF PURPOSE—The purpose of this work is to make an interpretative study of old-time Negro preaching as it is reflected

[3]

today in Macon County of Georgia—using the recordings of seven sermons.

THE RELATION OF THE RECORDINGS TO THE BOOK—Old-time Negro preaching is important without a doubt, but Dr. James Weldon Johnson declares, "the old-time Negro preacher is rapidly passing."[20] And this fact leads to the distinctive nature of this project: the recording of the sermons.[21]Although the type of preaching under consideration does pass out of existence (as it definitely seems to be doing), students of American homiletics, students of Negro dialect, of public speaking, and of other fields of scholarship, and the general public may use these recordings as basis for further study and understanding.

Without taking cognizance of the recording machine, Dr. Johnson declares of Negro sermons: "There is, of course, no way of recreating the atmosphere — the fervor of the congregation, the amens and hallelujahs, the undertone of singing which was often a soft accompaniment to parts of the sermon. . . ."[22] The recordings, even though they are unable to reproduce *all* of these aspects, go a long way toward a true presentation of these characteristics.

CHOICE OF MACON COUNTY IN GEORGIA—Throughout, the study has been confined to Macon County, in Georgia, because conclusive proof has been given by Arthur Raper, an able sociologist, that among Negroes the closest parallel to pre-Civil War days (during which time old-fashioned Negro preaching flourished on the big slave plantations) is to be found in the "Black Belt."[23] Since the Reconstruction Period, and up to the present time, the Negro Christian has become more and more like the white man; the former belief in the sinfulness of dancing and card playing, for example, is being discarded.[24] Only in the "Black Belt" do we still have situations that are very close to the Negro's slavery days: the slave plantations with master and slaves have become plantations with landlord and croppers; here alone have the Negro's earliest (old-time) religious practices been kept almost intact.[25]

Within the "Black Belt," "the conditions in Green and Macon counties, besides offering an interesting contrast, are illustrative of the 'Black Belt' as a whole."[26] The phrase "besides offering an interesting contrast" has reference to the fact that Green County is typical of that part of the "Black Belt" which has made the greatest progress and has, therefore, become most un-like the old slavery days; on the other hand, Macon County is typical of that part of the "Black Belt" which has clung most closely to the conditions of the old days.[27] It is reasonable to expect, therefore, that also in Negro preaching Macon County offers

[4]

better samples (least change from conditions of the old days) of old-fashioned Negro preaching than does Green County.

THE ORIGIN AND DEVELOPMENT OF THE STUDY—This study of Negro preaching was accepted as a worthwhile project in view of these facts: (1) the Negro represents almost a tenth of the United States' population; (2) the church is the Negro's most important institution; and (3) old-fashioned preaching (although waning) still is the most vital factor in the church.[28]

The initial survey uncovered much interesting information on the Negro and many allusions to Negro preaching; but, more significant to the investigator, it revealed that no detailed study with recordings had been made of genuine old-fashioned preaching among Negroes. From the beginning, it was felt that only by means of the recording machine could these sermons be put down accurately. Shorthand could not be depended upon. Yet, the sermons had to be taken down as delivered because this type of minister does not (often cannot) write his sermon. It was agreed, then, that the recording machine had to be used.

The following plan was followed:

1. Study literature pertaining to the folkways, religion, beliefs, etc., of the audiences in the Negro churches in Macon County.[29]
2. Attend church services to
   a. record a representative number[30] of sermons;
   b. observe the practices of each preacher as to gestures, etc.
3. Confer with each preacher and some of his members to learn the minister's training, preparation for a particular sermon, etc.
4. Make the interpretation of Negro preaching on the basis of accumulated data.

The original plan of procedure was followed closely, despite many difficulties.

A unit of the University System of Georgia, the Fort Valley State College, purchased a Victor recording machine; and the college president kindly made the equipment available for recording Negro sermons over a period of three months.

Fortunately, Macon County is only a few miles from Fort Valley State College, where the author, during the summer of the recordings, was teaching a class in the Summer School's English Workshop. The students in this group were teachers from the high schools and grade schools of Georgia, and many of them came from Macon County.

[5]

They knew where the churches were located, whether or not the churches had electricity, when preaching was "held,"[31] the denominations of the various churches, the ministers' names, etc. This was very important, but even more important was the fact that these summer school teachers were known in the various communities in Macon County. Having them as members of the visiting party made it less likely to destroy the normalcy of the preaching situation.[32] Rural teachers in Georgia often attend church services regularly; therefore, these teachers from Macon County were a part of the church audiences and were not considered strangers or outsiders.

This English Workshop Group (and the author's wife) became the planning board for the recordings; Negro Preaching in Macon County became their project.[33] First, it was agreed that since, of the 130 or more Negro churches in Macon County, 78 were Missionary Baptist, 20 were Primitive Baptist, and 15 or 20 were Methodist,[34] the six sermons to be recorded might be: 3, Missionary Baptist; 2, Primitive Baptist[35] and 1, Methodist.[36]

The "Preaching Group" (as it was soon labeled by students in summer school) was well-organized before starting out for a particular church. The group for a Sunday's work usually consisted of four helpers; a larger number would have been too conspicuous. One student was to interview the minister after the sermon.[37] (The minister and the members of the church were never advised beforehand of the recording of the sermon, for obvious reasons.) Another student took pictures[38] of the church (interior and exterior) and of the minister and the congregation. A third student, with the author's wife, was responsible for written descriptions of the minister's gestures and pertinent occurrences during the services, as well as the order of services and the words which were lost in the recording in the changing of discs. A fourth student assisted with the recording apparatus. (These assignments were carried out as inconspicuously as possible.)

The group left Fort Valley early on Sunday mornings and journeyed to the chosen church in time for Sunday School. Usually the investigator had to teach Sunday School (not a new experience for him) and the other members of the "Preaching Group" mixed with the church people and made friends. After these preliminaries, it was generally an easy matter to obtain permission to make the recording.[39] Then the apparatus was set up out-of-doors and out-of-sight; only the microphone was visible to the audience during the recording. When there was a minister's study near the pulpit, it was used to house the apparatus; when it rained, the apparatus was set up inside the group automobile, which was driven close to the rear of the church.

After the sermon was recorded, invariably the recorder was asked to play back the services and the sermon. The minister and the audience (now no longer religiously emotional) laughed and enjoyed hearing themselves. Frequently someone remarked, "Dat's jest whut he sed!" Others considered it "wonderful" that a member of their race could make records.

It is not likely that the recording tended to destroy the normalcy of the preaching situation to any great degree. Once or twice there was some artificiality at first, but the ministers and the audiences always accepted us or forgot about our presence when the "spirit" touched them.[40] The recordings catch the spontaneity of the preaching and the reaction of the audience.

PLAN OF INTERPRETATION—The original, full-fledged, unique type of Negro preaching in America ("old-time" and "old-fashioned") existed during slavery, approximately from 1732 (the period of the great influence of Whitefield's preaching upon Negro slaves) until 1832 (the period of the reaction against Negro preaching following Nat Turner's slave insurrection).[41] From this hundred-year-era until the present time, the unique type of Negro preaching has been undergoing a change; however, some of the original characteristics and manifestations are to be found, in varying degrees, in Negro preaching today. The sermons recorded in Macon County can be compared and contrasted in important characteristics with the preaching of the original period according to the following plan:

1. Throughout this work the author has sought to approach the subject of old-time Negro preaching with the highest degree of respect, never with a desire to ridicule. A Christian from his youth, a product of a Negro home that believed in the old-time religion, one who was inclined to enter the ministry, and a member of the faculty of a church college, the investigator could approach this subject only with reverence, humility, and sincerity.

2. The Macon County Sermons are presented as they were recorded. (For obvious reasons, the true names of ministers, churches, and towns are not used.)

3. A discussion of the two basic causes of all old-time Negro preaching follows: evolving out of this discussion are the peculiarities or manifestations of old-time Negro preaching.

4. Using the characteristics or manifestations of old-time Negro preaching as a scale or standard, the author will interpret (by comparison and contrast) the Macon County Sermons as old-time Negro preaching.

5. The basic aim of the author is to show that in allowing

second-class citizenship to warp the Negro's old-time religion, the United States is abandoning *her* old-time religion: freedom for *all* the people—"All men are created equal and from that equal creation they derive rights inherent and unalienable, among which are the preservation of life and liberty and the pursuit of happiness."[42] "Give Me That Old-Time Religion"—both the Negro's *and* America's.

The results of this procedure are offered as an interpretation of old-time Negro preaching that should give every American citizen a new determination to help extend democracy to *all* the people—for "He's [*God's*] Got the Whole World in His Hands."

II.   Voice Crying in the Wilderness

SERMON I: "THOU SHALT LOVE THE LORD THY GOD. . . ."[a]

ACTIVITIES BEFORE THE SERMON:

1. *Song*: "My Faith Looks Up to Thee." Led, without musical accompaniment, by Rev. ————[b]. The congregation stood to sing the last verse.

2. *Prayer*: By Brother ———— ————. (The congregation hummed the last verse of the above song during the first part of the prayer, which was delivered in the rhythmical fashion.)

THE PRAYER

DEAR LAWD, we come befo' Thee and ask Thee ter stand by us. Thank Thee for ev'rything Thou's did for us. Christ, assemble between these four walls; git in the hearts uv men and women, boys and girls. Thou art God an' God alone.

Since the last time we's bowed, we's done things what we ought not uv done, an' we's left things undone what we ought uv done. Rule over Heaven and earth; rule over these people down here, the sick an' afflicted and weary. And bind us one to another.

Go with that one who gwine to preach de greater life today. Ask you to 'member the church. Brang us to pray. Lawd, have mercy on us.

Now, Lawd, when it come our time to die, pray You receive us into Thy kingdom an' give our souls a resting place. *Amen.*

3. *Song*: "I Love Jesus."[c] Led by Rev. ————; after which he moves into the pulpit and takes his seat there.

4. *Song*: "Come, Thou Fount of Every Blessing." Mrs. ———— plays the piano; choir and congregation sing.

---

[a] "In those days came John Baptist, preaching in the wilderness. . . . And saying. Repent Ye: for the Kingdom of Heaven is at hand. For this is he that was spoken ot by the prophet Esaias saying, *The Voice of One Crying in the Wilderness,* prepare ye the way of the Lord, make His paths straight. And the same John had his raiment of camel's hair, and a leathern girdle about his loins; and his meat was locusts and wild honey. Then went out to him Jerusalem, and all Judaea, and all the region round about Jordan, and were baptized of Him in Jordan, confessing their sins." MATTHEW 3:1-17.

[b] Interviewed, Rev. ———— related that he had been married for 29 years, had been a school teacher for 33 years, a preacher for 22 years, had attended high school at Paine College, Augusta, Georgia, and (to the author's surprise) had attended summer school at the Fort Valley State College to audit the writer's course in English Composition.

[c] Note how the songs and prayers all point toward the sermon to come.

5. *Hymn*: "Father, I Stretch My Hands to Thee." Led by Rev. ————. (Services are now "Turned over to the pulpit.")
6. *Responsive Reading*.
7. *Song: Continuing*, "Father, I Stretch My Hands to Thee."
8. *Prayer*: By the minister (now in the pulpit).

THE PRAYER

WE THANK Thee this morning for the opportunity extended towards us. Thank Thee that Thou hast saw fit to have us continue here in Thy vineyard to work out our soul salvation. Thank Thee that Thou hast left a written record, guide, and assurance that we have at Thy right-hand-side a friend, a friend-in-deed; at Thy right-hand-side a scarred Savior; at Thy right-hand-side a Mediator and Redeemer—but standing to receive our souls.

Thou have widen the way for us. We're knowed by our acts as did the disciples. They knowed Him by breaking of bread, giving livin' circumstance; to those we does meet, may we realize by our acts, by being born again; become living witness of Him.

Paul said to the Corinthi'ns, brothern, that—that He came at Peenakost, and, last of all, "I saw Him myself." May we *see 'im* in our daily lives; may we *see 'im* in our conversions and may we *see 'im* as we go about our daily occupation.

Now we pray Thee, bless the Man of the Hour, the Man of God, the one that Thou has at present in this foreign part of the vineyard. When we are called from here to another world, Jesus did promise to sinner on cross, may we kneel at Thy feet and cry, "Redeemer!" Amen.

9. *Song*: "Where He Leads Me I Will Follow." (Sister ———— "passes out" fans.)
10. *Scripture Reading*: Rev. ————

"There were seven brethern, and the first took a wife and dying, left no seed. And the second took her and died; neither left he any seed. And the third likewise, and the seventh had her and left no seed. Then all the women died also. And it is written, therefore, when they arise, whose wife shall she be of whom? And Jesus ansering sayth unto 'em, 'Do ye not ere. Besides, ye know not the scripture neither the call of God, for when they shall rise from the dead they marry not nor give in marriage, but are as the angels are in heaven."[d]

---

[d] The 1611 King James Version reads: MATTHEW 22: 25-30: "Now there were with us seven brethren: and the first, when he had married a wife, deceased, and, having no issue, left his wife unto his brother: Likewise the second also, and the third, unto the seventh. And last of all the woman died also, therefore in the resurrection whose wife shall she be of the seven? for they all had her. Jesus answered and said unto them, Ye do err, not knowing the scriptures, nor the power of God. For in the resurrection they neither marry, nor are given in marriage, but are the angels of God in heaven."

11. *Announcements*: Rev. ————

Members need to be complimented for supporting the Revival which closes today. There was much bad weather. Men and women came every night. Many others would have come if not for bad weather. Our duty to assist few that did attend, in financial support of revival. . . . Without further remarks, go into discussion.

THE SERMON

"THOU SHALT love the Lord thy God [*Reading from the Bible.*] with thy whole heart, [*Pauses for a count of nine.*] with your whole soul, with your whole mind, and your whole strength"* [*Pauses for a count of fourteen.*].

"Your whole heart, your whole soul, and your whole mind, and your whole strength." Forceful words of the Saviour. Th' word "whole" in itself carries a very strong meaning. The word "whole." When we think about this: That we must love the Lord with our *whole heart*— the word directed here as *all* of our heart—Th' word "all" means "whole"; th' *whole* of our heart. So Paul reads, "whole", with *all* our hearts.

Er—when we think about that, we think about how strong was the Master's behest here, command here, as he answered that very important question: "Which is the greatest commandment?" The persons who asked this question didn't want information; they wanted to criticize.

He give them their way and He answered: "Love thy neighbor as thyself."

𝄋 𝄋 𝄋

"Moses gave the Ten Commandments; God gave them to him on the Mount. You say you come not to destroy but fulfill. You say how the Ten Commandments given to Moses as guide to Children of Israel and, therefore, I want to know from you which is greater of these, Master?"

He answered. (We've heard you, oh Israel!) "The Lord our God is th' only one God, only one God, only one Law-giver." He's th' same God now. Same law—passed down generation after generation —was given Moses in his day, same for this changing age.

This is the most changeable stage of man's history. Never known time when things change so fast. What is today, not tomorrow. Same with tomorrow. We try to live up and be regular. When we get there

---

* This text seems to be based on two Bible passages: (1) "Thou shalt love the Lord thy God with all thy heart, and with all thy soul, and with all thy strength, and with all thy mind. . . ." LUKE 10:27; (2) "Thou shalt love the Lord thy God with all thy heart, and with all thy soul, and with all thy mind." MATTHEW 22:37.

—think we are all right—when we get there, find we're not all right. Keep us constantly changing. Ladies know more about that than men. Ladies try to git up to last of fashion. Especially when they have scarce means and have to work hard to git money to buy the latest style. And when we get money enough to pay, the style's changed.

Our text says, though times and conditions change, the Law is the same: "Thou Shall Love the Lord Thy God with Thy Whole Strength." Say further, "Thy Neighbor as Thyself."

Th' word "whole," strong sign. Don't leave anything out. Gets every bit of us. Go directly into th' answer our Christ gave. First, "the *whole* heart." Now, what is the heart? Let us think now what th' heart means to our life, to our body, to this whole system. What does th' heart mean? Th' heart is the seat of life; th' heart is the meat of life. It is the generator that generates and makes possible the flow of blood that feeds each member of the body. It is — depend on — life existence —every part of body. Each part functions as it receives blood. Should the heart fail, some member of th' body fail to render its service. Ask doctor for diagnosis. Something fail to function. Feet fail to function; hands fail to function; head fail to function; arms fail to function. Don't do the full share of work; th' body fail. Want to know the reason? Physical diagnosis shows sometimes some member don't git enough blood. Blood too rich. Blood not rich enough. Some remedies are given by the doctor to remedy the blood stream. I said the *whole* heart, not the physical heart, but the spiritual, *whole* heart.

"Love" is a splendid word. The dictionary gives us some meaning, and all that. I hate to think how we can gather out of language a sufficient definition of "love." *Love* is unlimited. It's unlimited. If we settle on a fixed definition, we rob the word of its greatness. The writer John strived to make a effort to describe love. He said this: "God so loved th' world that He gave His only begotten son." Didn't the disciples love? Love depends on our ability to go forth. Therefore, he said, we should love with *all* our hearts. We should put *all* we are in our effort to *love* God—*all* our intellect, *all* our intelligence, *all* our mind, *all* our understanding, *all* our knowledge.

Subject to growth, subject to growth, subject to growth. Greater idea of things, stronger conception. We should *grow* in intelligence, *grow* in intellect, *grow* in mind, *grow* in understanding, and *grow* in the love of God. Seems very common that we often see people *grow* in knowledge and wisdom and understanding and *grow away* from God. Knowledge and wisdom and understanding should help you to *grow near* God. The more knowledge, more ideas, more understanding should make you love God more. It gives you a better understanding of our Master when we can bend to the will, comply to the behest of our Master. *All* we know, *all* we grasp, *all* we get control of should render us *nearer* to the Master.

Service of power, service of knowledge, service of ability, use to uplift Him and spread th' kingdom of Christ and His accomplishment. As the Sunday School lesson bears witness, it's ours to spread, to make greater, more important and more impressive th' knowledge of our Christ. Better prepared to give forceful information, better information, and a better understanding. We should put our strength and power in the service of God, our *whole* strength, our *whole* mind, our *whole* heart.

Since these are the facts, we come to the conclusion: As we go forward in life we should go forward toiling for the Master, using all our knowledge, all our wisdom, all our intelligence, all our mind, all our understanding in making His Kingdom on this shore bright and shining, in the vineyard laboring wherever His cause gives opportunity, among sufficient new influence to help those under sway to love the Lord, a living influence to lead th' wanderer *to* th' fold of Christ and not *from* it. There are those of influence, those who claim to know Christ and claim to live His reputation, they conducting their life and acting so that they lead others *away* from Christ.

In this enlightened day, times has changed ways. There is a little song that says something like this: "Times change. . . . Do whatever you please; there is no harm." But you can't find a way around th' Savior's strong answer and still be followers of Christ. Th' Savior say that the time and condition doesn't change the law: "Thou shalt love the Lord thy God with all thy heart, with all thy soul, and with all thy mind."

But is *love* enough? Can love alone do the work? No! Love alone is not enough. In th' 13th chapter of First Corinthians there is no praise given to love alone. The apostle enumerates: love *does not* do certain things and there are certain things, it gives you to understand, certain things love *does do*—according to the second dip of his pen. Read that chapter in First Corinthians.

Yes, love is not enough. Even in our marriage love is not enough. Love can't do it all. It must have skill to live, to grow. If the measure of love experienced in matrimony isn't sufficient to give skill and knowledge to live together after marriage, it isn't sufficient love. Sufficient love not only teaches confidence or relation sufficient to get th' yoke together or to face matrimony, but it gives you skill and knowledge to live together after marriage.

God speaks of love. Love that is sufficient to get you in church, have you sign your name and take your obligations, isn't sufficient love if it doesn't hold you there. If it isn't sufficient to lead you through the ordeals of everyday life, it isn't sufficient. The Savior said: "Thou shalt love the Lord thy God with all thy soul, and with all thy mind, with all thy heart, with all thy strength."

We resort to Him whenever difficulties come into our lives.

✓ ✓ ✓

Parent love isn't enough. See a mother with her child in her arm, with a child in her arm. Will give her life for him. Why, mother, if thy love for th' baby isn't sufficient to have you give th' right guidance, th' right trend and thought to put before that child, it isn't sufficient. Sometime love as we've gotten, help us to spoil rather than care for your children. Jesus Christ say to us here that th' degree of love make all things possible. Love must see through eyes of children and guide them to Christ through th' simple pathway. Adult should be able to guide through th' general carriage of life. A parent's whole heart must be fixed on Christ, so that she can dictate the right policies for correct guidance of th' child. Love alone is not sufficient to make a good child; must have skill for growth.

Love alone, love alone, love alone isn't sufficient. Love for our God and for His soul—it isn't sufficient. If it isn't strong enough, it isn't forceful enough, it hasn't a strong enough hold on us to guide us in the way that our Savior would have us go, why, it isn't sufficient; it isn't sufficient.

It's true of us, my brothers and sisters, that we are failing to serve God with our whole heart, our whole soul, and our whole strength. Or, in other words, we—we are not fully fixed on God. For if we are fully fixed on Him and He fully fixed in us — as He said, "If you love Me and keep My Commandments, Me and My Father and Son will dwell with you and you with Us." And He dwelling in us—the very fact that He dwells in us give us sufficient strength, and knowledge, and information for all of the things and all of the necessary things of life.

And, therefore, my brethren and sisters, comes to us this morning this thought: That we must love God if we want—supremely—if we desire to be successful in this life. In our home life, in, in, in our community life, in our vocational life, if you want to be saved, must love God with all your heart, with all our soul and all our mind and all our strength and carry Him in our home life and admit Him into our home life, into our community life, and into our vocational life. That means, wherever we are, and whatever we are following or doing in life,

[14]

in all our relations in life, to carry our Christ with us. And we will have Him with us if we love Him with all our heart, and all our souls, and all our minds.

And what does it mean to us? In conclusion, what will it mean for us? It will, it will give us strength sufficient; it will give us strength sufficient to labor through the day. It is sufficient to lead on to the way. It will give us strength sufficient to save both ourselves and those over whom we have influence. Let us remember, my brethren and sisters and friends, that we are His embassengers. We are His helpers. And, Christians, we—He have set us aside, that we might hold on. Hold on by keeping alive the thought and the good will and opinion of the Lord and Savior Jesus Christ. Above all, to keep alive in the mind of the present world the idea that God is, that God is—to ignore this is impossible—and that all things are possible to Him as ever.

In all our changes we must love Christ with all our minds, all our hearts, and strength, and He'll guide us in these changes of life. If th' world believe on Christ, the changes won't be, won't be—if we hav' Christ in us—so radical; won't be, won't be so different. We'll be the same in Christ. All these other things will be forgotten. If Christ is within, change won't be so different; Christ th' same in th' heart.

✓   ✓   ✓

Of course, we can have intelligent homes. Of course, we can. God don't disapprove of our culture. He don't disapprove of us living up to the measure of the time. Certainly not! He placed things here for us and, He, He delights in seeing this. But, my brothers and sisters and friends, when we drift away from Him, when after He has given us all these opportunities—when He has given us opportunity for school, and churches and homes and made it possible for us to gather the riches of the land we had our way—we should not forget that with all this we should love Him with all our heart, all our souls, with all our strength, and our neighbor as ourselves. To do this you'll be handing down to the world that God is an unchanging Lord. It's easy for the world to change. And as He loves and as He guided and as He protected, and as He cared for the men and women of the past ages, He'll care for us. The same God today as He was then and He changes not.

May the Lord help us to—er—get this thought in our minds: That in all the changes of life, in all the changes of life, my brothers and sisters and friends, in all the changes of life — get that — He hasn't changed yet, hasn't changed yet.

The times haven't finished yet; they're still changing. Scenery

[15]

today will be different tomorrow. The sceneries in our life will be different in the life of these boys and girls here. Conditions will be different when they are men. Will be much different than what they are now. And when you and I as parents of today try to so set in the heart and mind, to so set in the hearts and minds of those children that God, that God is the same and ever is, and they see us going forward as living example, we must strive to serve with all our heart, and with all our souls, and with all our strength, and with all our mind, all that we are.

Make things just a little bit plainer: as we grow more intelligent, we serve God better; as we gather more of the world's goods, we serve God better. Get the idea! As we become more influential and men honor us and look up to us and rely upon us—all that we are—we love God more. We don't get away from Him, don't get away from Him.

See that I can take a stand for myself, relying upon God in all things. Let my, let my family life be high or let it be low; let it be elevated as it will, I still rely upon God and have them to know I trust in Him.

May the Lord bless us and may He bring us safely to Him.

↗ ↗ ↗

SERMON II: "GOD'S MYSTERIES UPON THE MOUNTAINS"[a]

WE ARE very happy to bring greetings from Atlanta. We had great service over there for twelve nights. You know about it. I'm tired.

And we going to talk this morning—we very glad to have our visitors out with us from the Fort Valley—er—High School.[b] And we going to talk this morning from the—we told that they're *taking* the sermons from different churches. We going to talk this morning from this text, the 10th chapter of the Book of *Joshua* and the twelfth verse; the 10th chapter of the Book of *Joshua* and the twelfth verse.[c] We find our text, let me repeat: "Sun, stood thou still upon Gittia and thou, moon, go in the valley. . . ." The subject: God's Mysteries Upon the Mountains. We are very happy to have present—er—talk—we going to speak this morning—er—talk about God's Mysteries—er—upon Mountains—not *mountain*, but *mountains*.

There are so many men—some our great philosophers—have tried to dig out all the mysteries of God. Gone off to school and studied and all lika that, but there haven't been no man able to—to—to learn all the mysteries of God. Past man's finding out. So high, can't go over; so deep, can't go under; so wide, can't go around.

I—I tell you, I's going up the road the other day and crossed a great river. On looking down the stream, thought came to me. I looked in the water and thought came to me: If all this water was ink, it wouldn't hold 'nough ink to write out the mysteries of God. Yet, has been some men tried to change God's word, to change God's word. There have never been a man—he go to school and get his diploma, and all like that; degrees on mathematics and, and theology and what not and—now we witness, never hear a man gwine to schools to git his diploma on God. Every time you read the Bible, you git more. You can talk 'bout Mr. Shakespeare but, see—and what not—never

---

[a] The minister was 36 years old, had two children, attended the public schools and spent one summer (1941) at the Georgia College of Central City. He had been the pastor of the Mt. Zion Church for eight years; was the pastor of three other churches, having been "called" to a large church in Atlanta three days before the above sermon was recorded. During his service at Mt. Zion, he built a pool for baptizing, and remodeled the church inside and outside. He said, "I was called by God to preach the Gospel, in my early childhood."

[b] He refers to Fort Valley State College, which once was a high school.

[c] "Then spake Joshua to the Lord in the day when the Lord delivered up the Amorites before the Children of Israel, and he said in the sight of Israel, 'Sun, stand thou still upon Gibeon; and thou, Moon, in the valley of Ajalon.' " *The Bible*, 1611 King James Version, JOSHUA 10:12.

[17]

been a man could know all about God. God terrible case—to see works of God. Reread text. Now, going to try to discuss few minutes, mysteries of God. I tell you, no man ever been equipped enough to learn, to know all about God's mysteries.

The fust mountain we going discuss here this morning—God's mysteries—going to be, the fust mountain, Jesus preached one day upon the mountain one of his great sermons. Preached the "Be Attitudes": "Blessed are the meek, for such is the kingdom of Heaven; Blessed are the poor in spirit; Blessed are the pure in heart, for they shall see God; Blessed are the merciful, for they shall obtain mercy." Jesus upon the mountain one day talking with his disciples: "Blessed are the, are the peacemakers, for they shall be called the children of God."

You know, I tell you, it's a fine thing to be a peacemaker, not a peace-breaker. Ain't dat right? Dat's a good way, I tell you. I don't give a dime, I wouldn't give a dime 'bout men talkin' what somebody said on dey dying bed, when dey were dying. I don't care anything about that; I want to know, what did that person say or what did he do while he live? Ain't dat right, my love? While he was clothed in his right mind, while the blood was running warm in his veins — I want to know—who did he go and help? My love! Did he give out a lending hand? That unfortunate man, that unfortunate woman, my love? That's a good way, I tell you. The Bible tell us, "Well shall know them by their fruits." Ain't dat right, my love? And the onlest way that we can serve God is by serving our fellowman. Jesus said, my love, "Call men unto Me," my love.

And He was out preaching on the mountain the "Be Attitude": "Blessed are the meek for they shall inherit the earth." What the word "meek" mean? Haven't you seen a lot of people, seem lack dey jest meek in spirit—ain't dat right?—meek in heart? They were so humble —ain't dat right?—so perfect. They were jest meek. . . . I tell you, you know, I think more the Lord bless us, more humble we ought to be; ain't dat right? The Master said on one occasion, the Bible said, "He that humble himself shall be exalted and he that exalt himself shall be abased." I don't think we even have nothing to brag about, even what we have. I don't think people ought to brag about praying, brag about how we can sing—ain't dat right?—or brag about how he can preach, my love. Because we prove this morning in the Sunday School lesson, ain't but one man can preach (dat's de man dat been ordained—ain't dat right, my love?), is qualified to preach the gospel. . . . How can he preach except he be ordained, my love? We got a whole lot of people going 'round here talking 'bout, "We ordained him; we ordained him."

Dere never been a man have been able to ordain. God only one who can ordain.

White man talk with us, by way——. But it's a mystery; God's work mystery—in—deeper than this world. God's word, put here and been passed, a mystery.

Now let's see here. I find Jesus one day was on the mountain, on top of it, and we find Moses—find Elijah—and Ahab went upon the mountain, and they got up there to cry to God, when God had sent a famine on the land and in the land and had dried up the rivers and the grass had withered down and the wells had gone dry. Lord, fine thing sometime to try your God; ain't dat right, my love? And Elijah said, "I tell you what we do; let's go up on the mountain, try our God. The God that I serve has never lost a battle; the God that I serve, He don't neither sleep nor slumber." Oh, Lord! Let's call on Him this evening.

Quickly they built the altar on the mountain . . . and built a . . . around the wall; you know about it. And they began to cry to God, called Baal all day and Baal—from morning until high twelve—and Baal wouldn't answer. And finally Elijah told them, "I want you to tear down your altar . . . [*The rhythm overcomes the sense here.*] path." God I serve move you. "Tear down your altar." I feel like a child of God this morning. And he begin to build the wall. We got twelve stones, twelve stones representing twelve apostles, the twelve tribes of Israel. Began to build the old altar. Ah, Lord! Begin to call on the mighty God. Tell me, God rain down fire and it leaped up the wall. Must go on. Ahhhhhhhhh, [*Sings it.*] *Lord!* Tell me, men, Elijah saw—let—praise God—me tell you, saw on the mountain—ain't dat right?—on the mountain. Let's see. Goin' to discuss the next mountain. Must soon close this argument.

Next mountain goin' to discuss, Lawd, the mountain, the mountain Mebo. You know, one day, Moses had led the people on the mountainside. Moses was their pastor. He had led the people of Israel a long time. And God said, "Come up here; I'm going to take you away from the work; Angelic hosts of angels will be your pallbearers." And Moses led them across the Red Sea. And they got tired of hearing Moses. One day they called Moses, say, "I tell you, we want to hear God talk some," and, "Come up on the mountain."

And Moses told 'em, "I tell you, cry for water." And Moses smoted the rock — you know about it — and call 'em rebel. (Find about dat word "rebel"; dat's a bad word.) "Come up here, you rebels, and drink."

And . . . God told him, "You been a good leader and . . . want you come up on the mountain; want let you to review that land, prom-

ised you long time ago, land that so good to see; that land—." Carry
Moses on Mount Calvary; cast wistful eye. Great mystery. And God
pulled back the curtains, called up the dead. Moses said, "Sweet breeze
of the dead, a lyric breeze." Organizer. Look at him lookin' on the
mountain! One day God kissed Moses' life out of his body. Ah, tradition don't tell me where Moses was buried, but he's buried somewhere.
Oh, Lord! And time moved on. A great mystery on the mountain.
Lawd!

The last mountain goin' bring to your mind is the Mountain of
Transfiguration. Ah, Moses has been daid over 1,400 years. You know,
the Lord came and got Moses, burdened by Jesus Christ. Moses ask the
Lord, "Do as you promise." Jesus had to go on, on the mountain. The
Mountain of Transfiguration. . . . Had to go on some business; had to
go on Calvary. Ah, Lawd. And on the Mountain one day, while he was
there, Moses 'peared up there with the Lord. Elijah came up there with
the prophets, told 'em, "Feed the people; feed the four thousand."
Jesus. . . . And Jesus. . . . Some of 'em fell down as dead. While they
were looking—ah, Lawdy!—lifted up deir eyes, saw a man praying in
Jesus. Jesus only. Heard a voice from Heaven . . . , "This is my beloved
Son; hear ye Him." Ah, Lawd! "You ain't got to hear talk any 'em no
more; you gonna hear my Son." My Lawd!

May I close this argument, my Lawd, on mysteries on th' mountains.
Last thought and last outline, Mount Calvary. Oh, I'm jest thinking,
my brethren, had not been the influence of Calvary, man had no salvation, world woulda been lost. Ah, the world swolled up 'gainst man;
the seven seas swolled up 'gainst man. Lawd, telephone wire done come
off the post, torn down. Lawd! Gonna make, one day—it—. Last
mountain, Mount Calvary. Man had no salvation. I kin see 'em goin',
"I must go to Calvary." Ah, Lord! "Captain's been waiting for me,
Captain been looking for me, Captain have been waitin' on me four
thousand years ago." Oh, Glory. . . ! Going to Calvary, upon the mountain. Last thought, Mount—Mount Calvary. Look at Him this morning
on Calvary. Two thieves hang beside Him; try, tries to make His death
disgraceful. Thief beside Man on Calvary; of God's mysteries on mountains. Tried to make Him a bad man. Oh, Lawd! On Calvary dying.
Great mystery on the mountain. Look at Him dying on Calvary. Thief
on the right; one on the left. Two thieves, one representing the Jew, the
other representing the Gentile. Oh, Lord, on the mountain. One on
the left said, "If you be the Son of God, come down." Oh, Lordy!
One was on the right said, "If you be the Son of God"—my, listen
what he said—"Oh, Lord, I heard about you being the Rose of Sharon
and the Lily of the Valley." My, Lord! "When Thou come into Thy

kingdom, my Lawd, remem—." Think about that humble prayer that the thief prayed on the cross. "My Lord, Oh Lawdy, when Thou come in Thou kingdom, oh, remember me!" My Lawd!

Kept on dying. He never stop dying: "This day, this day"—Son of God—"Shalt thou be with me in Paradise."

Heard a feller say in Atlanta the other day. [*Talking voice now.*] Sunday School, Sunday morning, said—that word "shalt thou," the word "shalt thou" and "shall thou" much difference—that he doubt that the thief was on the right side of the Savior. Last sentence, "Thou shalt, thou shalt, thou shalt," short. Let nobody fool you; He told the thief, "You will be with me; where I go, you also." Great God! Mysteries on mountains. Great mysteries—act—sin—men—and blood.

Centurion he stand around cross, said, "Truly, truly, this must be the Son of God." Another subscription on cross. They wanted Him to change His sign. He said, "No, what I said I said; I said what I have said."

Great mysteries. If people think about responsibility Jesus take, world would be better. Persons git to learn to bear one another's burdens. Trouble run to friend and he comes to it. If we get to Heaven, we must learn to bear one another's burden. Jesus—spirit arise—said, "Take your burden to the Lord and leave it there." God help us. Go off, talk, rejoice, be glad.

Our subject: God's Mysteries Upon the Mountains; God's mysteries upon the Mountains—not Mountain, but Mountains! The Tenth Chapter of *Joshua*, the twelfth verse.[d]

✦　　✦　　✦

---

[d] Some activities in the audience during the sermon: (1) a "Sister" in the right "Amen Corner" of the Church started bowing her head and mourning; (2) a "Brother," on the opposite side, thrust his hand outward as if he were throwing a ball and shouted, "Preach it!"; (3) fanning was continuous throughout the sermon; (4) two mothers were present with small babies; both babies kept perfectly quiet during the sermon.

Sermon iii: "John the Baptist—A Voice Crying in the Wilderness"[a]

It's very pleasant to be present here with you all today. Short service if possible. Got me kinda run-up; Communion at Smith Chapel, to preach Anniversary Sermon. Not feeling good. Ben on road, two weeks of service. Jounreyed all night to git home. Don't feel good; got headache. You all peach-struck; you all tired; been "gwine to it." Since you been "gwine to it" and am tired and I been "gwine to it" and am tired, don't 'spect too much. Omitted Sunday School. Kinda late; hafta bear with you 'cause I know you ti'ed. [*Reads from the Bible in such a manner that one hardly can understand a word.*]

> "In those days came John Baptist, preaching in the wilderness—[*of Judea*].[b] And saying, Repent ye: for the kingdom of heaven is at hand. For this is he that was spoken of by the prophet Esaias, saying, *The voice of one crying in the wilderness, Prepare* ye the way of the Lord, make his paths straight. . . . [Matthew 3:1-17.]
>
> "Then was Jesus led up of the spirit into the wilderness to be tempted of the devil. And when he had fasted forty days and forty nights, he was afterward an hungered. And when the tempter came to him, he said, If thou be the Son of God, command that these stones be made bread. But he answered and said, It is written, Man shall not live by bread alone, but by every word that proceedeth out of the mouth of God."[c] [Matthew 4:1-4.]

John was a preacher, baptizing folks. John the Baptist [*Loud cry of a baby in the audience.*]—and he was preaching to folks telling them about repentance of sin. Men don't lack you to tell them that.

Revival meeting about here. Been helping a man who gwine to help us. Gave me swell time down there. Only one thing: didn't have the spirit you got. [*Amens.*] I knocked 'round there. He will help us. We don't want to treat him no way but royal. If you want to be helped, have to help somebody. We wont to put him on a good revival. He got a home right there at home next to mine. If he don't treat me right,

---

[a] Reverend ———— gave his age as 55. He was married, had two children; attended Americus Institute, Americus, Georgia; 30 years a preacher; 25 years a pastor; 9 years at Holly Grove; pastored four churches. He said his aim in preaching is "to save souls."

[b] These words, like many others in this passage, he omitted. He often mumbled. It was discovered later that he could not read very well.

[c] It appeared that the minister read on and on until he struck something in the Bible that appealed to him, something that would serve as his subject; entirely extemporaneous.

he's right there where I can hear what he say. [*Chuckles.*] We start now to make our aim. Five dollars or eight dollars ain't gwine to speak to no good preacher. Ten dollars ain't gwine to speak to no preacher. He gwine to preach! Every time I bring a man here, he better preacher'n me. [*"No, he ain't," from the audience.*] That "white" man, Reverend ————, he looked at me — mulatto. I told him, "Don't look for me; I gotta go and represent Holly Grove."[d] Last Sunday, Father's Day; we had grand time; we done, around there, pretty well.

Bring it up in a "chump" and git through wif it. [*Refers to today's sermon.*] Our big day come on Second Sunday. Charter truck from Albany; be at Raymond[e] Second Sunday; 60 or 65 men, load it up. Beaver Creek; plan to be there. If you don' have nothin', I pay for it. I ain't sayin' you come; I just telling you, be glad to meet yer. I'm just saying, if you can come, come bring truck. I know some you dis'prove ridin' in a truck. [*"No, no," from the audience.*] All the brothers git together, git truck, see? 'Range to git truck. Hard road all way; paved all way to Raymond; straight road on through. I be there when you git there.

John was a preacher; preach 'pentance of sins. I [*have taken in a*] number of devils since I been here. Whether they converted or not, I don't know. I like that they sit down. But you'll do. Talk to me now. [*Asking for audience response.*] Them little black places dere ain't no good if you can just sit down. [*Humor; refers to the black faces of the audience.*] Consecrate myself now. [*Get serious.*] Get fair with you. I ain't got no need to come here; no one's a Christian here. Benches can't say, "Amen." You all can hear, can't yer? But John was a preacher, and he went down there by himself. Wasn't no crowd down dere when he got dere.

Jesus said, "Lift Me up from the earth and I draw all men unto Me. And I draw all men unto Me." In the life you live—some us lives mighty—lift Him up. We live it while we at the church, in the church, in your songs, your moans, and your groans. Lift Him up. Let's see— er—John went down there and lift Him up. Jesus came to him and talked to him and when the Tempter came to Him, "If Thou the Son of Man, turn these rocks to bread."

He answered, "Man shall not live by bread alone." Testing Jesus, showing Him all the good things, calling Him in question. Ef he done

---

[d] Rev. ———— had been helping the other minister in the latter's revival, but today he had broken away to serve Holly Grove. The audience liked this and said so with many amens, etc.

[e] The minister refers to another one of his churches.

got hungery, "Then make bread outta them stones lying around the mountain, jest like yer see 'em. Look at 'em!"

Thenk He got hungry, and they say to Him, "If Thou be the Son of God, command that these stones be made bread." Ain't that what he say? Preach it out there with me. I know what I'm talkin' 'bout; you too!

They thought that a fast change Him and carry Him their way. Some folks, if dey carry you their way, it's all right; aint got nothin' to do for you if dey can't. After done been to wilderness, fast and pray. "Fast" mean don't eat, don't drink. After that, at a certain time, He got hungry. He thought [*The Tempter did.*] dat a fine time, fine time, fine chance to change Him—change His idea, change His mind— and he didn't stay 'way! You know, some folks belong to the church; long's dey can't carry you dey way, dey have nothin' for you to do. Ain't dat right? Now dat's de Lawd's truf! But as long as dey git you to do what dey want, dey wid you.

After he'd taken Him on the pinacke of dat temple, then He got hungry. He got—let me tell you, He don't eat, don't drink—after that, at a certain time, He got hungry, see? He got hungry. Then he[f] say that "this is my time." We're on our way.[g] "Hungry; got nothin' to eat, but He says He's the Son of God." He said, "If you Christ, you outta prove it! You talk and don't prove it. Doing! He said that He God's Son; He always been with His Father; He hungry; got nothin' to eat and got no money and, quite natural, He'll yield to it." (You know, sometimes a fellow take things off people he wouldn't do it, but it's conditions. Conditions make you do things that you wouldn't do. If conditions didn't have us so 'tight', have us going, don't you know you wouldn't work all day and all night Saturday? [*Amens.*][h] Our conditions! Conditions! You look right at yer God sometime folks. God! Jesus look right at that rock. Rocks! Rock's something hard; something you can't bite; danger to swallow. (Conditions make you do things that you wouldn't do, don't you know.) Rock's hard; bust fellow's brains out. "Turn to bread; make bread out of these."

Jesus said, "Man shall not live by bread alone." That condem them by every word. [*Digression on "word."*] Not the word of Greek, Latin, grammar, Moody; not a word of source from anybody but God. The Word of God is food. The Word of God is shelter. The Word of God is water. The Word of God is protection—can't tear it down. The

---

[f] The Tempter.

[g] He means the sermon, the emotional part, is getting underway.

[h] It was peach-packing season and most of the audience had worked until very late Saturday night, really until Sunday morning.

Word of God, come out of the mouth of God. Might have all kind of recreation prepared, sot, put in hearing of folks; won't do no good. (Dis is plain stuff.) I'm sayin' to you that John—er—here are words spoken by the Savior. One that fixed us, have say in our souls. Makes you cry sometimes. [*Amen.*] Thunder is—. You at good place, too, th' church.

John, forerunner of Jesus Christ, born of Elisha, come before Jesus Christ advertising Jesus Christ. One hundred years before His coming, Ezekiel—David say likewise. Daniel says he saw Him as a stone tore out of a mountain. "I'll give Him all power." Ezekiel saw Him as a wheel; Ezekiel saw Him as a wheel comin' from—teeming. One Ezekiel saw Him; kept spying things—spectacle of force. Wheel in a wheel, little in big, Matthew — Luke — John — He's coming. John then grew up; maturity come up.

Don't know how much done in a run of a day. Lotta cussin' done in a run of a day; lotta disaster done in a run of a day; so much disaster done in a run of a day; no end to lying in the run of a day. Here's a day; another day. Grow—one day—days seem—. John Baptist preached in wilderness; say he go there by himself, holding up Jesus. Preached only one text. I'm got to git 'nother text every time I come here. Give up world; give 'self to God. Then you see Him; then you see Him, shall find the kingdom of Heaven at hand. He talk about Jesus; he talk about Jesus.

I know what I's telling you 'bout. "The Rose of Sharon, Knight of the Mornin' Star, come down to be ruler of the day. Kingdom of Heaven is at hand; Jesus not far off; always there to come to your need." That was spoke about by the prophet, the one crying in the wilderness: "Prepare ye the way of the Lord; make His paths straight; prepare the way for Him." Oh, brother, we ought to walk in such a life that somebody else ought to be prepare' through you for the Kingdom of God, the Kingdom of Heaven.

Heaven! I feel like it's a very splendid place. Heaven! I feel like it's the best place ever I have known. Wherever you at—in your state, in your field—when dat spirit of God hit you, you feel like you in Heaven right dare. You—ain't you never got happy? By yourself? You just done forgot everything and—and God knows you just feel like you in Heaven right then and there. [*Amens.*] Heaven is a spiritual place, spirit place. And Heaven make His paths straight—er—first why—.

Some folks say, "I'm a straight man myself; I'm a straight woman." Oh-oh-oh-oh, just follow on down the line; you just go her way; you'll find out whether she's straight or no. You'll find out whether she's straight or no, brother. You just deal with a man; you'll find out; you'll find out he's crooked as can be. Don't make 'em no crookeder'n him. He—. A straight man or woman don't care what time, when or where they are, they want to do right, want to walk out-right, plain before the world. Not ashamed of their lives; "I'm living straight." I ain't talking about walking straight and calmly, but your life! Straight! Straight! I ain't talkin. . . .

Come to advertise John. The famed John had a raiment with camel hair on it, brother. John advertised. Saw—John had his raiment —God—girdeth around. He went down there like Jesus was when He was, when He was—didn't have nothin' to eat. He said, "I make you, I prepare something for you." Jesus said, "I feed you when you hungry, clothe you when you naked—locust and wild honey, something for you to eat." And then I heard Him say—. Kinda a thing [*Refers to locust.*] that grow, maybe like a bug—I don't know. Then He come here and say—Bible say "locust"; that [*is all*] you need [*to know*]. Feller say, "Son, go to Heaven; sweetmilk and honey dere."

[*Son says,*] "Don't lack dem. So [*I will have*] nothin' ter eat." Didn't know what *he* gwine ter eat! Nigger oughta be knocked in head. "Don't lack 'em!"

Ah. Jerusalem, repent! Jews was in Jerusalem; Pharisees, Saddu-cees, all of them there. Preach! (I'm preachin' to everybody in here today. Sinner here, I'm preachin' to dem; Christian here, I'm preachin' to dem; hypocrite here, I'm preachin' to him.) So John was lifting up his voice—no group around—er—and they heard how Jerusalem and — they out-roused the parties of the Jews 'round there, crowded with crowded with—. They heard that . . . gone to Jerusalem, from Jeru-salem. They heard that a loud voice down there. I think God want you to lift up your voice. David said, "Lift it up; cry aloud—the earth— we must lift up our voices." Lifted up his voice; he didn't set no point on no money—on his preachin'. Nothin' but holding up Jesus, and then they heard him. And they turn aside and saluted and he saying such a powerful thing; they never had heard that before. They didn't know nothing about it and saluted the King. And then they saluted the—God—on dey mind, on dey mind. Some people ain't wont to preach unless they git lot of money. Conscience reasoned with them. "And then I heard that strange music down there, strange voice. I don't know what the matter down there and, down in the wilderness; ain't never been nothin' like dat before. Let's go down there; see what de trouble; let's see what dis thing mean." Dey done fine, didn't dey, brothers? Come on out, 'round about, go down. Remember, they want —. Yes, dey did! Turn aside, went to John and called him in questions, didn't they? Yes, they did! Asked him if he be the Christ or "Shall we look for another?" They asked John; John said . . . They asked him questions; they asked him questions.

John said, "I am not Him but just a voice."

They asked Him—didn't they, brothern?—"Who is you? Shall we look for another?"

"I am not Him. That coming after me is a perfect man, upright man, a man won't do no wrong, and I'm not worthy to stoop down to—I'm not worthy to bear His shoes." Luke, the Lord's disciple, last chapter taken from . . .[1] passage. I heard John say they went out to Him to get all rich, 'round and about Jordan. Ah, and was. . . . They asked John; John said. . . . This great preacher—when they got down there, John preach so forceful, got into the thoughts, hearts, all over. Saw themselves; saw not fittin' to die; repented of sins. They took Him down and baptized Him. John baptized Him down in Jordan.

Jesus said, "I come to, to you for baptism, generation to free from the wrath to come. I come in. . . . Generation of vipers now in Jordan. Have mercy. I heard your influence in town, heard talk, children of God, or I'm a liar—you—but you—." (Don't 'wake nobody; let 'em sleep right on.) Uhmmmmmmmmm! "I looked down the mountain, my brethren—" (Don't 'wake nobody.)—on wrath to come." God's judgment done warned 'em a long time, warned 'em a long time. Oh, Jerusalem, have mercy now. Oh, Jesus, have mercy now. Flee from the wrath to come; bring forth fruit for repententance. Abraham, our father, Father of Faithful. God talked to him, Abraham, one time and told Abraham—said to Nickademus, "God bless you in your field; your band shall multiply and seed shall multiply and number shall multiply like the sands." Nobody can number 'em, sands of the seashore, brother.

Lord! Lord! Now look at Him now, brother. I heard him talk—John—I said—and so—Abraham—and so and said to—hewn down tree—. "God is able, God is able—strong—to raise us, chillun of Abraham, God is able"—ain't dat right, brethren? "Save de soul!" Ain't dat right? Ain't [we] got to pray to git to Heaven if we want to? Stones out of rocks. Able, able and now also able—I wish I had time ter arger dis thing—to act—. Every tree bring good fruit, don't it, brethren? Every tree bring not forth good fruit, hewn down. Oh, Lord, cut you down in the morning; git the right action. Ah, now,

---

[1] He uses "er" to cover up the exact location of the passage, which he either did not know or could not recall. But a lack of knowledge must not break his rhythm of delivery. Thought, expressed in logical words, is not to be expected here—nor is it necessary for the minister's purpose

chillun, git the right action, git the right action. Oh, Lord, cut you down in the morning; cut you down in the noontime! Have mercy! Heard his say that coming after me One baptize you in fire, Holy Ghost. Burns, and when it [*Holy Ghost*] gits to burning, can't hold your peace! Burn up lies, burn up undermining, burn up sin! Let you see the truth again. Shall heat you, sinner.

Ah, who is the wheat? Lord, Lord, who is the wheat? Been born again. What do it? Let make fine flour. Gather, put in barn, keep from bad weather. If live right, if do right, Lord gwine to gather you after a while; keep bad weather off; keep rain off. Won't do to gather too soon; gather at certain time. Cut dat wheat! Lord! All carry to mill; keep dat mill prepared. Fine flour. Lord ain't gwine to cut you down till yer git right; Take you in kingdom; see after you. No rain, [*Audience answers by repeating each of these.*] no bad weather, no trouble, no sorrow, no crying—Lord!—no more lying been said about you, no more tattlin', no more going hungry, " 'cause I'm the bread of life." [*Hums a song; change of pace.*]

Lord, have mercy, my Father. [*Talking now.*] I—listen at him [*John*] talking and baptizing. All them people repent. He [*Jesus*] come about 70 miles—I don't know how far it was He come down that little stream. Stepped over into Jordan where John was. Looked up river, saw Jesus coming. "Saviour!" Appearance didn't look lack other folks. "My Lord." Thought of God. "Look yonder; let Him git your attention." All look over Jordan. Saw Jesus; see Him when He git down there.

"Don't know Me?"

John knew. "Behold the Lamb of God. Yonder He come; yonder He come, Judaea. Yonder He comes, Jerusalem. Yonder He come, Jordan."

When He git down there, Jesus said, "Baptize thou Me."

John said, "I need to be baptized of Thee."

Jesus: "Suffer it to be so now, John." All wept. "It's the will of my Father; I got to be baptized."

And John took down and baptized, down in Jordan, "Son of God, Saviour and Master, I baptize Thee in name of Father, Son. . . ." Baptized in Jordan; went down in the water. John—see, see him pulling Him up. God turned back the curtains of Heaven, come from a pint of God's glory and flew down to Jesus where He was and sat on His shoulder. Brothers, my God and yours. God put the seal and the stamp on baptizing. "I repent, Father, Son and Holy Ghost." Heard the voice speak out of Heaven, "This is Thou"—up in glory—, "My Son, My Son, My Son." Devil stand—now—there. You can't baptize the Devil to save your life. Stand on banks till you come out of water and pin on your mind for my sake [*sic*].

Forty days, forty nights—I told yo' what fasting mean. They got hungry. Bible said they tempted them. They—call Son of God, commanded stone be made bread. Testing — Jesus said, "Man, man shall not live by bread alone." Ain't dat true, man? [*The audience chants: "Man shall not live by bread alone."*] Man, God's word good. Hungry soul, hear somebody sing and pray. Certain, man can't get filled till he harken.

Uncle Sam calling for me; mighty war on calling for me. Dis last remark to you. Sit on a high hill, sit on a high hill—East and West— Lilly of the Valley—. Things of the world, things of the world, things of the world. This world—. Yes—oh, Jesus! Oh, Jesus! Sundown—. Pinackle of temple—. Lilly of the Valley—. Beautiful things. "All this is mine, all this is mine, all this is mine. It is mine, it is mine, it is mine." Oh, Lord! "I tell you what you do now, if you just fall down and worship me."

"Get behind!" My Lord! God got His eyes on you. See all you do. Midnight! Save Jesus,[j] Save Jesus. Died on Calvary Hill. Save Jesus, save Jesus, save Jesus. Hint to the wise. Save Jesus. Get free. Save Jesus. Leper—save Jesus—take up your bed and go home. Save Jesus. Writing on the ground. Save Jesus, Man to depend on when trouble come. Put truth to him [*Devil*] and he go away. Truth breaks down things; truth washes down things. Last day—disciples—this Friday— took Him this night, took Him this night—all night long—now before Pilate. Judas, as he betrayed—little money—Judas as he betrayed, told 'em with a kiss. (Kiss ain't so good.) Judas, as he betrayed Jesus, betrayed with kiss. Mighty man.

Hold it [*the spirit*], hold it! Sometimes makes you cry, sometimes makes you cry, sometimes makes you pray, sometimes makes you moan, sometimes makes you right-living. If it makes you cry, I'll be with you, will not forsake you. Mother cry. Father fine. Everybody thinks you git it. Hold it. [*Moaning.*] Go with you to graveyard. He makes you your dying bed. Mercy! Hold it. [*Sings.*] I been had hold Him a long time; He ain't never let me down.

'Tis on cross, Friday evening. Lord! Right there Sunday morning soon, Sunday morning soon [*Christ*] rose out of the grave. Soon, soon, [*Sings it.*] soon [*Shouting in the audience.*][k] watches 'round grave; felt like dead man on to himself. Oh—oh, knocked off dying smile;

---

[j] Observe how "Save Jesus" becomes a refrain.

[k] Climax begins.

put back in one corner of grave. Angel sitting on Heavenly grave holding God's hand. Sat right there; nobody in the grave; saw it standing gaping open. He not there; somebody done stole Him away. I see Him go back. John go down to grave, go down to grave, go down to grave, go down to grave. Look-a-yonder, look-a-yonder; who do you see? Who you see? Jesus! Jesus! "I looked for Jesus, but shook and tremble." Jesus! Rocks began to roar. Jesus! "Got to tell my brother." Jesus! "I'm going before day."

Ahhhhhhh! Ahhhhhhh![1] [*General confusion.*]

Got my . . . in your soul. Got to cry sometime. Know I been born again. Git off by 'self and cry. My soul, [*Audience moans, "My soul."*] My soul have Saviour. Have trouble and tribulation; sometimes afflicted; have to crawl into your home. Farewell; Farewell! [*Uniformed ushers come to administer to the shouting ladies.*] For motherless child, nowhere to go, nobody to go to. Fatherless child. . . . [*Leaves pulpit and comes down to the audience.*] My! My! Don't you feel lonely sometime in world by yourself? Give me your hand. [*Picks up a tune on "Give me your hand." Audience joins in singing.*] Lord, give me your hand. Won't He lead you? [*Talking now.*] Won't He take care of you, chillun? Be consolation for you? My, my Lord! I done tried! I know He *do* care of you, preserve your soul, and den what I like about You, carry you home. Here rain wouldn't fall on you. Beautiful land. Gwine to sing and open de doors of the church.

◆ ◆ ◆

---

[1] Climax.

I am glad to be present; happy also to see you present, your presence. Regret very much for being somewhat late; however, we hope to work out of this gradually.[b]

We invite your attention to the reading of the Book of Proverbs, the 24th chapter, beginning with the 30th verse:

"I went by the field of the slothful, and by the vineyard of the man void of understanding; And, lo, it was all grown over with thorns, and nettles had covered the face thereof, and the stone wall thereof was broken down. Then I saw, and considered it well; I looked upon it, and received instruction. Yet a little sleep, a little slumber, a little folding of the hands to sleep: So shall thy poverty come as one that travelleth; and thy want as an armed man."

This is our text, Proverbs the 24th chapter, beginning with the 30th through the 34th verse. From these verses the theme suggest itself to our minds is this: The Danger of Neglect.

Solomon here is very plainly and clearly bringing to us an observation of the slothful man. He also points out here that where negligence has been made that the fields and the walls are all in bad shape. He began here by saying, "I went by the field of the slothful." It's dangerous to be slothful; it's a great sin to be slothful. The sin of slothfulness is a great sin. He said this same slothful man was a man that was void of understanding. It's pathetic to be void of understanding.

He passed by the vineyard; therein the weeds and the thorns, and the bushes have grown over and covered the wall over. It simply speaks that the vineyard had been neglected. The stone wall was broken down. Solomon saw and considered it well: "I looked on it and received instruction." It's reasonable to look at the negligence of a friend or a neighbor and receive instruction—to see wherein they have failed; to see wherein they have neglected their farm and their duties in life. So, therefore, this theme presents itself: The Danger of Neglect.

In thinking of how dangerous it is to neglect, first of all, we think of most calamities and accidents are caused by neglect. Whether they be in the air, on land, or on the ocean, they are all caused by neglect.

---

[a] Reverend ———— said he received a "divine call" to preach and has been preaching since he was 17. He attended school at Simmons Theological Seminary, Louisville, Kentucky, and at Morehouse College, Atlanta, Georgia. He pastors three churches besides St. Luke. He is a bachelor.

[b] He is new at this church, this being his 4th sermon as the pastor.

When we think of the fameous [*sic*] flyer Amelia Earhart, who some time ago attempted to fly across the blue waters of the Atlantic Ocean. . . . Something went wrong. That plane went down in some unknown place in the ocean. Million of dollars was spent in search for her, but until today she's unaccounted for. But it happened because of neglect.

Then I think of the plane that Dr. L. K. Williams, the President of the National Baptist Convention of the United States of America, Incorporated, had taken from Chicago, Illinois, to Detroit, Michigan, where he was slated to make a political speech. Because of unreasonable negligence, that plane caught fire and went down and Dr. Williams and others met with their death. Because of negligence.

Then I think of a few years ago on land, on the Little Southern Railroad, between McDonald and Atlanta. The Southern train wrecked and it wrecked at what we call Camp Creek. And that wreck until now is known as the Camp Creek Wreck. When the train passed through Jenkinsburg, a town back a few miles this side, the engineer was warned there. Because of rain, he was warned that the trestle was in bad condition. The engineer cursed and said, "I'm due in Atlanta in 'so many' minutes." He pulled out. When he came to the trestle, the trestle gave way. More than fifty lives were lost. He was well-warned, but he neglected the warning that he met at Jenkinsburg. So, it's dangerous to neglect.

And then I think of the *Titantic* [*sic*], that great ship that started out from Southampton. That ship that had Captain John Smith as its captain and had all of the luxuries that a luxurious heart could desire. Had everything for their pleasure and their comfort thereon. They were well-warned as they left Southampton of the icebergs that were way out there in the ocean. But the reply was that "This ship is sink-proof; no iceberg will be able to sink this ship; this is the *Titantic*, the greatest ship that this country has ever built or known." But they went on and neglected that warning. But somewhere out near the mountain where those hurge [*sic*] icebergs had tumbled into the ocean that ship struck those icebergs. And, finally, the water found its way into the ship. Somebody, as they were riding, said, "I believe this ship is sinking here."

They said, "No! This ship is the *Titantic*; it can't sink."

But finally they said, "Yes, but the lower deck is almost full of water and it's going down." Finally, the captain give out orders to cast out the lifeboats and for the women and children to get on the lifeboats that they might be safe. And that great ship with those valuable things went down in the water. Because they neglected to take the warning. Christian friends, it's dangerous to neglect.

Neglect in any way produces a corresponding loss. I might make [a few] examples of a few things where neglect produces a loss. If a merchant neglect his business, he'll go bankrupt. If the gardener neglect to hoe the weeds, the plants will cease to grow; his crop will be cut; he will not be able to get much vegetable, wherein he neglected to hoe the weeds. If proper food and clothing is neglected, then the health will fail. Too many people go into bad health by neglecting proper food and clothing. Proper clothing is vital to good health but some clothing is not necessary for a healthy body. But neglect causes a great loss, loss of health.

Many people go into bad health by improper clothing, ventilation. I remember once reading a story of a man who went into a closed room, shut out all of the ventilation and heated the room at a high degree. Finally, he found himself suffering from heat. Then he opened the ventilators, the doors, and the windows and let all the fresh air in he could. And the consequence were, he developed double pneumonia and died. Then, for sanitation to be neglected, then that, means the health will fail also.

For the mind to be neglected there will be no education. And where ignorance predominates, there is always a great loss. Solomon said, in Proverbs, two—twenty-nine, two, "When the wicked beareth rule, the people mourn."[c] So, then, it produces a great loss.

Where conscience is neglected there will be heathenism, cannibals and prisons. What do we mean when we say, "Conscience is neglected"? The conscience, to my mind, is a court within itself. We mean by a court within itself that conscience is a thing that will try you, will convict you, and then pass judgment on you. For a conscience to be a whole court within itself, we see conscience as a judge in the judgment seat; then we see the prosecution attorney at the bar; then we see the defense attorney at the bar; then we see the solicitor general producing the state evidences on the case; we see the twelve jurors in the box; and then we see both state and defense witnesses taking the stand; and all these make up conscience. Conscience will try you, convict you, and pass judgment on you. Any time you are tempted to go wrong, they all stand close by. Every time you are prompted to commit a sin, they all tell you, "Don't do it."

The soul, neglected, becomes dwarfed and die. You see souls that have lost their spiritual shape. They're out of shape. They—maybe

---

[c] He is correct in the Biblical location.

with this illustration you see the condition of a soul that has been neglected. When the basketmaker works his white oak around in the yard, under the shade tree, once in a while he'll leave a piece of it laying out in the sunshine and the sunshine will so twist and so dry that piece of oak until it's impossible to put it back in any kind of shape. It was neglected; it wasn't put in the shade or in the water but it was left out in the sunshine. And that's the way it is with a soul that's been neglected. It loses its shape and it soon dies.

Then neglect weakens the power to decide. "I will," said a man one day who promised his companion on a dying bed that he would be saved before he died. He really meant, out of his heart and his soul, that he would be saved, but he put it off and waited too long. (*Pray for us.*)[d] So, it weakens the power to decide. He neglected the promise that he made to his dying companion. He neglected his soul to the extent that when death laid her hand on him and claimed him and carried him to sleep in the silent city of the dead, his last cry was, "I waited too long!" (*Come, Holy Spirit.*)[d] The longer we wait, the harder the task becomes.

Neglect produces a loss of sensitiveness. "What you mean by that?" I'm thinking of some one who wants to wake up at a certain time in the morning. They have an alarm clock. They'll set that clock to alarm at a certain hour and sure enough that clock will alarm and will awaken them out of their sleep. But they'll neglect the alarming of the clock. Not that they didn't hear it; not that it didn't alarm, but they neglect the alarming of the clock and go back to sleep and over-sleep themselves and stay there too long and be late getting to their job and lose their job. It's dangerous to neglect.

I think about people who move from the rural section to the city. The first few nights they're in the city, [*Begins accenting rhythmically.*] they're troubled with the noise, disturbed by the noise. Noisy cars, the trolley, the trains on the rails keep them disturbed for a few nights. Can't sleep sound, but they keep on. After a while, after a few nights have passed, they can just go on to sleep and sleep all night. [*Audience answers, "Sleep all right."*][e] Forgot about the noise; they forget about the rumbling and they sleep all right, undisturbed. Procrastination is a thief of time.

Neglect destroys interest. It destroys your interest in school; it destroys your interest in music; it destroys your interest in social affairs; it destroys your interest in the soul of man. And, in the word of God [*Sings it.*] neglect destroys these things.

---

[d] Preparing to move to the emotional part of the sermon.

[e] There is nothing religiously emotional in this thought, but the rhythmical delivery and the pause signal and stir the emotions; the people respond.

Salesman one day had a prospective customer and he failed, he neglected to call on him at the set time and he lost the sale, because he failed to call on him. Neglect in any way cause a great danger. Man one day as he traveled, one cold, icy day, he found a serpent on the ground. that was frozen. And this man had pity on him. He taken the serpent up off the ground and said, "I'll be a friend to him. I'll take him and put him in my bosom and warm him." The man taken the serpent, put him in his bosom and got him warm, but he neglected to take the serpent out when he was warm. He bit the man and the man died. It's dangerous to neglect.

A hunter one day been out in the woods, went out hunting in the rain and in the cold. (*Come, Holy Spirit.*) Went in home as it's customary for huntsmen to do, tired and wet and hungry. And as he went in, he sat his gun in the corner by the fireplace and neglected to take the load out of his gun. And, finally, a little three-year old child, playing about in the house, knocked the gun down and the gun discharged and shot the little child in the head, and it died. It's dangerous to neglect; it's dangerous to neglect. Neglect leads to ruin. Neglect lead to damnation. Neglect lead to loss.

Ah, I saw another man neglect to learn to swim. Stood on the banks of a river one day, saw all the child he had drown, because he neglected to learn to swim. Neglect will lead in the road of ruin to both time and eternity.

I can hear Paul saying one day in the Book of Hebrew, "How shall we escape"—ah—"if we neglect so great a Salvation?" Here's what he meant. He meant: "Is it any way around it?"

I can hear somebody answer 'im and say, "No! No! Ain't no way around it." I could hear Job saying one day, "There's no way to escape death, because your bounds been struck and you can't go 'round." Ahhhhhhhh, Glory! Dangerous to neglect, my friends. Then I hear him say, "Well, how will we get 'round then if we neglect to express Salvation?"

He said, "Well, it's so high, you can't get over; so wide, you can't go around; then it's so deep down, you just can't turn under it; no way 'round it." No way around this Salvation. Well, what do you mean now? Salvation said one day, "I am the way, the truth and the light"; He said, "I am an open door; I'm a door no man can shut, but you must come in by Me." He said to another crowd one day, "If any man come any other way, he cometh as a thief and a robber." My Lord. No way around Salvation. But I just kept on reading where He said to Nicodemus, "You must be born again." My Lord!

I said, "Well, now, men escape from the county chain gang; then,"

I said, "men escape sometimes from the jail houses; they escape from the state prisons sometimes and then every once in a while, somebody escape from the federal prison." My Lord!

But I could hear the word of my God ringing in my soul, ringing in my heart, good news and glad tidings, saying, "It ain't no way around Salvation. If you neglect this Salvation, ain't no way round it." No way around.

Dangerous to neglect. Somebody neglect their spiritual activity and they get cold and they get luke-warm. One reason why, one reason why we can't all cry the same cry is—er—[*Audience moans.*] we neglect our spirit [*Moans.*] and we get luke-warm. We neither cold nor hot and the Spirit can't find its way into our soul. I tell you, I tell you, if you let the Spirit find its way into your heart, It'll move in your heart and then it'll make you move. Ahhhhhhhh, Glory!^f Jeremiah said, "It's like fire shut up in my bones," and then, then, then he said, "It's like a mighty hammer." Oh, Glory! But I'll tell you what It'll do for you: It'll make an old man feel like a young man; if you are tired, it'll make you move anyhow. I tell you what it'll do for you: It'll make you forget about your burden; It'll make you forget about your heavy crosses; It'll make you forget about your trials. And then you'll say: "Whatever it takes, [*Loud accent by striking the speaker's stand rhythmically.*] I'm going on; I'm going in Jesus." [*Suddenly begins to talk; change of pace.*] Going on in Jesus.

Now my spiritual strength renewed,^g then I am going to remember that Salvation is free for all. It's dangerous to neglect It; it's dangerous to go by heedlessly. Salvation is to all men; Salvation is to men and mankind. And if we neglect this great Salvation, there is no way of escape.

May the Lord bless us, may He help us, and may He save us when it comes our time to die. Amen.

ᛏ   ᛏ   ᛏ

---

f Climax.

g Refers to the effect of the emotional part of the sermon.

SERMON V: "WHY WE COME TO CHURCH"[a]

I'M GLAD we could come together again to pray and thank God, observing His will. Praise His name. The reason we come together is to sing, pray and talk about God. We come to this house fer de purpose of singing, praying and knowing that God is the Keeper. Yer hear His word; His word is good. You satisfy ter enjoy home and here, wherever God puts yer.

Yer know, I'm dis way. I believe in doing everything where it ought to be done at. I believe when you have a car, don't put no gas in no-no radiator; it don't belong dere. Put de water in de radiator and the gas in the tank whar it belong and it'll do good. Put things whar dey don't belong, won't do no good; it'll do harm. Put everything in its own place.

And so as we assemble together, we couldn't honor a better man, greater man than He is. Greatest hero ever sat on the throne. He has great power throughout all ages. And the sweetness of His disposition in the hearts of many have caused us to have hope. He's the only man. . . . Only one fer us.

And whatever fer you all this morning, just hold yer cups, and whatever fer yer all, yer git it. Kinda like a mail-carrier or post office: give yer whatever fer you. So jest keep everything waiting and we'll see what's gwine to come ter you.

Now [*Rev.* ———] follow and gwine [*continue*] the service fer you. The Lord say, "Open yer mouth and I'll speak fer you." See what the Spirit gwine do. Tryin' to preach the Word of God. Pray His will be done.

✓   ✓   ✓

---

[a] This and the following two sermons should be grouped together because of the unique manner in which they were delivered. The occasion was "Union Sunday" (the one Sunday when other churches come to join a particular church in putting on a "big meeting") at this Church. Hundreds of people were inside and outside the church; persons had come from as far away as Philadelphia. Three of the best preachers were to speak. But, and this was unusual, six or seven "good" preachers sat in the pulpit at the opening of the services, none knowing which three would be chosen as speakers of the day, until a Union officer made the announcement while presenting the first speaker. The second and third speakers must use the same text that the first speaker uses; no one knows this text until the first speaker announces it in his sermon. This is an excellent situation for speaking that is almost impromptu.

The first minister was married to his second wife; he finished the third grade in school; had been preaching for 28 years. "Called of the Spirit" to preach; had four churches. He was blind, which might account for his not giving a full text and sermon. He never quite approved of the use of machinery in the church.

[b]Yer know, when us git hooked up here together, it's like a city and a town — ain't it? — when yer turn on de light. It's down in de corner stores and all behin' 'em and all over the house. It shine everwhar. Child or God'll shine anywhar you put it. Yer may git 'im bowed down, but he gon' shine anyhow! He don't care nothin' 'bout no trouble, child. He gonna shine anyhow! Ain't got no bread, but he'll shine anyhow! Ain't got no clothes, but he'll shine anyhow! Don't care how much yer talk 'bout 'im, he'll shine right on! Lay down at night; yer may . . . , but he'll shine right on! Git up in de mornin' he'll shine everwhar he go! Ever time yer look at 'im, he's shinin'! Ain't dat right?

. . . Now, we on our way home.

✦   ✦   ✦

---

[b] The first minister continued later, following the delivery of the next two sermons.

I don't—haven't felt good all day. Gonna "make it" all right. If I "make it," all right; all right if I don't. Preachin' out of my "rep"... . If I ain't "made it" now, 's too late now.

The text, 28th chapter of Elijah,[b] 1st verse. Going to read you a section. Elijah said, "And all the people. . . ."

There's so many doctrines and strange things. Some think one right; some another. But when God wake you up, you don't have to think. Only one thing: to preach; preach the power of God. Jesus said one day, "All power is in My hand." (May knock this thing down; I don' know.)[c] The Bible is called the Book of Books. Ain't dat right? Now, I want yer to follow me pretty close. . . . Don't lack what I'm saying, go on and talk anyhow. Help me out some. Don't git back. 'cause yer got me "in a tight."[d] Ain't gwine help a man "in a tight," he don't need yer when he git out. Ain't dat right, brethren? Oh, yeh!

Now as I said, this here the only book to give you a true record of God's word. You can read . . . Moody, Calvin. . . . If you want the true record of God and Christ, you gotta git the Bible. Oh, yes! Now you all know that; don't look at me; open yer mouth! It's the only book, I said, that give you a true record of God and Christ, and the Bible is right! Ain't dat right, brethren? I don't care who—it's right! The Nigger handlin' it may be wrong, but the record is right! That's the way I believe about it. The record is right; I don't care what nobody say; what they do. They as . . . as the Spirit of God moves 'em. And the Spirit of God didn't move over 'em, dey did poor work. The record's

---

[a] Reverend ———— said that he had "never been in a classroom in his life." Asked how he started preaching, he replied: "Felt the Spirit in me; kept worrying me; wouldn't give me no rest. Spirit had to get out." He has been preaching for 43 years. He has three grown children and married his "last" wife a year ago. He pastors four churches.

[b] He evidently has reference to the story of Elijah found in 1 Kings of the Bible: (1) "And in the thirty and eight year of Asa King of Judah began Ahab the Son of Omri to reign over Israel: and Ahab . . . reigned over Israel in Samaria twenty and two years. . . . And it came to pass, as if it had been a light thing for him to walk in the sins of Jeroboam the Son Nabat, that he took to wife Jezebel and the daughter of Ethbaal . . . and went and served Baal . . . and Ahab did more to provoke the Lord God of Israel to anger" (1 Kings 6:29-33); (2) "And Elijah . . . said unto Ahab . . . there shall not be dew nor rain these years, but according to my word. And the word of the Lord came unto him, saying, 'Get thee hence, and turn thee eastward, and hide thyself by the brook Cherith'" (1 Kings 17:1-4); (3) 1 Kings, chapters 18-22.

[c] Refers to the microphone in front of him.

[d] In difficulty; must get the audience "happy."

right; the Nigger handlin' it may be wrong, but the record's right! Ain't dat right?

The words of the text were spoken by Elijah, the Man of God. Now I wanta contralate [*sic*]; that is, Trust in God. Now if you trust in God, it don't make any difference about the money. Hell may raise and the devil excite, but Jesus dun left on the record that "I'll save my heart's delight." Now, God wouldn't forget His angels, brethren.

Now, Fred, I want you ter help me out now, 'cause I'm in a "tight." And—I don't know—dere's peoples done come for one thing and some come for annuder. Some uv em' done come here looking for mistakes. Well now, I know dat feller ain't gwine be disappointed, 'cause I'se full uv dem.[e] [*Laughter.*] Ain't dat right, brethren? I can't go nowhere unless the Lord God lead me. . . .

The words of the text was expressed by Elijah, the Man of God.[f] And—there was a kingdom. . . . Wife. . . . Kings fighting on the field, Elijah and Ahab. There was a king, wasn't dere, brethren? And he married a woman by the name of Jezebel. And . . . Ahab . . . he married. . . . Ahab, he done turned to his wife, and he cried. . . . Because he was king, she told him, he could have his way.

Remember what Isaiah said, "Yonder come a King . . . goin' ter reign. . . . Ain't never been a king 'cept God. . . ." His King's gwine rule in Judgment.

(I believe I git on this horse this evenin' soon.) [*He means, get everybody aroused, including himself.*] I saw 'im—gittin' time I git movin' along. Ahab went down and tried then to find Naboth in the vineyard. Naboth in his vineyard . . . where he found his father. Naboth said, "No, Lord, I can't labor in the vineyard." But bye and bye old Ahab got mad and went on home. Ain't dat right, brethren? While Ahab had gone home, his wife—he got in the bed, he wouldn't eat nothin' and he wasn't, wouldn't drink nothin'—his wife said to him, "What's the matter with you?"

He said, "I went down to trade with Naboth concerning his vineyard and he wouldn't trade. I offered him 'so much' land; I offered him even 'so much' money." Ehhhhhhh! [*Wild disorder in the audience.*][g] Ahab couldn't get the vineyard.

---

e Refers to the recording of the sermon.

f From this point on, there is so much response from the audience ("Preach it," "Amen," "Gwone, man!" etc.) and so much rhythm, accent and noise that only a few of the minister's words make sense when written down. The excitement is suggestive of that of a crowd during the most exciting moments of a football or baseball game. But the minister and his words are the center of things; the preacher carries the ball.

g There is nothing in the words of the story to arouse the emotions, but the ideas suggested and the rhythmical and spectacular delivery cause emotional outbursts.

Jezebel said, ". . . Don't worry. . . ." Had him taken down the hill and stoned to death. Ain't dat right, brethren? And when Elijah saw . . . was stoned to death . . . He . . . taking Ahab . . . taking Elijah. . . . Ahab had to tell him to go on down in the vineyard. Ain't dat right, brethren? And Jezebel, when she had taken Ahab . . . taken Elijah . . . taken. . . . Take care of his business and leave. When she got on down—old Ahab walking about . . . vineyard and saw Elijah. He said, "Are you really there? Have you found me?"

Elijah said, "Ahab, dat's all right, my God has fought many a battle; ain't never lost one. . . ." You know, God say, "I'm God now . . . , fought on Mt. Zion . . . , lookin' both ways at the same time. I'm God now and I'm Heaven. I'm . . . Champion . . . I'm Commander!" Ain't it right, brethren?

"Old Ahab," as Elijah come down and said, "Old Ahab, . . ." (I got to hurry on and be out the way now. ["*Take yore time, Reverend; ha, ha, ha!*"] People here from Atlanta, Albany, and on out to Cincinnati.) Well, old Ahab—Elijah went down and said, "Oh, man ain't gwine git no rain." Elijah went on, Ahab tried to find him. . . . Ain't dat right, brethren? Ahab. . . . Elijah. . . . But Ahab couldn't find him. Well, bye and bye, God knows where he was. . . . Ain't dat right, brethren? He knows your days; He knows how long you is come; He knows how long — when to pick you up. He knows when to put you down. He told Elijah, "Now you go show yourself to Ahab and I'll give yer the rain; I'll give you the rain and he can't get none,[h] [*Suddenly stops the mad, rhythmical pace and begins talking calmly; it's like the quiet after the storm.*] until he git it from you." [*Pauses, while the audience takes over, bubbling with emotion.*] "Oh, yes! Go show yourself to Ahab and I'll give 'im some rain. Can't give 'im none until y'all show up." Ain't dat right? Oh, yes, sir!

Ahab, you know, he come out and God went on in front of Ahab. And Elijah and the three lambs come on behind. ["*Talk, talk!*"] He met Obadiah. Here's what he done. He met Obadiah. He said, "I knowed 'im." Ain't dat right? And he said, "Ain't dis my Lord?"

Elijah said, "Go tell Ahab I'm on the line." Ain't dat right, brethren?

Obadiah said to 'im, "If I go and tell 'im, de Lord's gwine take care of you, and when Ahab come to find you and can't find you, I guess he'll kill me."

I hear Elijah tell Ahab, "It's sho is God's will, Jehova of whom I stand; I'm gwine show myself to Ahab today." Ain't dat right, brethren?

---

[h] Can't get any rain.

When he met 'im 'round, when he met 'im Elijah told, Ahab said, "Ain't you de one dat's trouble Israel?" Ain't dat right, brethren?

"Ahab," Elijah said, "No, I'm not the one; you in your father's house that was breaking the laws of God. And the God you have's Baal. And Sodom came down here. He got feet and he can't walk; he got a mouth and he can't talk." Ain't dat right, brethren? He got to stay there until you coome and get 'im. And, oh, dat God, he won't do. Ain't dat right, brethren? And Elijah he stood there. And I wanta tell you what he wanta do. He's a child of God. Ain't dat right, brethren? ". . . Open my mouth; I tell 'im I'm a Child of God." Ain't dat right, brethren?

Baal, Baal is the god and—I said the God of Heaven, the Crown— got 450 men, and ain't but one them. . . . Gwine wake up in the morning. Get yourself together. I'm thinkin' right now, Sodom of. . . . Ain't dat right, brethren? Ain't too many to try yo' God. He said, "I'll feed you when you get hungry; I'll water you when you get thirsty." And dey got them out on the ground. They counted about 850 agin one man. Ain't dat right, brethren? And dey begin to call on 'im, "Oh, Baal." I heard. . . . Baal ain't said nothin'. Ain't dat right, brethren?

And Elijah said, "Call a little louder; he might hear you." Then Elijah called on his God. He rained down fire, and Baal's men tried to get away. Elijah said, "Ketch 'em; don't let 'em go." Ain't dat right, brethren? Talkin' about de One. Saw 'im in the battle; He never lost a one. "I'm the One; my word is the light to your feet and a lamp to your pathway. Trust God and I'll be to you anything—Heaven. I ain't gwine away." How long? How long must I work in the vineyard? ["*Preach it!*" *etc.*]

When you worshipin' up a man, ain't nothin' but Baal. Ain't dat right, brethren? When you worshipin' up anything, ain't nothin' but Baal. When you worshipin' up that fine car you got, ain't nothin' but Baal. "Go down and tell men that they must—they kin go to Heaven if dey wants." Ain't nothin' but Baal.

How long? How long must I work in the vineyard? [*For arousing the audience, "How long?" is now like placing a match to gasoline.*] Now God has said, "I am the way, the truth and the light." And God has said that "No man can come to Me"—my Father—"by any door. . . ." [*Words lost in shouts:* "*Stay on dat horse,*" "*Yes,*" *etc.*]

Yonder He come. . . . God Almighty. . . . Thunder, your con- science; lightning in yore hand. . . . Said, "Everybody is gwine ter pray now!" [*This was the climax, the point of highest audience excitement.*] Ain't dat right, brethren? God Almighty! Ain't [*He*] never thundered in yore conscience? Ain't [He] never tore up the plot of ground in yore heart? You gwine 'round here. . . . Sometimes you think one crowd's right and sometimes you think the other crowd's right. And everywhere you go and hear a good meetin', you come back and say, "Them people's right." But how long? . . . Every man is followin' God . . . , callin' God's word. . . . Now don't you? [Pauses. "That's all right." "Yeah!" etc.] Dey don't mind goin' to a burial; know dey Dad's got the key. Dey don't mind goin' in de grave, 'cause dey God done got de. . . . I don't mind deep waters! I don't mind enemies talkin' 'bout me! The Lord can hold me. . . . Ain't dat what He said?

How long? How long? [Pauses. "Dat's all right!" etc.] Tears up the plot of ground of your heart! Put you ter talkin' plain. . . . Knocked Paul down between Jerusalem and Damascus when Paul was a servant of God! That could be said. . . . Paul didn't. . . . [Talking now.] He said, "No man knows a father but the son! No one knows the son but. . . ." ["Everything's all right, Rev. Amos." etc.]

"How long?" said Daniel in the lion's den. . . .

Look here, old man Ahab . . . tried to kill . . . hang old man Modekiah! Ain't dat right, brethren? Old man . . . he couldn't bow down to 'em because it was wrong. Ain't dat right? Way bye and bye the same gallows that Haemon built for Modekiah, he got hung on it himself. Ain't dat right, brethren? And when he hung old man Haemon he had ten sons and they hung dem. It's a bad thing to bother with a Child of God. . . . And the wind hadn't blown. [In his stride again now.] It thundered and no one hadn't heard! The lightning hadn't played a lengthy game across the muddy cloud! Heaven hadn't been burned or hell even warmed up, or even organized. . . . ["Talk now!" "Ride it, Amos." etc.] (Go on, on this thing now.) [He means that, emotionally and rhythmically, he is in his stride. A woman laughs in a high, hysterical voice; everyone seems literally happy; no tears here. This is festive; the audience seemingly admires the preaching as an art rather than a religious message.] Heaven. . . . [From here on, coherence is entirely lost in a whirlpool of emotional ejaculations.]

Sermon VII: "Elijah, the Man of God"[a]

The Lord be good ter us. The text we jest heard was whut yer call "sound doctrin'." Dere wasn't no 'duced mixture in it a-tall. That's whut yer call "right straight from the shoulder." Now, you know, when Reverend ————wuz talkin', showin' yall somethin' happen in de days of old, the oldest temptation. . . . And dem days was, de days of old, jest like de is now. Dere's a crowd wonderin' was Elijah's God, God, and dere's one they wus sayin' dat dey god wuz de God. Folks in dis world de same way now. Isn't it so?

Eh, you know, ye come on down in Christes day when He wuz crucified and put in the grave and the Roman soldiers, yer know, yer know, wanted to to be sure that dey see Him not come out of the grave. And, but, yer know, dey went to sleep that night. When God, when God Almighty's Son got ready to come out of the grave, He busted the grave and blinded dem men and put 'em to death, God bless yo' souls, and come on out. Ain't dat whut He does? And when He come out, you know when He come out, dey tell me dat—er—dem mens, you know—er—didn't see 'im.

I remember when I was called to preach. Dere wuz one crowd preachin' He didn't rise and dere wuz annuder crowd preachin' dat He did rise. . . . Er, my belove', but one day, my belove', [*In stride now.*] I come jest to readin' in de Bible whar it said. . . . [*Coherence and words lost in the rhythm and audience response.*] And I got worried again. I was like the folks comin' from. . . . I said, "Now, whut is God?" I said, "Now, one man said to me, 'You got ter work out yer soul's salvation' and I hear annuder preacher sayin', 'Now, it's by grace, it's by grace, not accordin' to yer work, but accordin' to His own version, the grace given us in Christ Jesus.' " And I sit right there. I come 'st doin' like Job. Jest like . . . [*we*] folks will do. I sit on my little "do nothin'" and wait on time. [*Laughter.*] . . . Got me a three-legged stool and I sot right down, my belov', until God, my belov', visit me one night. And He come to me one night, my belov', I seed a bright light, my belov'. Lit the whole room up. I seed a light shinin' all 'round me, belove'. A little man speak ter me agin and led me ter de church. . . . "Preach de Gospel; . . . great faith in God—Christ, preachin' de

———
[a] The minister was 24; with no formal education. He had been preaching for eight years, and was married for four years. He pastored one church. His sermon tells how he was called to preach.

Word of God." And I wuz wonderin' 'bout dat thing. When I knowed anything, my belove', God done placed me on de wall, done put somethin' down in me. I come'st ter preachin' fer dese old . . . [*Christian*] Folks. And I said, "When de world wuz in grope darkness; when de world. . . ." [*"Hold yer horse, boy!" Women shout for joy. etc.*] Ever since dat day I been standin' right here, my belove'. Ain't been sittin' on dat fence no mo', my belov'.

My belov', ole—ole man Elijah said, my belove', when he got worried, my belove', went out and set on the fence, my belove'. . . . Ain't it so, my belove'? And . . . promised him and said, "Oh, Lord, dey've done kill all our God's folk. . . ." Ain't it so, my belove'? [*Coherence lost in frenzy.*] . . . Just about dat time . . . , "Ten thousand knees has never bowed to Baal . . . ," my belove'. . . . Ain't been worried no mo', my belove'; I'm so glad, my belov', dat God done visit me, my belove'. . . . Talkin' 'bout a savin' God. . . . Oh, God. . . ! On bended knees, won't He tell yer what to do? [*"Preach, sir!" etc.*] . . . My belove'. Yer know, somethin' have to happen—God have ter let somethin' happen! [*"Tear it up!" screams a woman. etc.*] My belov'. . . . And ole Paul said he had a great God. . . . [*"Hold yer horse, boy!" "Talk, hon',"*[b] *yells a woman. "Pull 'em down!' etc.*] The whole world. . . .

. . . The great God of Zion, my belov'. . . . Ole Paul, Abraham's grandson come. . . . "Got six men; dey can't eat and dey can't walk. . . ." Ain't it so, my belov'? . . . All mens got worthy . . . [*sic*] Don't have to be worried 'bout dat no mo'. Paul put dat god out of business. Ain't it so? Reverend ———— dun put 'im out of business. Ain't it so? Ef yer ain't got no eyes, yer can't see dat. Ef yer ain't got no yers, yer can't hear it. Ain't it so, my belove'? He dat got sum yers, let 'im here. . . . Reverend ———— knows. "Ef they believe in God believe also in me. . . ." Almighty God. . . . Ain't dat so? But dey tells me jest before dat happen ole Satan, dey tell me, put de Lord in jail. . . . I'm talkin' 'bout God and His darlin' Son. He is comin' down. . . . "I'm born to die." God bless yo' souls. . . . [*"Dat's good 'nuf!" "Good luck, boy!" etc.*]

✓ ✓ ✓

---

[b] Honey.

SERMON VIII: "PRAY!"[a]

THE TEXT is found in the 5th verse of the 35th chapter of Genesis.[b]
[*He pretends to read from the Bible and from this chapter in Genesis,
but he is really dealing with the story of Joseph, found in the 37th
chapter of Genesis.*]

It's a proud privilege that we have the pleasure to enjoy. Thousands
of people dying by guns, pistols, and other ways. But they are gone.
Some of us could be gone too. Some of us is mean enough to be gone.
[*Laughter.*] We fool around, break peace, feud and won't do right. With
all dis disaster on de world, people ain't concerned a bit. Dey doing
worser.

I done been in de pulpit for four weeks; I been preachin' fer 'em.
(You know I ain't lazy—'till I git lazy.) [*Laughter.*] It don't take all
dat hard preaching ter be saved. I sed to dem Friday night, "De Lord's
gettin' ti'ed of our wicked ways." Don't you know, nobody come to de
mournin' bench now but little chillun? I feel lack de mothers and
fathers, mothers expecially, send 'em dere outta de way, look lack to me.
Dey is comfort' seats; won't be worried wid 'em back yonder. It's lack
dat everywhere I been.

You know how I's feelin'. Tried my best ter git mens here to
preach, so I could sit down and listen. But dey backed out. I gotta go
on four more weeks in de service. De day month, you won't be able to
turn 'round on dat yard out dere. Be here early, to git seats. He's de same
God now. (Goin' ter take my time. Ef I don't raise no bristles, it's all
right wid me. I leave for Alabama next week ter preach.)

I gwine speak today from the 37th chapter of Genesis, the 16th
Verse: "I seek my brethren. . . ."[c] Joseph's jealous brothers. The subject:
Pray! [*The penny collection is taken and the minister lifts his hands
over the money and blesses it*: "*Blessed be the cheerful giver, for he shall
be made fat.*"]

Ef any more comin', we ain't waitin' on 'em. Dey ain't gon' wait
on 'em in dat great gittin' up mornin'. [*Laughter.*] Ain' gon' worry

---

[a] See Sermon III, footnote a, for facts concerning this minister.

[b] "And they journeyed: and the terror of God was upon the cities that were
round about them, and they did not pursue after the sons of Jacob." This second
sermon confirms the suspicion that this minister was unable to read well, a fact
which makes his sermon indeed remarkable.

[c] This time he is correct. The entire verse reads: "And he said, I seek my brethren; tell me, I pray thee, where they feed their flocks."

yo' patience. I been here long enough fer you to know whether I kin [*preach*] or **cain't**.

Ef we ever needed prayer, it's now. I ain't expectin' dumb people to sing, but even dey got ways to make signs. [*The bus arrives outside and people pour into the church.*]

Joseph's brothers sold him as a slave. Jesus said, "Man ought always pray." A man kin work and git over-het, high heat, and faint. Jesus said, "Don't faint; keep prayin'." Ef a man see he gettin' over-het and keep on and fall out dead, I don't think he's in his right mind. Ef you git over-het one time and keep on. . . . How crazy I'd be ter stay here and keep on preachin' till I fall out.

Jealousy is a bad thing. Jealousy is a bad thing. . . . You know, a Christian gits jealous of you some time. That's right! Looks lack you gittin' a little closer to Jesus den him; got a little mo' power then him or her; dey git jealous of you. . . . That's what you call spiritual jealousy. Dey don't want you to do no more fer de Cause than they do. . . . (That's fine to have that. I don't care ef a bunch of yall did that.) 'Feared that one'll do a little more for Him. And ef all er us git dat kind a 'ligion and den do our duty, de church'd be better. Ain't dat right? . . . Some men can't work 'cause de so jealous. All dem don't witness jest make me think dey guilty. [*Laughter.*] . . . When you working, you jest worried in mind. Can't wait till he git home. [*Claps his hands.*] Dat's right! You can tell 'im dat Old Buck ain't been here, but he don't believe you. You women—same dog bit you. It's de same wid you. Some women, you can't please 'em 'bout nothin'.

Joseph's jealous brothers sold him as a slave. And dey'll sell you. . . . Well, how de do it? Dey'll go out and tell de other folks about you what wouldn't know it: "Lord, he shore is mean." . . . Day sold dey brother because, because dey was jealous and dey would like to git rid of 'im. And did git rid of 'im. But our Lord and Savior Jesus Christ had so much power that. . . It's a fine thing to do right.

. . . Our chillun now. A child's a man at twelve years old and a little woman at twelve years old. Dey begin to show up their manhood. Little girl—. But us ruin our little chillun. I'm—I ain't lying to yer. (Come inside, pappy; I want to talk to yer.) We adjust dat little child. "Mamma's little man," "Mamma's little woman." Whar he's a man at? "Mammas little woman." And when she begin to show it, you don't want it. (*Claps his hands.*) You done talked dat in him. Dat's whut you done done. (Yall don't lack dis argerment, but it's good! It's good! And yall know my way and manner; I don't change. . . .)

And old man Jacob had first Jesus. . . . The first prayer [*He refers to a prayer just given. This prayer was recorded, and the speaker co-*

operated by praying directly into the microphone. The minister did not seem to approve of this.[d]] In other words of speaking, some of us speak jest 'cost us got physical livin', good voice, know a little somethin' 'bout the Bible; we say it over in our prayer some time jest to be huard [*sic*] by men. But a prayer is a sincere desire. A prayer come up outta the heart, wid a meaning into it. Yeh, meaning.

Prayer is a light on the bench. When yore way gits dark in this world, travelin' thru in a Christian manner, prayer will shine and den prayer will show you ter git out uv it. Jest use prayer and God— exercising prayer—will lead you out.

The flock, I say. You are a flock. You are a flock uv Christian people. Dat's right! I know sometime tarrer grow 'mong de wheat. Christians are the wheat. So He say, "I gather my wheat. . . ." Tarrer, it burns you. Tear it out. Gits it out from 'mongst the wheat. Can't stand it. You know, it must git out. But the wheat is goin' stay right dere. So it is wid a Christian when de's pure. He'll stay right whar Jesus put 'im. ["*Amen.*"] Some people is tryin' to show you that he's wheat. [*Getting into his stride now.*] But without the Bible, he's gone on out again; go out wid de win'; go out wid de win'; go out wid de win'. So you are the flock. Den, we. . . . the preacher oughta feed you. Ain't dat right? He oughta feed yer wid whut? De Gospel! De truth! Feed yer wid righteousness! I think a feeder, er, ah, oughta feed every sheep. Feed yer. . . .

Yo' own kin folks sometimes kin be your worst worry. Yo' own kin folks do you mo' harm den anybody else. Sometimes we think our best friend is our next door neighbor. (Don't dodge me now.) And sometimes de yo' enemy. ["*Amen.*"] and yo' best friend is over yonder, over yonder somewhere. De, de idea bout it, if dey wuz thieves, dey wuz thieves. . . . De wouldn't let 'em stay here and eat out and let 'em have nothin' ter eat. Dey'd be lookin' out for 'em. . . .

And, so, he was a good sheep. And while feedin'—and his brother —are not goin' back fer—dey, dey, dey, dey fell out wid 'im. And the . . . was rich with the son of. . . . Dey, dey, and, and with the son. . . . And Joseph brought unto his father. . . .

I don't care how humble, how submissive you are, you gwine make a mistake sometimes, because Jesus said, "There's no perfect person on earth." He's right! I don't care how you do, what you do, you gwine err. [*He pronounces this often mis-pronounced word correctly.*] Sometime. Den you kin have the chance to git right. Ef you never do

---

[d] Reverend ———— was, at first, not in favor of our making recordings in his church. The deacons, led by the man who gave the prayer in question, had decided to permit the recordings despite the minister's hesitancy. Also, the prayer had aroused the audience; professional jealousy?

wrong, you don't have no right to pray. Eh? He left His Word, "He that's already clean don't need to be made clean." Not a woman tomorrow gwine take what de wash—gwine take, ain't gwine git dem clean garments and wash 'em. Huh? No, no, honey. (I know whut the spirit's for; I ain' foolin yer. I'm puttin' it jest as plain as you got eyes to see.) Dey, dem, dat wuz clean and ironed and laid back, dey ain't gwine bother dem. But whut dey gwine git [is] dose soiled clothes. Clean clothes. "But whut you gwine git 'em fer?" Because dey dirty; need cleanin'. Ain't dat right? And ef a heart's not right, yo' mind ain't right and yo' conscience ain't right, its a filthy heart, filthy mind, filthy conduct, filthy action, filthy every way. You need to be cleaned up. And prayer will clean you; prayer will clean you. And prayer will show you whar you wrong. I dare you ter pray. Daniel prayed three time a day. . . . He found out that prayer wuz the thing to do. Prayer will reach the Holy Spirit. Prayer. So he, er, er is speakin' with you.

Now Israel loved Joseph. . . . And he tried to serve Jesus. He loved him, Joseph. He loved him. . . . And we ought to love one 'nother as Joseph. . . . We ought to love one 'nother. It's safe that we do. Ef we love one 'nother lack God would have us love one 'nother, dee wouldn't be so much confusion in dis land, wouldn't be so much crime, wouldn't be so much fightin' ef we loved one 'nother.

. . . Joseph, had had a dream one night. [*Now in stride. Rhythm often overcomes coherence.*]. . . . God got a way to let you know. "I'm God." ["*Preach it!*"]. . . . He had a dream one night; didn't he, my friend? . . . And he got up in the mornin' and he look so much in different. He changed—God worked on the soul and He changed 'im up so, makes 'im look different. He make a ugly person look pretty well. Can't He make you pretty, so to speak? . . . . He changed his walk; He changed his condition; He changed his life. ["*Preach it good now!*"] Made him git rid of baggage. He said, "I'm gwine lay dat life down and pick up another life."

In conclusion, brethren,[e] . . . (I'm stayin' by my subject. . . .) And Joseph had a dream. When God give the command, his 'pearance changed. . . . And I heard 'im say, "A clean children."

. . . I thought, I think, my friends, ef you don't have no hopes, hopes in the Fourth Sunday Meetin'—. Everybody pays their fare and git on board, don't yer? Dat's whut I want you ter do now. Git on board and let's pay yer fare: "Amen" and "Thank God" or whatever comes to yer. ["*Preach it good!*"]. . . . See dat feller out dere? He look

---

[e] One reason why a second recording was being made of this minister's preaching was that during the first recording the expression "in conclusion" had misled the author to believe the sermon was closing, with the result that all discs were used up before the climax of the sermon. (Songs, etc., *were* recorded.)

so fat; he look so pretty, and de Spirit won't tech him nowhere?[f] [*Laughter.* "*Amen.*"] Now, brethren, God want us. . . . Don't let dat happen to yer.

Abraham. . . . Eh, chillun. . . . [*Audience intones a moan.*] "Had a dream last night. When I dream last night. . . . Dreamt last night that. . . ." Know what shielded him, my friend? I seen Him. . . . a shield over here one Sunday mornin'. He was takin' on board. And I dream, chillun. . . . [*Audience intones the last two words.*]

God wants his church to stay together. He wants us to love one 'nother. Wants us to stay together. . . . Let me tell you; a hypocrite cannot stand up in the Cause against a Child of God; he's bound to fall. But I'm fixin' to stand right up ter it now, brethren. I don't care what the world say. Day go 'round. . . . Anybody can dance dat wants to dance. . . . Tear it up! [*Tear it up!*" *repeated by the audience.*] (. . . In my argerment!) . . . Whole lots of these black folks won't bow. . . .

The very one you hate in this world, the very one you walk around, the one you gwine scorn, chillun, is the very one gwine fan the flies outta yo' face. That feller you got ter order into yer home, he's gwine walk pass yo' door because he couldn't pass another way. Ehhhhhhhh! . . . Dey ain't had no idea dat dey'd have to come to bow to Joseph. 'Cause dey wuz on a high peak, dey had a high mind. Ain't dat right, brethren? Lawd God Almighty! Dey look at 'im and say, "We'll never bow. He'll never come to rule over us." Didn't dey, my brethren? Oh, John! I heard 'im say in my mind, "A dream is jest another dream." Hum-m-m-m. He told it to his brothers. Said he could stop the sun and the moon. But they can starve him. . . . And they let him starve, my friends. . . . Said, "I'll be with him," my friend; "I put some water at his bedside." In my country, the more you have, the more enemy you have. Hmmmmmmmmm, ehhhhhhhhh, hmmmmmmmmmm! [*Three distinct musical notes. To be repeated again and again.*][g]

Let's keep in my mind, brethren. . . . , "Shall they enter a mother and thy brother and ye come to bow down or serve to thee, the earth." And his brethren. . . .

"Even my brethren?"

He said to him, "His father or servant. . . ." Ain't dat right, my friends? Yes sir! A lot of things that we tell a feller, he forget it. But we are servin' him. . . . Have mercy, my Father. Look at 'im now.

And while movin' on, brethren, his brethren—and God heard— said (his son, his brethren went to sleep, his father's son. . . .): "Oh,

---

[f] He pointed through the window to the author.

[g] Only the recording can describe this accurately.

Father, I don't want dat ole dreamer to go wid us. Oh, Father, oh, Father, keep him home; we don't wont 'im."

. . . Sometimes you have to tell a person somethin' and you know dey don't lack it. . . . And he ain't gwine pay yer no attention. . . . I see Joseph gwine to his brethren. . . . On top uv the mountain jest before the sun go down. And take the partin' message of God's Word. . . . Dey worried. Don't it worry you, my friend? . . . . Ain't it true, my brethren? . . . . Hold the line! Hold the line! ". . . . Oh, Joseph, Oh, Joseph, I want you to go down. . . ." God Almighty! God Almighty! ". . . . And I want you to bring some of your folks." Ain't dat right, brethren? . . . . And Joseph told his brothers. . . . But Jesus told 'im, "Can't do you no harm." [*"Preach it, sir!"*] . . . Ain't He all right, brethren?

Ehhhh, Lord. [*Intoned.*] I jest feel lack saying sometime, "I lost both of my hands, both of my hands; let me git my hand. [*Intoned.*] Need ter look for 'em." Don't you tell 'im something sometime? Have mercy, my Father!

I seed 'im comin' at the foot of the mountain. Heaven! [*Intoned.*] . . . Have mercy now, my Father! . . . I seed 'im, brethren. My Lord! And he closed the gate. . . . I seed 'im about this time looking. [*"Looking."*] When you ask God for a blessing; don't you look for it? Looking. [*From here on, the audience repeats this word whenever the minister uses it.*] Looking! Watch some uv us miss our blessing; we run off before God git there. Looking! Sittin' there looking for Him, brethren. . . . Heard one say, "I tell you whut we do. Let's take that coat off Him and let's go kill a little sheep and let's put that blood from that sheep. . . ." (Anything livin' or human got blood in it. Can't live without blood. You know when a man's cut. . . . , he must bleed. Ain't dat right, my friends?) . . . And dey took that coat off and they rolled it in that blood. And then they let him down. ". . . . Let's perish 'im." You know that, brethren. ". . . Hide 'im." They thought that the only way the blood cry against. . . . But, brethren, any little thing you do to one 'nother is gwine come against you, get you, my brethren. Oh, Jesus! I looked down the road. . . . And trade was sure. They went out and sold him.

Pray! [*"Pray!" from the audience. This word from now on is also intoned whenever the minister uses it.*] Pray! A praying man or woman won't do you no harm. Pray! (I believe yall done give out! I been preachin' so long. . . .) [*"Preach it!" "Preach it good now!"*] Pray! in Jesus, and . . . when you feeling bad, pray right on. When you feeling lonely, pray right on. Pray! [*Sings it.*] Pray! Pray! God will answer your prayer when you pray out your heart, won't He?

. . . He rat at yo' hand; He rat at yo' feet; He rat at yo' mouth. Pray! Pray! You pray in your bed. You pray riding your automobile. You pray when . . . Pray! Pray! . . . When you start praying, de people'll come in, won't de, chillun Pray! . . . Jest sit down and lock the door. [*"Yeb" comes in regular after-beat time to the minister's rhythm, from one man in the audience; this fills in the time in the minister's rhythmical pauses and sounds like a man driving a mule, trying to make him go faster and faster.*] So jest don't lock de door. Go on your knees. . . . I say, don't lock de door. For prayer's sake, brethren. . . I say, don't lock de door. For prayer's sake, brethren. . . A prayer's a light fer yer. . . . Pray! Pray! Lord! Lord! Can't make a good deacon undoubt yer a prayin' man; can't make a good Mother of the Church undoubt yer a prayin' woman. You can't do nothin' unless you a prayin' person. Pray! Pray! [*Climax. A woman screams and shouts. Another woman calls, "Preach it ter us!"*] . . . . Daniel prayed three time a day. . . . Ain't it so, my brethren? . . . And Jesus said to 'im — ain't dat right, my brethren? . . . : "Hallowed be Thy name." Jesus, His name had charm over death. Spit out. . . . Eh, Lordy! Ehhhhh! [*Pauses.*]

[*Talking calmly now.*] You ought to pray. [*Falling action. The emotions are calming down, but unwillingly.*] Pray! to overcome yer enemy. Pray! . . . . At your feet. Pray! . . . Lack yo' prayin' know how. Pray! Pray! Till you see Him for yourself. Prayer'll make you move, won't it? Prayer'll make you shout! Prayer'll make you cry! Pray! Pray! when it's raining. [*"Yes, God!"*] Pray! when it thunders! Pray when de moon shines! Pray! when everything's all right! Pray! when de sun's arisin'! Pray! when you in Jail, jest keep prayin'. Paul and Silas jest kept praying. Pray!

✓ ✓ ✓

III.   Let My People Go

In speaking of the preachers of the Reformation Period, G. C. Lee makes this pertinent observation:

> . . . It is impossible either to understand their work or to recognize their comparative merits without viewing them in connection with the people among whom they worked and the great movement in which they took part. For the preacher and the people are bound up together most intimately, so that there is no more accurate test of the depth of the religious life of a community or an era then the sermons that are delivered in public worship. . . . His [*the preacher's*] message is influenced and shaped by the influences that affect his auditors. . . . He may at times be a leader; he may be able to mould the minds of his hearers; but he is rarely able to rise far above those to whom he ministers.[1]

If this be true of ordinary preaching, it is even truer of the folk-like and emotional old-fashioned Negro preaching. To understand the sermons recorded in Macon County, one must consider the origin and development of the basic ideas and characteristics of this preaching.[2]

This leads to the two basic causes of old-fashioned Negro preaching in the "Black Belt" before the Civil War, and in Macon County today: (a) the mixing of the early American and the African religious practices; (b) the need of a people in bondage for a medium of escape.

The sermons of the previous chapter still ringing in his ears, the reader will be led (1) to consider historically each of these two basic causes, how each has played a vital role in the creation of old-time Negro preaching; (2) to examine a list of the characteristics of the original[3] old-time Negro preaching. In the chapters to follow, using this knowledge of the original old-time Negro preaching as a standard, the author will discuss old and new influences in the Macon County sermons.

I.   The Early-American and African Heritages

The strange rhythmical preaching of Sermon vi[4] is puzzling. Indeed it should be, for the preacher is a living example of the sudden crossing of two religious cultures: one, greatly advanced; the other, quite primitive.[5]

Part I seeks to show that the mixing of American and African backgrounds of religious practices produced old-time Negro preaching. This will be done (1) by considering the very earliest American background (until the coming of Negro slaves); (2) by considering the African religious background of the slaves; (3) by showing the actual mixing of the cultures; and (4) by observing the advent of the Negro church.

THE AMERICAN HERITAGE—It appears that there was Christian Civilization in America (on the Island of Greenland) as early as the 12th century.[6] But America had little pulpit eloquence until the 16th century, although it is said that Columbus's first act, in 1492, of kneeling to thank God for a safe journey might be considered as preaching of a sort; Columbus was performing the duty of a preacher at that time. It is known that, on returning to America in 1494, Columbus brought with him twelve priests.[7]

In the 16th century, Spanish Catholic priests wrote America's first real chapter in pulpit eloquence.[8] This was a chapter of humble missionary teaching.

Mention should be made of the coming of various orders of Catholic missionaries (Dominicans, Jesuits, Franciscans), but it is the 17th century that marks the significant period in the development of the American heritage of preaching, especially as it was to influence Negro preaching. (Negroes were first brought to America in 1619.[9]) In this century there were two centers of preaching in America: in Virginia and in New England.

Preaching activities in Virginia[10] are very important, because this state fell within the "Black Belt" section, where were many newly arrived African slaves.[11] The following is a list of religious practices which first impressed the Negro:

1. The church was considered the means of purifying devils.
2. Governer Dale had the authority to put to death any person who spoke against the Holy Trinity . . . or who uttered blasphemy or unlawful oaths.
3. It was the law that a person should be publicly whipped three times for behaving disrespectfully to any minister in the settlement.
4. A person who was persistently absent from Divine Service was punished with a fine, with whipping, or six months in galley service or even death.[12]

The Negro slave faced this type of religion in the beginning. But he had his own African religious heritage.[13] Even if the African did not bring his old religious practices to America[a] he certainly did bring with him his religious temperament. As Dr. Park concludes, "The temperament is African, but the tradition is American."[14] Professor Good speaks even more specifically when he says:

> Negroes have not lived in this country long enough to destroy the customs of the race developed in Africa. They hand down from generation to generation many of the customs and superstitions of the race, though most of them are greatly modified by life in the United States.[15]

Dr. DuBois tells us very definitely that the American Negro's religion was influenced by African practices:

> It [the Negro church] was not at first by any means a Christian Church, but a mere adaptation of those heathen rites which we roughly designate by the term Obe Worship, or "Voodoism." Association and missionary effort soon gave these rites a veneer of Christianity, and gradually, after two centuries, the Church became Christian. . . . , but with many of the old customs still clinging to the services. It is this historic fact that the Negro Church of today bases itself upon the sole surviving social institution of the African fatherland, that accounts for its extraordinary growth and vitality.[16]

It is significant that Herskovits[17] says the African influence in America is strongest in the South and especially in Georgia.

THE AFRICAN HERITAGE—What was the African temperament? To answer this question one must consider the characteristics of African religious life.

The conception of God comes first to one's attention. The African thinks of God as one who "has created his people and then [has] gone off and left them to the mercies of the spirits, good or bad."[18] (This suggests a basis for superstition in the African heritage.) The following quotation shows that all Africans believe in God:

> Standing in the village street, surrounded by a company whom their chief has courteously summoned at my request, when I say to him, "I have come to speak to your people," I do not need to begin by telling them that there is a God. Looking on that motley

---

[a] Contra John Hope Franklin, *From Slavery to Freedom*, Knopf, New York, N. Y., 1947, p. 40. The University of Chicago published, November 1949, Lorenzo Dow Turner's *Africanisms in the Gullah Dialect*, which uncovers the use of 4,000 African words, names and numbers by Negroes in the United States today.

assembly of villagers,—the bold, gaunt cannibal with his arma-
ment of gun, spear, and dagger . . . — , I have yet to be asked,
"Who is God?"[19]

They believe in God, in one God.[20] But they think that this God is
"absent and indifferent to his people, having left them to spirits."[21]

The African's belief in spirits shows the possibility of an imaginative and superstitious temperament. He believes in many kinds of
spirits. Mary Kingsley says of these spirits: "Their number is infinite
and their powers varied as human imagination can make them."[22]
In many instances, the spirits of the African's religion are concerned
with death. In some places, "it is also customary to bury implements,
weapons, etc.,"[23] for the use of the departed and the various other
spirits with whom his spirit will unite. This great belief in spirits
tends to produce almost constant fear in the Negro:

> Living thus in the presence of multitudes of spirits, which are
> disembodied and therefore ubiquitous, and which seem to retain
> their consciousness and memories of past experiences, the Negro
> is in constant terror lest he may be harmed by some spirit, whom
> he may have injured while in embodied human form. This con-
> stant element of fear has wrought greatly upon the emotions of
> the Negro. . . . , thus explaining in part his highly emotional
> temperament.[24]

Thus, fear and a highly emotional nature become elements of the
African temperament. But the main cause for the Negro's fear and
highly emotional nature are to be found in his system of fetich:

> If one's God is an absentee God, having left one to the mercy
> of the spirits, and if one is surrounded by many multitudes of
> such spirits, good or bad, which may do some good or work one
> great harm, it would be the natural bent of the human mind to
> find a way to establish friendly relations with the good spirits
> and to ward off the power of evil spirits. This the African does
> through his system of fetich. A fetich is any rag, string, stick,
> tooth, piece of wood. . . in which a spirit has been coaxed to take
> up its abode.[25]

The African associates death with the evil spirits. He rarely ever
believes that death comes of a natural cause. When a person dies, the
family begins to search for the evil persons who caused the spirits
("who-dooed" today) to bring about the death. When the culprits are
located, "they are murdered or sometimes given the poison ordeal which
is usually effective in proving their guilt, for they die, and is not that
positive proof that they were guilty?"[26] This custom is important. It il-

lustrates how the chief can easily trump up a charge against any person whom he fears or hates. The ambitious man is afraid for his life; the man who dares to change existing conditions is killed. Therefore, another element of the African temperament was to accept the existing order, to refrain from speaking against the evils of society.

Another aspect of the African's religion which tended to subjugate the people was the position of the witch doctor or medicine man, "so called because he concocts the fetich which is used to cure sickness and drive away evil spirits which cause disease."[27] He is next to the chief in power; he has the power of life and death over everyone in the tribe — with the exception of the chief.

In the African's religion there is little emphasis upon morals, because God is absent.[28] This becomes significant when it is observed later in this work that some Negro ministers today seemingly are without morals.

Weatherford shows that the African developed emotionally because he lived in the Banana Zone, where men did not need to work and plan in order to live.[29] He states:

We should expect then that those persons who lived in the hot climate of Africa where fruit and vegetables grew in abundance would normally be less developed mentally than those who lived in a climate where foresight and the struggle for existence favored those who had a higher degree of intelligence and eliminated all other. . . . The coast tribes of the equatorial region and the tribes of the humid river deltas have through long centuries of ease and sloth developed a race of low mentality. . . . This lack of mental stimulus had a very decided influence on emotional reactions. . . . Where the mind has little variety of activity it develops a feeble power of self-control. The native emotions, therefore, have primary away and are left uncontrolled by the higher and stabilizing reasoning faculties.[30]

Of the mental traits of primitive man, Boas says, "Lack of logical connections, lack of control of will, are apparently two of its [*the mind's*] fundamental characteristics in primitive society. In the formation of opinions belief takes the place of logical demonstration. The emotional value of opinions is great and consequently they quickly lead to actions."[31] And Davenport shows that this primitive mind becomes illogical and superstitious, and fear thus enters as a dominant influence.[32] "The progress from brute to man is characterized by nothing so much as by the decrease in proper occasions for fear."[33]

There were many reasons why the African should be highly emotional and possessed with great fear. There were wild beasts, insects, crocodiles, diseases; he felt helpless in the the face of the powers of nature.

Thus, his form of government, environment, and religious beliefs made it impossible for the African to gain recognition . . . as a speaker and leader within the tribe. The chief ruled his tribe, but even he was unable to achieve recognition beyond the domain of the particular tribe, because of the difficulties of communication, the wars, the jungle, and the fear of the natives.[34]

The African environment was most important in preparing the Negro for his future religious adjustment in America — with fear, superstition, imagination, and death being dominant characteristics. His African environment, says John Murray,[35] "was entirely barbaric . . . the gloom and darkness of the jungle . . . cannibalism. . . . Fear and superstition were jungle rulers. There was nothing more final, depressing, and unnerving than *death* . . .;[36] his imagination and interest in religion were stimulated. The jungle background of fear tended to develop the *emotionalism* and *superstition* of the Negro to such a high degree *that it far over-shadowed his ability to reason.* As a result, *shouting, singing, emotionalism,* and *bombastic display* made a powerful appeal to the Negro. Since the African audience delighted in emotionalism, the early *speeches were largely emotional* and *seldom followed a logical pattern.*" As a result of this environment, then, the African's religious beliefs developed accordingly:

1. that spirits guided and punished their actions;

2. that there was a Supreme Being.

3. that there were evil spirits, which religion and the medicine man could drive away.[37]

The Negro in Africa had (1) a tribal government; (2) little chance for self-expression[38] (no one dared question the chieftain); and (3) little opportunity for logical speaking because *people in bondage* were given little opportunity to deliberate over their problems. Thus, both because of the lack of freedom of speech and the barbaric environment and superstition which strengthened the intense emotional nature of the Negro, African speaking became *rhythmical, emotional,* and *bombastic* (which pleased the African), but *logical appeal had little influence* in changing his ideas. And *every Negro was an active participant* in religious expression and worship.[39]

The African's speech occasions and his speeches as such, were few: (1) preparing for war; (2) birth; (3) marriage; and (4) burial. These were ceremonial occasions and *"shouting, noise, dancing,* and *festivity* prevailed at these times."[40] The medicine man and the chief were often the most popular speakers.[41] There are practically no records of speeches, with the exception of a supposed speech by an early African named Adahoonzon.[42]

The Negro slaves, then, who found themselves in the midst of early American religious practices and beliefs, possessed also an African religious heritage. This summary might be made of the African heritage:

1. "Shouting, speaking, and persuasion actually existed in the heart of Africa. . . .
2. "The tribal form of government and the rigid customs tended to prevent the rise of many speakers in a tribe.[43]
3. "The African audience was highly emotional, uneducated, superstitious, and imaginative.
4. "The purposes of speeches usually were to impress and to persuade.
5. "African speakers were effective in their delivery and in securing results."[44]

It is reasonable to assume that these early characteristics of African speaking have left their mark on Negro preaching;[45] the African had some background when he was brought to the New World. Now, to see how the African heritage and the developing American heritage combined to form the American Negro's original old-fashioned preaching.

PREPARATION FOR THE MIXING OF THE AMERICAN AND THE AFRICAN HERITAGES[46] — During the early years of slavery, a transitional period in Negro preaching, the American Negro slave, just from Africa, was too afraid to lift his voice. Millions of Negroes[47] had been taken from Africa and had been thrown into a new environment. The temperate climate of America replaced the torrid climate of Africa; woods and forests replaced the jungle growths; government of the tribe was destroyed entirely; slavery and serfdom replaced the uncertain but independent life; broken English replaced the native African language. The slave had been brought from a hunting and fishing stage of civilization, which was thousands of years old (as was the civilization of the early Britons a long time before the coming of the Romans) and had been thrown suddenly into a new world, a new civilization, which boasted the results of the contributions of thousands of years. This new American civilization (from Europe) was 2,000 years ahead of that of primitive Africa. The slave was told to find his place in this world.[48] And he did, but perhaps it was inevitable that in attempting to find his place in religion the Negro developed an African version of American religious practices.

If Africa had been a primitive civilization for the Negro, America offered him an even darker future. He might have disintegrated mentally

[59]

or revolted physically[b] — and perished.[49] But he possessed a religious temperament which gave "him *faith and a means of expression for his over-wrought feelings. . . .*"[50] The basic religious beliefs and superstitions of the Africans were easily converted into Christian doctrine, and in America the Negro came under the influence of the colonial preacher.[51]

What was this influence of the colonial preacher? Mention has been made of two American colonies in the 17th century in which preaching was centered: New England and Virginia. The majority of the slaves resided in the latter colony, and it is significant that the preaching of this colony *laid emphasis upon morality and social obligations and religious fidelity to the teachings of the established church.*[52] Politics did not enter the pulpit here (unlike New England), but many preachers in Virginia were *"leaders of men and communities"* and were not so much concerned with politics.[53] That was American preaching during the 17th century. But a new spirit was to enter the pulpit.

THE GREAT AWAKENING (1714-1770)[54] — The Negro slave had been learning much, but the preaching influence of the 18th century climaxed and crystallized Negro old-fashioned preaching. Why? Because a type of religious worship which was closest to what he had known in Africa became the vogue. There came a change in spirit and a deep discontent with the stereotyped and formal religion which had become the type; *fervent, powerful, evangelistic*[55] preaching[56] entered the picture. The influence of this kind of preaching spread. In 1735, a revival broke out which showed many of the extreme *physical manifestations* that were to become common as the movement continued; this extreme emotional excitement in religious worship was popularized in both America and in Europe by George Whitefield.[57]

George Whitefield "landed in Savannah [*Georgia*] in 1738. This was the first of Whitefield's work in America."[58] After he labored three months in Georgia, building and endowing an orphan-house, he returned to England to obtain priest orders for himself and funds for his orphans in Georgia. Bacon continues the story:

> Being detained in the kingdom by an embargo, he began that course of evangelistic preaching which continued on either side of the ocean until his death, and which is without parallel in church history. His incomparable eloquence thronged the parish churches, until the churches were closed against him. . . . Then he went into the open field in the service, as he said, of him "who had a mountain for his pulpit, and the heavens for his sounding-board. . . ." Multi-

---

[b] There *were* many revolts: "Over 250 slave revolts or attempted slave revolts took place in the United States prior to 1860" (John M. Lofton, Jr., "Denmark Vesey's Call to Arms," *Journal of Negro History*, vol. 33, no. 4, October 1948, p. 396). But the Negro slaves did *not* revolt enmasse.

tudes of every rank thronged him; but especially the heathenized and embruted colliers near Bristol listened to the unknown gospel, and their awakening feelings were revealed to the preacher by his observing the white gutters made by the tears that ran down their grimy faces. At last the embargo was raised, and . . . he sailed in August, 1739, for Philadelphia, on his way to Georgia. His fame had gone before him, and the desire to hear him was universal. The churches would not contain the throngs. . . . Seeing the solemn eagerness of the people everywhere to hear him, he determined to make the journey to Savannah by land, and again he turned the long journey into a campaign of preaching. Arriving at Savannah in January 1740, he laid the foundation of his orphan-house, "Bethesda,"[59] and in March was again on his way northward on a tour of preaching.[60]

George Whitefield was the greatest representative of the pulpit of the Great Awakening. It is said that a play, "The Minor," was written in England and played at Drury Lane to ridicule and burlesque his manner of preaching, but his success both in England and America was tremendous. Benjamin Franklin says that as many as 30,000 people were at one time swayed by his eloquence in an out-of-doors crowd in Philadelphia.[61] Franklin goes on to describe one of Whitefield's sermons: "His delivery . . . was so improved by frequent repetition that every accent, every emphasis, every modulation of the voice, was so perfectly well-turned that without being interested in the subject, one could not help being pleased with the discourse; a pleasure of much the same kind with that received from an excellent piece of music."[62] The following analysis[63] of the secret of Whitefield's power is suggestive of old-fashioned Negro preaching:

1. His appearance was impressive;[64] he was slightly above middle height.
2. His voice was rich and clear and had a wonderful range. Whitefield had perfect voice modulation. He himself said that the Christian world was in a dead sleep and that nothing but a loud voice can awaken them out of it.
3. His action was persuasive. He was instinctively dramatic in every gesture; he was a master at playing upon every emotion of his hearers.
4. His power of vivid description was adapted to his audience.
5. His intense conviction and his sense of being Divinely commissioned were persuasive.
6. His delivery was without a manuscript.[65]

This was the new type of preaching which the Negro slaves heard. The influence of Whitefield's mode of preaching even spread to "cold"

New England. White New Englanders found themselves moved by such emotional preaching. In fact, if the shouting heard on the records of Macon County seems strange consider the following description of the reaction of a New England audience to a sermon by Jonathan Edwards:

> As the sermon proceeded many of the people slid forward on the edge of the pews, in their intense interest. The *shrieks* and *out-cries* arose from the different parts of the congregation. Some *nervous* individuals[66] actually gripped the pews to keep from sliding into the hell that Edwards had pictured directly underneath them. . . . And there was actually so much confusion that Edwards had to request the people to remain silent so he could finish his sermon.[67]

Such were the religious influences with which the Negro came into contact during the 17th and 18th centuries: (1) an emphasis upon morality and social obligations and religious fidelity to the teachings of the established church — no emphasis upon politics in the church; (2) extremely emotional preaching.[68] This was in keeping with the Negro's African religious practices to no small degree. But how did the Negro get a chance to hear early American preaching? Why did the slaves become Christians?

ENCOURAGING THE MIXING OF THE AMERICAN AND THE AFRICAN HERITAGES — At first, the Christianizing of the Negro was not given much consideration. But much work was soon carried on by such organizations as the *Society for the Propagation of the Gospel in Foreign Parts,* which was established in London in 1701 "to do missionary work among the heathen,[69] especially the Indians and the Negroes."[70] The movement spread to the New Country. "In 1784 Bishop Porteus published an extensive plan for the more effectual conversion of the slaves, contending that 'despicable as they are in the eyes of man they are, nevertheless, the creatures of God.' "[71] Upon such a premise the Christianizing of the slaves progressed — first, in the Colony of South Carolina, under the Reverend Samuel Thomas of Goose Creek Parish, where slaves were taught the scriptures and were baptized.[72] And on "up until the time of the Revolutionary War, the religious welfare of the Negro followed that of the whites."[73] The Negro was being taught and instructed in the ways of the Christian religion, but he took no active part in the church, although organizations such as the Quakers, the Baptists, and the Presbyterians later "accepted the Negroes as human beings and undertook to accord them the privileges of men. . . ."[74]

It was the religious beliefs of the Methodists and the Baptists that gave the Negro religious expression,[75] because the preaching of these groups appealed to his emotional nature; "and it was not until the time of the emotional preaching of Whitefield (1714-1770)[76] that large conversions were made among the Negroes. The preachers of the Methodist and Baptist churches carried their personal message into every town and hamlet. The itinerant preachers visited the log and mud cabins and placed the Negro on a plane of equality, and at the same time *appealed to his deep emotional nature.* This religious movement and revival captivated the Negro, gave him a new social position, and became the impelling force in assisting him to adapt himself to conditions in America.["77]

It is not strange that the slaves welcomed Christianity (especially of the Methodists and the Baptists[78]), for "to these Africans, cut off from their country and their former tribesmen, it gave a historical tradition, a literature, and a background all at once. They were too far scattered and dispersed to retain much of their language, myths, and traditions, or to keep alive their African culture. Now Christianity with its wealth of historical tradition was there. Both the Old and the New Testament offered much with which they could immediately identify themselves. . . ."[79] The religion offered to them [*to the Negroes*] was embraced with little hesitation or question. And from this somewhat grim Protestantism of the 18th and 19th centuries the Negro's religion of the present day derives."[80]

There was but one step remaining to complete the evolution to old-time Negro preaching: to let Negroes themselves preach Christianity as they now understood it. This, too, came to pass. The Methodists, Presbyterians, and the Baptists soon permitted Negroes to expound the scriptures; however, to many sects, this was "violating laws of long standing, prohibiting Negro ministers from exercising their gifts."[81] But the fight to permit the Negro to preach was won. By 1763, Jonathan Boucher could say boldly: "It certainly is not a necessary circumstance essential to the condition of the slave that he be not indoctrinated. . . . You may unfetter them from the chains of ignorance, you may emancipate them from the bondage of sin, the worse slavery to which they could be subjected; and they shall be delivered . . . into the glorious liberty of the children of God."[82] And thus, in time, the Negro preacher too found his place, as if in fulfillment of the Bible itself:

Whosoever shall call on the name of the Lord shall be saved.
How then shall they call on him in whom they have not believed?
And how shall they believe in him whom they have not heard?
And how shall they hear without a preacher?[83]

THE OLD-TIME NEGRO PREACHER — Indeed, the Negroes did get their own preachers. As James Weldom Johnson points out:

The history of the Negro preacher reaches back to Colonial days.

[63]

Before the Revolutionary War, when slavery had not yet taken its more grim and heartless economic aspects, there were famed black preachers who preached to both whites and blacks. George Liele was preaching to whites and blacks at Augusta, Georgia, as far back as 1773, and Andrew Bryan at Savannah a few years later. The most famous of these earliest preachers was Black Harry, who during the Revolutionary Period accompanied Bishop Asbury as a drawing card and preached from the same platform with other founders of the Methodist Church. Of him, John Ledman in his *History of the Rise of Methodism in America* says, "The truth was that Harry was a more popular speaker than Mr. Asbury or almost anyone else in his day."[84]

Black Harry had learned to preach by going about with Bishop Asbury. As Woodson points out, he "learned from him [*Bishop Asbury*] to preach more forcefully than Asbury himself."[85] Woodson continues with an interesting description of Black Harry and an amusing incident about him:

Harry was "small, very black, keen-eyed, possessing great volubility of tongue, and although illiterate so that he could not read," was one of the most popular preachers of that age [*the age of the original old-time Negro preaching*]. Upon hearing Harry preach, Dr. Benjamin Rush pronounced him the greater orator in America. Desiring Harry to accompany him in 1782, Bishop Asbury made the request, saying that the way to have a very large congregation was to give out that Harry was to preach, as more would come to hear Harry than to hear Bishop Asbury. On one occasion in Wilmington, Delaware, where the cause of the Methodist was unpopular, a large number of persons came out of curiosity to hear Bishop Asbury. But, as the auditorium was already taxed to its fullest capacity, they could only hear from the outside. At the conclusion of the exercises, they said, without having seen the speaker: "If all Methodist preachers can preach like the Bishop, we should like to be constant hearers." Someone present replied: "That was not the Bishop, but the Bishop's servant that you heard." This to be sure, had the desired effect, for these inquiries concluded: "If such be the the servant, what must the master be?"[86]

The authenticity of this story cannot be vouched for, but it would seem that this old-time Negro preacher did have his good points as a preacher.

As the story of Black Harry shows, these old-time Negro preachers were encouraged to go to greater extremes emotionally because the white people seemed to enjoy this method of preaching,[87] John Jasper, "the typical representative of the old school"[88] of Negro preaching, "became famous because of his sensational methods and because he was exploited by members of the white race."[89] Jasper often spoke along with white ministers[90] and the more sensational he was, the more recognition he and the Negro audience received. He was best at funerals, where "his vivid and spectacular eloquence resulted in an uproar of *groans, shouts, fainting women,* and *people who were swept to the ground to lie in a trance-like state sometimes for hours.*"[91] How the whites must have leaned closer to hear Jasper tell of his conversion to religion:

> I was seekin' God six long weeks — jes' cause' I was sich a fool I couldn't see de way. De Lord struck me fus' on Cap'tal Squar', an' I left thar badly crippled. One July morning' somethin' happen'd. I was a tobarker-stemmer — dat is, I took de tobarker leaf, and tor'd de stem out, an' dey wan't no one in dat fac'tory could beat me at dat work. — 'Fore I kno'd it, de light broke; I was light as a feather; my feet was on de mount'n; salvation rol'd like a flood thru my soul, an' I felt as if I could 'nock off de fact'ry roof wid my shouts. — just den de holin-back straps of Jasper's breachin' broke, an' what I tho't would be a whisper was loud enuf to be hearn clean 'cross Jeems River to Manchester. One man sed he tho't de fact'ry was fallin' down; all I know'd I had raise my fust shout to de glory of my redeemer.[92]

A summary of Jasper's preaching is a summary of all old-time Negro preaching of this period:

> Jasper had the ability to make a story *familiar* and *vivid* to an audience by putting it in language easily understood by the listener. Jasper was always *familiar* and *concrete* in his use of material. Often his sermons consisted of the *stringing together of picture after picture,* but at the same time he was keenly logical and tactful, and often made frequent use of *humor* in delivering his sermons. It was, however, in the face of opposition that he most excelled since his keen *invective* and *satire* were skillfully used to crush opposition. . . . Effective speech is that which brings results — even though its form may be crude. Jasper's *oratory swayed, impressed,* and often *convinced* those who came to ridicule. He possessed a great imagination combined with logic although his source of information was, for the most part, restricted to the Bible. Doubt never troubled the mind of Jasper, for the literal word of the Bible was his test, and he implicitly believed in the Bible as the word of God. With unshaken faith he enthusiastically preached from his sincere convictions, for who could doubt the direct word of God?[93]
>
> Jasper was of the old school of preachers who spurned the new pulpit manners. He sang the old revival songs, and he steeped himself in the teachings of the Bible. He preached from a stock of sermons, often repeating them over and over. Jasper is typical of many of the earlier Negro preachers who felt the call to preach and heeded the call.[94]

[65]

Jasper's delivery was ungrammatical and awkward, and he deliberately made his sermons spectacular.[95] He stuck to the old methods of speaking, and to the old dialects and manners.[96]

That was the old-time Negro preacher. He was illiterate; he reflected the African heritage. Rules of logic and education did not hamper him; his sermons were the product, for the most part, of his imagination. For him, classical standards of rhetoric did not exist;[97] his speeches were *imaginative, emotional,* and *filled with imagery;* word pictures became the keys to the minds of the Negro audience. The speaker's information came from life-experiences; therefore, his speeches possessed concreteness drawn from experience, not abstract ideas from books. This use of imagery and concrete illustrations is illustrated in the following sermon in which Jasper speaks of the plagues which God sent upon Pharaoh, the Egyptian ruler:

I tell yer my brudderin, dis skeme did de business for P'haro! He cum from ridin' one day' and wen he get in de pallis de hole hall is full uv frogs. Dey iz scamperring' and hoppin' roun' tel dey farly kivur de groun' and Pharo' put his big foot an' squash'd em' on de marbul flo'. He run inter his parler tryin' ter git away frum 'em. Dey wuz all erroun'; on de fin chars, on de lounges, in de pianner. It shocked de king til' he git sick. Jes' den de dinner bell ring an' in he go ter get his dinner. Ha, Ha, Ha! It's frogs, frogs, frogs all arroun'! Wen he sot down he felt de frogs squirmin' in de char; de frogs on de plates, squatting upon de meat, playin' ovur de bred, an' wen he pick up his glas ter drink de watur de little frogs is swimmin' in de tumber. Wen he tried to stick up a pickful his fork stuck in a frog; he felt him runnin' down his back. De queen she cried, and mos' fainted an' tol' Pharo' dat she wud quit de pallis befo' sundown if he didn't do somethin' ter cler dem frogs out'n de house.[98]

John Jasper used ideas within the experience of the audience. He is an actor dramatizing the story of Pharaoh. The stage is set with frogs, plates, dinner bells, bread, meat; every object is familiar to the audience. At the same time he tells a simple story about Pharaoh, who takes on flesh and blood and lives. "At the same time Jasper in his sermons would philosophize and point out the practical moral which would benefit the congregation."[99]

It was John Jasper who linked old-time Negro preaching with the newly organized Negro churches, "which brought a more polished and educated ministry. His death marked the close of the old type of Negro oratory. . . ."[100] (The close of the *original period* of old-time Negro preaching, it should be said, for the sermons of Macon County prove that this type of Negro preaching has not yet disappeared entirely.)

[66]

THE ESTABLISHMENT OF THE NEGRO CHURCH — A sign that a new development in Negro preaching was entering was the establishment of the Negro Church.[101] The original old-fashioned preaching had been closely connected with and conditioned by white people.[102] The beginning of the Negro Church was one of a series of steps that were to end gradually the great period of old-time Negro religion and to bring to a close a long line of old-time Negro preachers.[103] The Civil War, freedom of the slaves, Reconstruction, and education were to be the great factors in the decline of original old-time Negro preaching.

SUMMARY — The strange rhythmical, extremely emotional, vividly narrative, simple, Biblical, epideictic, at times almost incoherent preaching of Sermon VI[104] and the puzzling audience response and reaction, do not require far-fetched and ultra-profound explanations. These are merely the manifestations of the mixing of American and African heritages of religion. Old-fashioned Negro preaching (whether the original type of this preaching[105] or the Macon County type) is the result of the mixing of two religious cultures: African[106] and early America.

2. A PEOPLE IN BONDAGE

HEAR the Sermon VI records[107] played again; this time, think with the minister; join the audience, as it follows the sermon, to respond as the congregation does. You might not, for this preaching is *of* and *for* a peculiar type of people — a subdued, a suppressed people.[108] This leads to the second basic explanation of all old-time Negro preaching: *it is the expression of a people in bondage.* It is partly an escape[c] mechanism.[109] During the period of the original old-time preaching (slavery days), and in Macon County when the records were made for this study,[110] the Negroes were in bondage.[111]

SLAVERY DAYS — The Negroes were a persecuted people during the days of slavery; the very word "slavery" suggests that, and the history

---

[c] The author is aware of the opposition to this psychoanalytical approach. Irvin Kristol, for example, says that "orthodox psychoanalysis and religion will never agree on truth. The issue between them is simple and clear-cut. Religion asserts 'that the understanding of psychoanalysis is only a dismal, sophisticated misunderstanding, that human reason is inferior to divine reason, that the very existence of psychoanalysis is a symptom of gross spiritual distress. . . . Psychoanalysis, religion might say, comes not to remove insanity, but to inaugurate it' " (*Time Magazine,* November 14, 1949, p. 65, quoting and summarizing Kristol's statements in *Commentary*).

The author takes this position: in old-time Negro religion, there is some religion and there is some emotional release.

of American oratory has been made more glorious by the eloquence of men who fought the inglorious institution of slavery. But it was impossible to suppress the emotions of these Negroes whose very existence in Africa had centered in the unlimited expression of their strong emotions through their equall as strong imagination? The slave was ordered to do this, not to do that; he was whipped; all his former institutions and his culture were destroyed for him; as a slave, he could not even lift his voice to express his dissatisfaction. Like steam confined in a kettle of boiling water, the slave's emotions had to escape or explode — or both. In the case of the slave, both occurred: (1) *escape* by means of religion (the original old-time religion); and (2) *explosion* in the form of slave insurrections (which marked the end of the original period — about 1732 to 1832 — of the old-time religion).

Whitefield's emotional preaching did more, perhaps, than anything else to encourage the slave along the road of mental escape from his conditions. "The emotional preaching of Whitefield brought to the Negro a religion he could understand, and which could stir him to self-expression. He responded to it with enthusiasm, allowed his imagination to run riot with it, loved it with passion. *It afforded him a mental escape from the wretchedness of his social position*,[112] *whether he was a slave or free*,[113] and it stimulated him to assert himself as a human being. More than any other force it aided him in adapting himself to the ways of Western civilization"[114] Whitefield merely suggested, but there were other white preachers who spoke directly to the slaves and told them to take their minds off worldly things. Observe these words of a sermon delivered to slaves (eager to make an adjustment) by a white minister:

Almighty God hath been pleased to make you slaves here, and to give you nothing but labor and poverty *in this world*,[115] which you are *obliged to submit to,* as *it is in His will* that it should be so. If, therefore, you would be God's *freemen in Heaven, you must be good* and strive to serve Him here on earth. I say that what *faults you are guilty of towards your masters and mistresses, are faults done against God Himself,* who hath set your masters and mistresses over you in His own stead, and expects you to do for them just as you would do for Him. And Christian ministers are commanded to exhort servants to be obedient to their own masters and to please them well in all things." Now, when correction is given you, you either deserve it or you do not deserve it. But whether you really deserve it or not, it is your duty, and Almighty God requires that you bear it patiently. . . . Suppose you are quite innocent of what is laid to your charge, and suffer wrongly in that particular thing, is it not possible [*that*] you may have done some other bad thing which was never discovered and that Almighty God, who saw you doing it would not let you escape without punishment one time or another? And ought you not in such a case give glory to him and be thankful that He would rather punish you in this life for your weakedness, than destroy your souls for it in the next life? But suppose, that even this was not the case (a case hardly to be imagined), and that you have by no means, known or unknown, deserved the correction you suffered, there is this great comfort in it, *that you bear it patiently, and leave your cause in the hands of God: He will reward you for it in Heaven,*[116] *and the punishment you suffer unjustly here, shall turn to your exceeding glory thereafter.*[117]

Slaves with less imagination than that of the Negroes, might have been influenced by such a suggestion of escape.

This message of the great reward after life, let it be emphasized, could not have been taken so literally if the people to whom it was addressed had seen, at that time, another means of escape. But, like the children of the Bible, they too were held in bondage, so "the Negro turned away from escape from bondage through revolt and insurrection[118] by holding in front of him his ideal of escape after death. . . ."[119] Yes, the Negro slave's future looked dark; he saw no other way out; thus, his intensely religious nature gave "him faith and a means of expression for his over-wrought feelings. . . . The basic religious beliefs and superstitions of the Africans were easily converted into Christian doctrine.[120]

Some may believe this situation existed only during the days of slavery — that the slave, a full-blood Negro just from Africa, *did* turn to old-time religious preaching partly as a means of escape from the unpleasant reality of his present life, but that slavery and full-blood Negroes ended in the United States with the Civil War, thus excluding Macon County from being a place of bondage for Negroes at the present time.[121] He should look at the record; he should examine the facts concerning the life of Negroes in Macon County today.

MACON COUNTY[122] — The conditions of Negroes during slavery days, like other aspects of the "Black Belt" country, have undergone change and modification.[123] But the conditions of the old days have remained most intact in Macon County.[124] The Negroes here, too, cling to old-time preaching partly as a means of escape. (The writer uses the word "partly," for he is well aware of the genuine religious aspect which is always present in old-time Negro religion.)

Since the plantation system was the heart of the "Black Belt" during slavery days, it is significant that Macon County "recently reached what seems to be the zenith of its plantation system."[125] Likewise, a picture of Macon County Negro life today is strangely like that of slavery

days. The slave plantations with master and slaves have become plantations with landlord and croppers.[126] During chopping and picking times,
crowds of Negroes go to the fields to work hard all day for little pay.
It is difficult work but, as in the older days, loud talk and singing of
spirituals pass the time away. This is share-cropping, and "the pernicious-
ness of share-cropping is a well-known fact of history."[127] It robs, de-
bases and pauperizes.[128] Such were the conditions of the Negro in Macon
County when the recording of the sermons were made. He was still in
bondage.[129]

Being in bondage and, like the slave, seeing no solution, he has
clung to the Negro's "Old-Time Religion,"[130] which is, in part, a religion
of escape from the realities of this world. So, in the religion of the
Macon County Negro "the *emphasis is placed upon personal salvation,*
and it gets little further, for any statement or activity which assumes
that every person is of worth . . . is tabooed because it threatens the
established relations between the races."[131] Therefore, *mercy* rather than
justice becomes the chief attribute of the Negro's God. "The accent
has shifted from *hell* to *heaven,* from *retribution* to *forgiveness,* from
fear to *hope.* Such a shift could be accounted for by the urgent need to
belittle present conditions, to hope for better things, to anticipate return for suffering endured, and welcome in exchange for rebuff."[132]
Richard Wright has put words into the mouths of "Black Belt" Negroes
who, in their escape from reality, cling to old-fashioned preaching:

> The preacher tells of days long ago and of a people whose sufferings
> were like ours. He preaches of the Hebrew children and the fiery
> furnace, of Daniel, of Moses, of Solomon and of Christ. What we
> have not dared feel in the presence of the Lords of the Land, we now
> feel in church. Our hearts and bodies reciprocally acting upon each
> other, swing out into the meaning of the story the preacher is un-
> folding. Our eyes become absorbed in a vision. . . . The preacher's
> voice is sweet to us, caressing and lashing, conveying to us a height-
> ening of consciousness that the Lords of the Land would rather
> keep from us, filling us with a sense of hope that is treasonable to
> the rule of Queen Cotton. As the sermon progresses, the preacher's
> voice increases in emotional intensity, and we, in tune and sym-
> pathy with his sweeping story, sway in our seats until we have lost
> all notion of time and have begun to float on a tide of passion. The
> preacher begins to punctuate his words with sharp rhythms, and
> we are lifted far beyond the boundaries of our daily lives, and up-
> ward and outward, until drunk with our enchanted vision, our
> senses lifted to the burning skies, we do not know who we are, what
> we are, or where we are. . . .
> We go home pleasantly tired and sleep easily, for we know
> that we hold somewhere within our hearts a possibility of in-

exhaustible happiness;[133] we know that if we could but get our feet planted firmly upon this earth, we could laugh and live and build. We take this feeling with us each day and it drains the gall out of our years, sucks the sting from the rush of time, purges the pain from our memory of the past, and banishes the fear of loneliness and death. When the soil grows poorer, we cling to this feeling; when clanking tractors uproot and hurl us from the land, we cling to it; when our eyes behold a black body swinging from a tree in the wind, we cling to it.

Some say that, because we possess this faculty of keeping alive this spark of happiness under adversity, we are children. No, it is courage and faith in simple living that enables us to maintain this reservoir of human feeling, for we know that there will come a day when we shall pour out our hearts over this land.[134]

This description strikes at the very heart of an interpretation of old-time Negro preaching and, in so doing, it reveals that all old-time Negro preaching is basically alike in *that it is in part a medium of escape from unpleasant conditions,*[135] which leads to the second basic cause of old-fashioned Negro preaching: the need for a medium of escape from an impossible world. DuBois described this modern bondage:

I have called my tiny community [*located in the "Black Belt"*] a world, and so its isolation made it, and yet there was among us but a half awakened common consciousness, sprung from common joy and grief, at burial, birth or wedding; from a common hardship to poverty . . . low wages; and above all, the sight of the veil that hung between us and opportunity. All this caused us to think some thoughts together; but these, when ripe for spirit, were spoken in various languages.[136]

Summary

The Two Basic Causes — The sermons which have been recorded in Macon County can be understood only in the light of the causes of the origin, evolution, and development of the basic ideas and characteristics of old-fashioned preaching. *The first basic cause of all old-time Negro preaching is the mixing of early American and African religious practices,* the results and manifestations of which are many and unmistakable (and without a knowledge of their historical basis, one views old-time Negro preaching as either comical or mysterious). *The second basic cause of old-time Negro preaching is the need for an escape mechanism by a people held in bondage.*

Characteristics of Old-Time Negro Preaching Evolved from the Two Basic Causes — A very important result of the discussion of the two basic causes of old-fashioned Negro preaching has been

the manifold suggestions and implications of the fundamental characteristics of old-time Negro preaching. It may be well to summarize these
characteristics systematically, using four of the classical constituents of
rhetoric as the basis of organization (invention, disposition, style, and
delivery):

INVENTION

A. PURPOSES

To persuade the sinner to "take up the new life" according
to the Bible, the real word of God.
To impress the audience, so that there will be an outburst
(escape) of emotion in shouting and frenzy.
To give religious instruction, according to the Bible.

B. SUBJECT MATTER

The Bible is the source of all ideas, information, and truths:
God is good; "the more we suffer in this world, the greater
will be our reward after death;" morality, social obligations,
and religious fidelity are to be emphasized; there are evidences
of fear and superstition.

C. MODES OF PERSUASION

Personal Appeal: the minister is uneducated but is "called"
by God; his word is the word of God; the preacher is usually
an impressive person, has a dramatic bearing and a melodious
voice.

Emotional Appeal: by means of rhythm, sensationalism, rhetorical figures, imagery, suggestion, etc., the minister puts the
audience into a mood to accept his ideas; this is the greatest
appeal.

Logical Argument: not as important as emotional appeal; the
best argument is that "it's true because the Bible said so."

DISPOSITION

There is no logical organization because there is little preparation. The emotions determine everything.

STYLE

Familiar, concrete, narrative, ungrammatical language; Biblical; humor; deals with *things* rather than with *ideas*.

DELIVERY

Awkward, spectacular, dramatic, bombastic; musical voice;
rhythmical and emotional; enthusiastic; sincere.

These characteristics are only suggestive of, for example, John Jasper's preaching. But, since his sermons were not recorded, his art is lost
forever. However, available information indicates the above picture is
close to the essentials of old-time Negro preaching. It might serve as

something of a standard for comparing and contrasting the characteristics of the sermons which were recorded in Macon County.

To democratic America seeking an explanation of the unique, old-time Negro preaching, the thundering reply is: "Let My People Go."

IV.   Fire Shut Up in My Bones[a]

WHAT ARE the purposes[1] and the methods of persuasion of Macon County preaching? Are these elements typical of old-time Negro preaching? What new influences have entered the picture?

PURPOSES — When Phillips Brooks said the purpose of a sermon should be "the persuading and moving of men's souls,"[2] he did not refer specifically to old-time Negro preaching. But old-time Negro preachers (like John Jasper and Black Harry) at least moved the *emotion* of men — even unto screams and shouts. Imitating the white ministers who addressed the slaves, the old-time preachers sought to persuade and to instruct their hearers along the road to an escape from this world by having them look forward to a future life; but their primary purpose was to impress the audience.[3] The purpose of Macon County preaching remains in the vein of old-time preaching.

Aside from the basically religious motive, the immediate purpose in the Macon County sermons is to impress and to arouse the audience — to cause shouting, excitement and emotional abandon.[4] Ministers and members refer to this climactic state as "getting happy," "letting the spirit have its way," "having a good time," etc. The ministers offer many indications and implications that "arousements" is paramount. One minister, pointing outside the church to the author working with the recording apparatus, gave an illustration of the unemotional condition; he did not approve of an unemotional congregation. He implied the purpose of preaching was to get the "Spirit" to move his hearers:

> "See dat feller out dere? He look so fat; he look so pretty — and de spirit won't tech him nowhere. . . . Don't let dat happen to you!" (VIII)[b]

On another occasion this minister is aware that his purpose is to "stir up" the audience:

> "Not feeling good; been on road. . . . Got headache. . . . You all tired. Been gwine to it. Since you been gwine to it and am tired and I been gwine to it and I am tired, don't 'spect too much. . . ." (III)

---

[a] The Spirit "is like fire shut up in my bones. . . . It's like a mighty hammer." (IV)

[b] Roman numerals refer to various sermons included in this volume.

[74]

Now what type of sermon should the audience not "expect" from this *tired* preacher? It should not expect a spectacular, strenuous "whoop-em-up" sermon.[5] The minister adds:

> "Goin' ter take my time. Ef I don't raise no bristles, it's all right with me." (VIII)

"Raising bristles" means shouting and "getting happy." And when the audience is "cold," the minister rebukes them because of their silence:

> "I ain't go no need to come her; no one's a Christian here. Benches can't say 'Amen.' You all can hear, can't yer?" (III)

Another minister refers to "arousements" as the purpose of the sermon:

> "Whatever fer you all this evening, just hold yer cups, and whatever for yer all, yer git it. . . . So jest keep everything waiting and we'll see what's gwine to come ter you." (V)

Another refers to this emotional purpose as "making it:"

> "I don't — I haven't felt good all day. Gonna 'make it' all right." (VI)

The ministers (II, VII, I, and IV) also sought, in varying degrees, to arouse the emotions of the audience. DuBois is correct when he says a purpose of the old-time Negro sermon was to produce frenzy or shouting, "when the spirit of the Lord passed by, and, seizing the devoted, made him mad with supernatural joy . . . , [*the effect varying*] from silent rapt countenance of the low mourner and moan to the mad abandon of physical fervor — the stamping, shrieking, and shouting, the rushing to and fro and wild waving of arms, the weeping and laughing, the vision and the trance."[6]

The recorded sermons indicate the purpose to persuade the listeners to become Christians, or to become better Christians. For example, after having stimulated the audience to shouting, one minister points to the happy confusion and tries to persuade non-churchmembers (sinners) to join the ranks of the redeemed:

> "Don't you feel lonely sometime in the world by yourself? Give me your hand. [*Sings it.*] Won't He lead you? [*Talking to the happy and responding Christians*:] Won't He take care of you? My — my Lord! I done tried! I know He *do* take care of you. . . . Gwine to sing and open de doors[7] of the church." (III)

It is obvious that the minister's purpose is to persuade sinners to become Christians. A good example of persuasion (and it illustrates the attempt to escape from reality) occurred effectively in the third sermon. The listeners were tired, having packed peaches throughout the

week—and until two and three o'clock that Sunday morning before coming to church. Yes, they are tired, sleepy, and bitter. The minister would
persuade them to believe that they suffer in this manner because of conditions in the South. He tells them that the Devil, knowing that Christ
was hungry, took the Master upon a mountain and tempted Him by
asking Christ to turn rocks into bread; then the minister says:

> "You know, sometimes a feller takes things off people, he wouldn't
> do it, but it's conditions. . . . If conditions didn't have us so 'tight,'
> have us going, don't you know, you wouldn't work all day and all
> night Saturday?" (III)

And this minister discusses love in persuading the audience to escape
from the troubles of this life:

> "If it [love] isn't sufficient to lead you through the ordeals of
> everyday life, it isn't sufficient." (I)

Similarly, another minister is preaching Christian character when
he says:

> "Though times and conditions change, the Law is the same: 'Thou
> shall love the Lord thy God with thy whole strength.'" (I)

He continues:

> "God speaks of love. Love that is sufficient to get you in church,
> have you sign your name and take your obligations[8] isn't sufficient
> love if it doesn't hold you there." (I)

The minister refers to *the great mystery* of God, in persuading his
audience:

> "There are so many — men some our great philosophers have tried
> to dig out all the mysteries of God. Gone off to school and studied
> and all like that, but there haven't been no man able to learn all
> the mysteries of God. Past man's finding out. So high, can't go
> over; so deep, can't go under; so wide, can't go 'round." (II)

More in the vein of the educated minister than the old-time
preacher, one minister attempts to persuade his audience to believe that
neglect is dangerous:

> "Neglect in any way produces a corresponding loss. I might
> make examples of a few things where neglect produces a loss. If
> a merchant neglect his business, he'll go bankrupt. . . ." (IV)

This minister, however, illustrates the three purposes of arousing,
persuading, and instructing. His sermon has two distinct parts:[9] (1) the
intellectual part, the purpose of which is to persuade, and (2) the "stir-

ring-up" part, the purpose of which is to impress and to arouse, as illustrated in his rhythmical deliver of these words:

> "I could hear Job saying one day, 'There's no way to escape death, because your bounds been struck and you can't go 'round!' Oh-h-h-h, Glory!" (IV)

He even suggests, in closing his sermon, that his purpose has been (in the stirring-up part) to arouse in order to renew *spiritual strength*; he speaks for the audience and for himself:

> "Now my spiritual strength renewed. . . ." (IV)

Another minister seeks to arouse his audience emotionally, but he also feels that the minister's purpose should be *to instruct* the listener concerning the Gospel:

> "So you are the flock. Den, well, the preacher oughta feed you. Ain't dat right? He oughta feed you wid whut? De Gospel. . . ." (VIII)

Such, then, are the purposes of old-time Negro preaching in Macon County. Most noticeably, to arouse, to "stir up," to excite the emotions as a means of escape from a wretched condition; this is not altogether a religious purpose. Persuading the sinner to come to Christ is still important. The purpose of instructing the audience unemotionally is present, especially in the preaching of the more highly educated Negro ministers. Raper was correct when he said that, in Macon County, Negro preachers usually have as the purpose of their sermons personal right-living and shouting: "It is unique to find a rural Negro preacher who understands and talks about present day community and social needs."[10]

Another ever-present purpose appears in all old-time Negro preaching in Macon County: getting as much money as possible from the audience.[11] The minister who makes his audience shout and have a good time is called "a good preacher" and such a minister is repaid handsomely in the "collection." Even his persuasion and instruction point up the conclusion that a good Christian meets his "obligations" — pays his "dues." The minister should not be criticized severely on this account; his pay is unbelieveably small. He himself often regrets the necessity of emphasizing money, as one minister shows when he says that John the Baptist was a real preacher, one who "didn't set no point on no money . . . nothing but holding up Jesus. . . . Some people ain't wont to preach unless they git lot of money" (III). Yet, this same minister (four weeks later) lifted his arms over the "collection" and said, "Blessed be the cheerful giver, for he shall be made fat" (VIII). Unlike the original old-time Negro preacher, the present minister is acutely conscious economically; he often appears to be seeking money primarily and souls second-arily; the original minister seems to have sought souls primarily.[12] This emphasis upon money, let it be stressed, does not lessen the original importance of emotionalism in old-time Negro preaching. If there is no "arousements," the people label the preacher as "no good"; such a minister is soon discharged or he is shifted to a smaller church. Money-raising ability is a mark of success.

Chart I indicates the purpose of old-time Negro preaching recorded in Macon County. TO PERSUADE refers to "winning souls to Christ." TO AROUSE refers to emotional escape; it is not solely a religious purpose. TO INSTRUCT refers to teaching from the Bible in an unemotional manner. TO GET MONEY refers to pleasing the audience so that they will give money freely.

All the sermons seek primarily to arouse and to raise money; persuasion and instruction are primary with but two ministers.

SUBJECT MATTER[13] — Phillips Brooks, "the greatest preacher in America,"[14] once said that "the real question about a sermon is . . . whether there ever was a time when the discourse sprang freshly from your heart and mind."[15] Such discourse contains the true ideas, beliefs, and convictions of the speaker. In the spontaneous, emotional Negro sermon (which springs from the heart and mind), the ideas represent the combination of the Negro preacher's African and American heritages of religious beliefs; the ideas direct the hearers to an escape (by

CHART 1.   PURPOSES OF MACON COUNTY SERMONS

SERMON	TO PERSUADE	TO AROUSE	TO INSTRUCT	TO GET MONEY
I	*	*	*	*
II		*		*
III		*		*
IV	*	*	*	*
V		*		*
VI		*		*
VII		*		*
VIII		*		*

means of the Christian doctrine of the Bible) from the trials of this world. The ideas of the original old-time Negro preaching were based on the Bible and emphasized the goodness of God, right-living, and suffering in this world in order to obtain a better life in the world to come. That was the original old-time Negro preaching. Are these same ideas emphasized in Macon County preaching? Are there new ideas?

These sermons indicate that many of the ideas of the original old-time preaching remain. However, with new influences have come new ideas; and many of the old ideas which remain are fighting desperately for their lives.

An old-time idea which is still important in Macon County Negro preaching is that the Bible is the source of all truths:

> "The Bible is called the Book of Books. Ain't dat right?. . . . This here [*the Bible*] the only book to give you a true record of God and Christ; you gotta git the Bible. . . and the Bible is right! . . . . The Nigger handlin' it may be wrong, but the Record is right!" (VI)

The minister's prayer expresses this belief when he says: "Thank Thee that Thou has left a written record, guide and assurance. . . ."[16] The ministers declare that the information found in the Bible is the truth, that it is the Word of God. Accordingly, the text and themes for sermons are usually taken from the Bible:[17]

SERMON I. "Thou shalt love the Lord thy God [*Reading from the Bible.*] with thy whole heart, with your whole soul, with your whole mind, and your whole strength."[18]

SERMON II. "We going to talk this morning from this text, the 10th chapter of the Book of Joshua, and the 12th verse: 'Sun, stand thou still upon Gittia and thou moon go in the valley. . . .' "[19]

SERMON III. The minister (who apparently could not read very well) mumbled words, with the Bible before him, about John the Baptist and the temptation of Christ by the Devil (MATTHEW, 3: 1-7; 4: 1-4).

SERMON IV. "We invite your attention to the reading of the Book of Proverbs, the 14th chapter. . . the 30th verse: 'I went by the field of the slothful. . . .' This is our text."

SERMON V. This was introductory (perhaps not a sermon in the usual sense of the word[20]); the preacher did not take a text.

SERMON VI. "The text, 28th chapter of Elijah, 1st verse. Going to read you a section. [*He could not read.*] Elijah said, 'All the people. . . .' " He evidently has in mind the story of Elijah, found in *First Kings, chapters* 16-18.

SERMON VII. The minister had to use the same text used in Sermon VI. (See explanation, footnote a, p. 37.)

SERMON VIII. "The text is found in the 5th verse of the 35th chapter of *Genesis*." The minister pretends to read from this section but actually refers to the story of Joseph, found in the 37th chapter of Genesis.[21]

But regardless of announced text, the sermon finally always finds the theme of a better world to come. And that theme is from the Bible. The Bible, then, is still the source of the old-fashioned Negro preacher's ideas.

"Daniel says he saw Him as a. . . ." (III)
"John Baptist. . . says he go there by himself. . . ." (III)
"David said. . . ." (III)
"I hear Paul saying one day. . . ." (IV)
"Elijah said. . . ." (VI)
"Remember what Isaiah said. . . ." (VI)
"Old man Elijah said. . . ." (VII)

This abiding-fondness for the Bible results in the Negro's knowing, even as a small child, many verses and stories from this great book. His speech, whether in the cotton fields or in church, is flavored with Biblical ideas. A minister's most informal discourse shows the influence of Biblical ideas. When one minister said casually that "If you want to be helped, [*you*] have to help somebody" (III), he was probably unaware that the idea was not original. The minister, consciously and unconsciously, takes into consideration this nature of his audience: that they know, almost as well as he does, the ideas which he presents. The ideas are not new but, like old friends, are dearer because of the close acquaintanceship. The minister calls for witnesses to the truthfulness of a story from the Bible:

"Day done fine, didn't dey, brothers?" (III)
"Ain't dat right, brethren?" (III)
"Ain't dat true, man?" (III)

These Biblical ideas (which are made a part of the Negro's very existence) beget in the Negro other ideas, the wisdom of which is worthy of consideration:

"[*If you*] Ain't gwine help a man 'in a tight', he don't need yer when he git out." (VI)

"I believe in doing everything where it ought to be done at. . . . Put everything in its own place." (v)

"The Nigger handlin' it [*the Bible*] may be wrong, but the Record's right." (vi)

"Some folks, if dey [*can*] carry you their way, it's all right; ain't got nothin' to do for you if dey can't." (iii)

"Sometimes a feller take things off people he wouldn't do it, but it's conditions." (iii)

"You just deal with a man; you'll find [*him*] out." (iii)

"Truth breaks down things; truth washes down things." (iii)

"A kiss ain't [*always*] so good." (iii)[22]

Why do the ministers and the congregation still cling to the Bible? Because "His Word is good" (v). Who, they say, would not want such a good thing: "Don't you want God's Word? Man, God's Word good; hungry soul, hear somebody sing and pray. . . . Man can't get filled till he harken" (iii). But when the Negro says the Word is "good," what does he mean?

Biblical ideas (as was true during slavery days) still help the Negro make both an emotional and economic adjustment in the United States. The Negro's highly emotional temperament resulted from his African background: fear of death and belief in a God (the belief in some powerful director of the seasons of the year and of the life in the jungles). The Negro's cramped economic, political, and social status as a "Black Belt" share-cropper (as was also true in Africa and during slavery in America) demands a means of escape for this emotional and superstitious temperament. Macon County preaching shows that Biblical ideas still aid in this mental escape from reality.

Since the conception of God is the center of any religion, it is well to consider the Biblical ideas of God that appear in Macon County Negro preaching. The Negro compares God to an all-powerful man who sits on a throne and protects the lowly (such as the Negro):

". . . We couldn't honor a better man, greater man than He is. Greatest hero ever sat on the throne. . . . And the sweetness of His disposition in the hearts of many have caused us to have hope. He's the only man. . . only one fer us." (v)

These are Biblical ideas to which a lowly, emotional people can cling. They give the Negro hope for the better life in the future, a pride in being a "child" of a man who is even more powerful than, say, the Governor of the State. The omnipotence of the Negro's God is stressed repeatedly:

"Thou art God an' God alone." (PRAYER, I)

"The Lord our God is th' only one God. Only one God. Only one law-giver." (I)

"God is able; God is *able*—strong—to raise [*up*]; chillun of Abraham, God is able [*to*] save de soul: . . . I been had hold Him a long time; He ain't never let me down." (III)

Therefore:

"We must love God if we want—supremely—if we desire to be successful." (I)[23]

The Negro likes to dwell on the great power of his God— a natural reaction of a people who are so powerless. [*God (and Christ)*][24] is the hero to the Negro that Stalin is to the Russian. Preachers wax eloquent in telling of God's (Christ's) great deeds. The story of the resurrection of Christ is a favorite:[25]

"When God, when God Almighty's Son got ready to come out of the grave, He busted the grave and blinded dem men and put 'em to death, God bless your souls, and come on out." (VII)

"Saw Him [*God*] in the battle; He never lost a one. 'I'm the One; my Word is the light to your feet and a lamp to your pathway.' " (VI)

Such a great God, naturally, knows everything:

"He knows your days; He knows how long you is come; He knows how long—when to pick you up." (VI)

Indeed, such a religion is "good."

But the attributes of God, based on the Bible, would not in themselves satisfy the lowly Negro. Almost every white man he knows seems to know everything and he certainly *is* all-powerful, in so far as the unfortunate Negro in Macon County is concerned. God, to please the Negro, must have still another attribute: He must be merciful.[26] And that is in keeping with the Bible. Therefore, the sermons show the Negro's belief in prayer, because a merciful God will answer prayer and forgive the sinner. Who would not serve and pray to such a good God?

"The Lord be good ter us." (VII)

"On bended knees, won't He tell you what to do?" (VII)

Just trust in Him:

"Trust God and 'I'll be to you anything—Heaven. I ain't gwine away.' How long. . . must I work in the vineyard?" (VI)

"Now if you trust in God, it don't make any difference about the money. Hell may raise and the devil excite, but Jesus done left on the Record that 'I'll save my heart's delight.' Now God wouldn't forget His angels, brethren." (VI)

Thus, prayer assumes a very important position:

"Can't make a good deacon undoubt yer a prayin' man;

can't make a good mother [*of the church*] undoubt yer a prayin'
woman. You can't do nothin', unless you a prayin' person." (VIII)

The praying man takes on an attribute of Christ when he bows and
prays for mercy: he humbles himself. Therefore, the "Black Belt"
Negro (frustrated), already humbled (almost to the nth degree)
escapes from the reality of his despicable condition and thanks God
for it all and begs Him for mercy:

"Lawd, have mercy on us." (I)
"Lord, have mercy, my Father!" (III)
"We thank Thee this morning. . . . Thank Thee. . . . Thank
Thee. . . . We thank Thee this morning for the opportunity extended towards us." . . . . . . "Dear Lawd, we come befo' Thee
and ask Thee ter stand by us. Thank Thee for ev'ry thing Thou's
did for us." (PRAYER, I).

These ideas show that the Negro has escaped[27] completely from
Macon County: (1) because he believes in life after death; (2) because
he believes his God is able to take him into Heaven (a real place); and
(3) because he is terribly afraid of death. The Negro never tires of the
idea of the Lord and His power over death:

"May the Lord bless us; may He help us, and may He save
us when it comes our time to die." (IV)
God will "go with you to graveyard; He make up your dying
bed. Mercy!" (III)

The preacher often dwells upon the emotion of fear in order to obtain
shouts by concentrating on the idea of death, with little attempt at
coherence:

"Felt a *dead* man—on to himself; oh! . . . Knocked off *dying*
smile; put back in one corner of the *grave*." (III)

Again the preacher uses the idea of death to arouse *fear* of this *merciful*
God:

"Oh Lord, [*He'll*] cut you down in the morning; cut you
down in the noontime! Have mercy. . . . God got His eyes on you!
See all you do!" (III)

Again, the minister, shifting from the *wrathful* God, returns to the
protection of the Almighty God against death:

"Dey [*Christians*] don't mind goin' to a burial; know de
Dad's got the key. Dey don't mind goin' in de grave, 'cause dey
God done got de. . . . L don't mind deep waters! I don't mind
enemies talkin' 'bout me! The Lord can hold me. . . ." (VI)

If some of these ideas of the Macon County Negro's preaching appear contradictory, it should be recalled that white ministers guided the Negro slave along this road of escape. Their aim was to make the Negro a docile slave. Even today Macon County preaching reflects this early Biblical instruction of "taking low" in this world and living a better life:

"Ef we love one 'nother lack God would have us love one 'nother, dee wouldn't be so much confusion in dis land; wouldn't be so much crime; wouldn't be so much of fightin'. . . ." (VIII)

Neither a slave-master nor a plantation owner could object to this preaching. If all Negroes acted accordingly, fewer chickens would be stolen; Negroes would work more and complain less of educational, economic, and social inequalities.[c] As one minister said:

"You satisfy [*are satisfied*] ter enjoy home and here [*church*] —wherever God puts yer." (v)

Or observe these ideas:

"Yer know—I tell you, it's a fine thing to be a peacemaker— not a peace-breaker. Ain't dat right? Dat's a good way, I tell you. I don't give a dime—I wouldn't give a dime 'bout men talkin' what somebody said on dey dying bed, when dey were dying. I don't care anything about dat; I want to know, what did he do while he live? . . . Who did he go out and help? . . . The Bible tell us, 'We shall know them by their fruits.' . . . The onlyest way that we can serve God is by serving our fellowman. . . . More the Lord bless us, more humble we ought to be. Ain't dat right?" (II)

"The Master said on one occasion—the Bible said, He that humble himself shall be exalted and he that exalt himself shall be abased!" (II)

"When we think about that, we think about how strong was the Master's behest here, command here, as He answered that very outstanding question: 'What is the greatest Commandment?' . . . He answered, 'Love thy neighbor as thyself!' " (I)

White ministers told the Negro slave that if he suffered "here below," his reward would be great in Heaven. Heaven became important to the Negro. So it remains:

"Go down and tell men that they must—they kin go to Heaven if dey wanta!" (VI)

"Dey ain't gwine wait on 'em in dat great gittin' up mornin'!"

---

[c] As recently as November 1949, the author heard a white minister tell an assembly of Negro college students that even a slave can be free *in his mind.*

[84]

"Now, Lawd, when it come out time to die, pray you receive us into Thy kingdom and give our souls a resting place." (PRAYER, I)

"When we are called from here to another world—Jesus did promise to sinner on cross—may we kneel at Thy feet and cry, 'Redeemer!' " (PRAYER, I)

And who would not desire a place like this:

"Heaven! I feel like it's a very splendid place. Heaven! I feel like it's the best place ever I have known. . . . Heaven is a spiritual place—spirit place. . . . No rain; no bad weather; no trouble; no sorrow; no crying. Lord! No more lying been said about you; no more tattlin'; no more goin' hungry. . . ." (III)

The step from the acceptance of these ideas to shouting is easy for Macon County Negroes. And emotional excitement is the final, happy, climactic step in the Negro's escape. He loves it and realizes its importance. Like the belief of the original old-fashioned Negro preacher, the belief of these ministers remains that the "spirit" must move you; something must happen:

"Yer know, somethin' have to happen. God have ter let something happen." (VII)

Another minister gives a classic description of the effect of the "spirit:"

"I tell you. . . if you let the spirit find its way into your heart. . . It'll move in your heart. . . and then It'll make you move. Ah-h-h, Glory! '. . . It's like fire shut up my bones. . . . It's like a mighty hammer.' I tell you what it will do for you. It'll make you forget about your heavy crosses; It'll make you forget about your trials. And then you'll say, 'Whatever it takes, I'm going on; I'm going in Jesus.' " (IV)

This minister says the Negro forgets about everything when he is "happy:"

"Wharever you at—in your state, in your field—when dat spirit of God hit you, you feel like you in Heaven right dare. You—ain't you never got happy? . . . You just done forgot everything. . . . Holy Ghost burns, and when it gits to burning, can't hold your peace! . . . Sometimes makes you cry. . . sometimes makes you pray; sometimes makes you moan. . . . " (III)

Sadness is a part of that strange state of shouting, which is a mixture of joy and sadness.[28] Of the sad note, the preacher declares:

"Got to cry sometime. Know I been born again. Git off by 'self and cry. . . . My soul. . . have trouble and tribulation; some-

times afflicted; have to crawl into your home. Farewell!" *Shouting.*
(III)

Nothing is impossible for the Holy Ghost:

"He make a ugly person look pretty well! Can't He make
you pretty, so to speak?" (VIII)

These excerpts demonstrate the similarity of ideas in Macon County
and in original old-time Negro preaching. The Bible is dominant.
From it flows the conception of Christianity which is necessary for
an escape from the trials of this life. The Negro preacher imitates
the white preachers of slavery days and offers religion as a substitute
for worldly needs:

"The Word of God is food! The Word of God is shelter!
The Word of God is water! The Word of God is protection!"
(III)

But not a word is raised against the sins of the landlords or the poli-
ticians of Macon County.[29] In only one instance does a minister *start*
to mention a white man, and then he recalled that he was "out of key,"
before finishing the statement. Speaking of the undesirable way in
which some people boast of their abilities, this preacher said suddenly:

"White man talk with us—by the way—. But it's a mystery. . ." [*Catches himself and returns to his subject of God's
mysteries.*] (II)

He was getting onto "forbidden territory."

However, the sermons in this study indicate that education and
general advancement have affected the religious ideas of Negro preaching. A transitional state exists—a movement *away* from the ideas of
original old-time Negro preaching *to* something new. Old ideas, faced
with education and enlightenment, are fighting to live. One minister
exhorts his audience to "love God as of old, for He and the Bible do
not change, even if conditions do change:"

"He's the same God now. Same Law, passed down generation after generation. . . . Same for this changing age. This is the
most changeable stage of man's history. Never known time when
things change so fast. What is today, not be tomorrow. Same
with tomorrow. We try to live up and be regular; when we get
there, find we not all right. Keep us constantly changing. . . . Our
text says, 'Though times and conditions change, the Law is
the same: Thou shalt love the Lord thy God with thy whole
strength. . . . Knowledge and wisdom and understanding should
help you to grow near God and not away from God.' " (I)

The following suggests a reply to the criticism that the old-time preacher does not appeal to the intellect:

"There's so many doctrines and strange things. . . . But when God wake you up, *you don't have to think*. Only one thing — to preach!" (VI)

The statement is significant. It demonstrates that the old-time Negro preacher and his audience are themselves cognizant of the fact that theirs is not *to think* ("to reason why") but *to act, to gesture, to rant, to shout* ("but to do") or *perish* ("or die").

The old religious ideas are being shaken. Many sinners used to fill the "mourning bench" (the seats for those who seek religion), but "nobody come to de mornin' bench now but little chillun" (VIII). A minister once could satisfy his congregation by repeating the same sermon. John "preached only one text, [*but*] I'm got to git 'nother text every time I come here" (III). And John "didn't set no point on no money. . . . Nothing but holdin' up Jesus. . . . Some people ain't wont to preach unless they git lot of money" (III). These are new ideas, which are destroying original old-time Negro preaching. Educated people try to give new grammatical meanings to God's Word: "Heard a feller say in Atlanta the other day — Sunday School, Sunday morning — said that the word 'shalt thou' and 'shall thou' much difference; that he doubt that the thief was on the right side of the Savior. . . . [*Refers to the crucifixion of Christ.*] Let nobody fool you; He told the thief, 'You *will* be with Me; where I go, you also" (II). Old and new ideas struggle for acceptance.

The old-time preacher knows that education is dangerous to the life of his art, to the "fire shut up in [*his*] bones" (IV). He never overlooks an opportunity to lambaste it. For example:

"There are so many men — some of our great philosophers — have tried to dig out all the mysteries of God. Gone off to school and studied, but there haven't been no man able to learn all the mysteries of God. . . . There have never been a man — he go to school and get his diploma . . . degrees on mathematics and theology, and whatnot . . . never hear a man gwine to schools to git his diploma on God. . . . You can talk about Mr. Shakespeare, but . . . never been a man could know all about God." (II)

The following quotation offers another disapproval:

"One Word! Not the word of Greek, Latin, grammar, Moody; not a word of source from anybody but God." (III)

Thus, the struggle between the old ideas and the newer ideas of Negro preaching continues.

But despite the old-time preacher's desire to keep the *old-time religion*, Negro sermons show characteristics which are entirely new. An intellectual discussion of ideas based on the events of this world is taboo, but the following minister dwells on a condition *in this world* in an unemotional manner:

> "It's a proud privilege that we [*have*] the pleasure to enjoy. Thousands of people dying by guns, pistols and other ways. . . . Some of us could be gone too. . . . With all dis disaster on de world, people ain't concerned a bit. Dey doing worser." (VIII)

This quotation indicates that the radio, the newspaper, or some other agent has brought these *this-world* ideas to the minister's attention.

The Macon County preacher occasionally hears a sermon by an educated minister. This minister explains words, refers to great writers and books other than the Bible; the old-time preacher imitates the educated approach. The following Macon County preacher explains, after quoting Jesus' words concerning locust and wild honey:

> "Locust is kind thing that grow, maybe like a bug — I don't know. . . ." (III)

He becomes impatient with this new approach and says he does not know, but he tries it again. He wants to show his exact knowledge of foreign places:

> Jesus "come about seventy miles — I don't know how far it was He come down that little stream. . . ." (III)

Again he admits his ignorance. But he seems strangely concerned. New influences *are* at work.

The most highly educated Macon County minister (IV) reflects many indications of the new influence on old-time Negro preaching; he does so in the intellectual part of his sermon (his sermon possesses two parts: the intellectual part and the emotional part). Punctuality in old-time Negro services is a strange requirement (old-time Negroes do not "hold services" on time as a rule); but the minister begins his sermon by saying:

> "Regret very much for being somewhat late; [*He had been on time, but the audience had been late.*] however, we hope to work out of this gradually." [*This was his second Sunday as the pastor of this church.*] (IV)

The old-time Negro preacher considers the literal meaning of the Bible sufficient for the theme of his sermon. The minister interprets the scripture to obtain his theme. First, he reads a passage from the Bible:

" 'I went by the field of the slothful, and by the vineyard of the man void of understanding; And lo, it was all grown over with thorns, and nettles had covered the face thereof, and the stone wall thereof was broken down. Then I saw, and considered it well; I looked upon it, and received instruction. Yet a little sleep, a little slumber, a little folding of the hands to sleep: So shall thy poverty come as one that travelleth; and thy want as an armed man.' "

Then he says:

"From these verses the theme suggest itself to our minds is this: *The Danger of Neglect....*" (IV)

And that became his theme throughout the sermon. But he did not draw his ideas to support this theme solely from the Bible. His ideas came from newspapers and from his experience: Amelia Earhart's disappearance; the death of Dr. L. K. Williams, "President of the National Baptist Convention of the United States of America, Incorporated"; a railway disaster; the sinking of the *Titanic;* a negligent merchant; a basket-maker; the man who continued to sleep after his clock alarmed; the country man who moved to town; a man who neglected to learn to swim (IV). The less emotional part of his sermon illustrates the effect of new influences on old-time Negro preaching in Macon County.

The subject matter or ideas of the sermons recorded in Macon County declare that old-fashioned Negro preaching is not dead there. Many of the original ideas of old-time Negro preaching are in evidence: the Bible is *the* usual source of ideas. The Biblical ideas of God, Heaven, and sin open the door to a religious escape from the world of reality. But the Civil Rights Fight, education, the radio, and newspapers are modifying the ideas of this preaching (not without opposition, to be sure); these ideas are entirely unlike the ideas of the original old-time Negro preaching. Unless "Judge Lynch" and "Jim Crow" finally win out in this "land of the free," the new ideas (which attend freedom, enlightenment, and man's humanity to man) are certain to triumph over the old ideas (which attend slavery, ignorance, and man's inhumanity to man).

In the purposes and in the subject matter of Macon County sermons, much evidence of the original old-time Negro preaching appears. The Bible remains the basis of everything; the African and early American heritages are still in evidence. But education and new influences are modifying both the purposes and the subject matter of old-time Negro preaching; it is destroying the "fire shut up in my bones." America's "fire shut up in her bones" (freedom for *all* the people) is slowly destroying the frustration aspect of the Negro's old-time religion ("the fire shut up in his bones").

V. The Man of God [a]

THAT OLD-TIME Negro preaching does persuade and move men's emotions cannot be doubted, in the face of the "amens" and "shouts" of the recorded sermons. Certainly the audience is "moved," but what are the methods used? Some Negroes declare that the magnetism and power of the preacher solely are responsible for a "good meetin'," that the minister's ability to affect the emotions of the audience accounts for the shouting and the frenzy. Few observers accept logical argument as an important element in old-time Negro preaching. The recorded sermons are evidence of both modes of persuasion: (1) through the character of the Negro preacher (Ethos),[1] and (2) through emotional appeal (Pathos); and (3) through logical argument.

THE CHARACTER OF THE SPEAKER (*Ethical Appeal or Ethos*) — The speaker is "the keystone of the speech situation, for every quality which we desire in the good speech must be in the speaker and every desirable effect of an able ministery or of a speech situation can be traced to the character—broadly speaking—of the speaker."[2] For the Negro preacher the concept of "character" as a means of persuasion[3] includes the total man; the old-time Negro preacher is not merely a speaker with a speech: he is the "Man of God" with God's message to men — the instrument through which the Father talks to His children.[4] Therefore, character as a means of persuasion will be considered (1) in the case of the Negro preacher in general, and (2) the Macon County preachers in particular. Does the old-time Negro preacher speak as an authority? Does he speak as an honest and good man? Does he seek the good will of his audience?[5]

The audience's conception of the Negro minister as a "Man of God" is obviously a persuasive element. Even before the preacher speaks, his listeners are in a receptive mood, for the old-time Negro preacher does not "just go to school" and then begin preaching; he is "called of God to preach." (This was true of the original old-time Negro preacher like John Jasper.) But what forces and influences develop this "man of God"? What is the nature of being "called"? What character qualities of the

---

[a] "Now we pray Thee, bless the Man of the Hour, the *Man of God....*" PRAYER (I)

[90]

preacher make him persuasive? How does the "Man of God" differ from other Christians?

The preparation of the "Man of God" often begins before birth. One colored woman, whose experience is not unlike others in the "Black Belt," told the writer that during pregnancy she prayed to God for a son, and promised to dedicate the unborn child to the work of God. This woman had been reared in a religious home; her parents believed in the old-time religion. Surely enough, the child was a boy, and Jerry's "preparation" began.

Even as a baby, Jerry (and his older brother) was carried to church, where he must have stared in amazement at the singing and shouting people about him. Then there were baptizings and revival meetings. From Jerry's very earliest recollections, he recalls most vividly this religious environment. The Bible was read at home; there was Sunday School for father, mother and the children every Sunday morning. (This often meant a 5-mile buggy ride in dust or mud — even when the family had labored in the cotton fields all week.) After Sunday School, the pastor delivered his sermons which never failed to "tear an audience all to pieces." After preaching, the people ate from baskets, and later, the young people held the Bible Study Meeting.

Jerry's mother remembered her promise to God. Always a good Christian, she now grew closer to God; she began to see visions and to dream dreams, "just like the people in the Bible." She became a dreamer, like Joseph, and often startled the family with the accuracy of her predictions. This is significant, because Jerry's father (who had first attracted the mother by playing a guitar at a country dance), although "converted," still liked to take a drink ("for his cold") and was not at all certain of the Lord's kindness to the Negro.

The fulfillment of the mother's predictions of future events prevented Jerry and his father from discarding the old-time religion.

By the time he was four, Jerry had become a "marked" child. He was a good Christian child, not "bad" like other children of his age. He had already begun to preach. He often stood on chairs and preached to the other articles in the room while his mother worked and listened with pleasure and satisfaction. Occasionally, during this period, the preacher visited the family and exchanged Bible verses with Jerry. (Everyone in the family knew many Bible verses. Each gave a verse before every meal.)

It was on one of these visits of the pastor (during a "revival meeting") that Jerry ran to the preacher and announced he "had a 'ligion." When the pastor asked how Jerry knew that he had "a 'ligion," the little boy said, "I can feel it."

"Where?" asked the minister.

"In my belly," replied Jerry seriously, showing his protruding stomach with one hand and holding out a large, half-eaten sweet-potato in the other.

Some of the family laughed, but the minister rebuked them with the words: " 'Suffer little children to come unto Me and forbid them not.' "

Jerry's mother took this confession seriously; this child was going to be a preacher. The boy had already become a Christian, but he had not yet received the "call" to preach. Even without the "call," the boy became active in the work of the Lord. When he was about six or seven, Jerry was helping his cousin pull corn (the cousin pulled the ears of corn and Jerry rode in the wagon). But Jerry was busy; he kept "preaching" to his cousin (who was about to be inducted into the army[6]) to "get religion" so that if he was killed, he would go to Heaven. This cousin, a "big sinner," soon "got tired" of this "preaching" and yelled at the boy, "Shut up preaching at me, you little yeller rascal; you are just like your mammy!" (The cousin is now a successful Chicago preacher, probably Jerry's first convert.)

Then Jerry too became a dreamer. He dreamed that he and another boy were standing before a gate. A man told the other boy to get on a large scale, as if to weigh himself. Down went the scale with the other boy on it (to hell, presumably). The man told Jerry to step up. He obeyed, and the scale stood still! Then, the scale struck like a clock, three times. Jerry wanted to know what that meant. The man said, "That's the number of years you have had religion, three years." Imagine that! It had been exactly three years ago that Jerry had told this minister he "had a 'ligion in his belly"!

Jerry's story spread, and he became "quite a figure" in the community. He was on the road toward becoming a "Man of God." When revival opened that year Jerry joined 10 or 15 other people (including his brother) at the "mournin' bench." The preacher told these "sinners" to pray to the Lord for forgiveness of their sins and that the Lord would give them a sign when they had "got religion." Night after night this continued. Converts would fall out, scream, cry, shout, and "come through" (get religion). Jerry sought such a conversion experience, one like the following experience of a "bad sinner:"

> "I don't know why it was I got converted because I had been doing nearly everything they told me I ought not to do. I danced, played cards and done just like I wanted to do. I don't reckon I was so bad but they said I was. In my heart I was good and felt that some day I would do better.
>
> "One day, when I was about 22 years old, I got up feeling

awful heavy. I went about my work and had started to washing when I suddenly began to feel worse and worse. I wasn't sick, I was just heavy. I began to say, 'Lord, I wonder what is the matter with me?' I stopped washing and went in the house and layed across the bed and there I saw Jesus. He turned my face to the east and said, 'Go and declare my name to the world and I will fill your heart with song.'

"While I was laying there I saw the city. It was the prettiest place that I ever saw. All the little angels were the same size and color and as they flew all their wings moved at the same time and made the sweetest music I ever heard.

"After I passed through this experience I lost all worldly cares. The things I used to enjoy don't interest me now. I am a new creature in Jesus; the workmanship of His hand saved me from the foundation of the world. I was a chosen vessel before the wind ever blew or before the sun ever shined.

"Religion is not a work but a gift from God. We are saved by grace and it is not of ourselves but the gift of God."[7]

But nothing like this happened to Jerry. Even his best friend "got a 'ligion" and loved to talk about his conversion. He said he felt as light as a feather. Jerry began to worry. There can be but one reason why Jerry did not "come through" (have a conversion experience): either he lacked the necessary emotion and imagination, or his father (who, however, was now a deacon of the church) had influenced him unknowingly.

Jerry's brother "came through"; this left Jerry the only "sinner" in the family. That was "bad." He prayed with renewed vigor now — in the buggy and under the persimmon tree — everywhere. He watched stars and asked the Lord to let them shoot if he "had it," but always the stars either did not shoot or the wrong star would shoot.

Matters had become serious; the revival was to close the very next day. On this last day Jerry made his first great decision: sign or no sign, he would "join up" tonight. This he did. He joined the church without feeling anything but horrible stage fright; not even a tear came.

But only Jerry knew this. The others were glad. (The mother was not "happy;" in fact, she never gave emotional signs of her strong religious beliefs — but she was a great speaker in those parts and often spoke until others were moved.) Jerry was baptized to his great amazement and fear. The men (all in white, as everyone else was) took him to be submerged into the river. He was again on the road of the "Man of God."

Then the "call" came. One day while his mother ironed and he was on the bed, Jerry suddenly felt an urge or a command to open the Bible and read the first verse upon which his eyes fell. He obeyed. To his amazement (but not to his mother's amazement), the verse was: "Go ye into all the world and preach My Gospel."

Jerry was 11 years old when the "call" came. He knew the Bible; he was a "good" boy; he had delivered so many "pieces" and talks in church that he was considered an able speaker throughout the community; everybody knew that he was "marked"; now that he had been "called," Jerry was ready to enter the pulpit, and *what he was*, became his most persuasive device. Jerry's words, regardless of his sincerity,[8] were accepted as "The Word of God," because Jerry was a "Man of God."

Jerry's story is suggestive of the background of many Negro preachers in the "Black Belt." It explains their unique position in the community.

Jerry represented the "good" Negro who became a minister.[9] The background of the "bad" Negro gives him ethical appeal because of the contrast between his new life and his old, "sinful" life. The people reason, "As bad as old Henry was, he surely must have been 'called' or he never would have become a preacher." Both types of preachers arc "called" and both have appeal because of what they are.

A questionnaire used to ascertain the nature of the preparation of the old-time Negro preacher contained the following statement: "Describe (without naming) two persons who exercised the greatest influence over your thinking on religious matters." A minister in the spirit of the old-time preacher, had this to say:

> "During my early childhood I was naturally exposed to all sorts of religious teaching. I remember first that 'Hell' (as it was termed) was actually under the ground and child-like I would not even dig too far into the ground for fear of striking it. We had picture cards; and the representation of Heaven was a bird's-eye-view of a city with great spires or steeples, all white, and angels flying about just as we represent birds on the wing. All this was pictured above something which looked like great clouds of smoke. This was exactly what I believed Heaven to be except I had in mind that where God lived, one would have to walk up golden stairs just as we go up the steps of a modern dwelling with a high terrace. As I remember, most of the sermons I heard had the flavor of the 8th chapter of Revelation, 2nd verse ['*And I saw the 7 angels which stood before God; and to them were given 7 trumpets*']. If you can, imagine as you read, this being literally read line for line, with a snort here, and a gurgle there, a wiping of the brow, a strained breathless wail at the end of each paragraph, with some two or three continually moaning a weird, subdued tone, someone half-praying in the same manner, and at the close of all a song such as 'I Heard the Voice of Jesus Say,' given

out by line and sung in the long meter. . . . I believed to unite with the church was a sure way of getting there. [*Heaven.*] As a child I believed that God was a large and powerful man who lived up above the clouds, in Heaven, and that He was able to see everything that was done. Through the Lord's Prayer I regarded Him as the Father of all. I had the 'Big-Stick' idea of God. I conceived Him as an angry taskmaster exacting with jealousy and harshness certain things of men and threatening to cast into burning brimstone and fire those who fell short. Next I conceived Him as a friend to those who were good but mean, inconsiderate to the rest. I believed that every child was born full of sin; that the sinner must go about mourning and praying until he heard a 'still small voice' declaring that his sins had been forgiven."[10]

The character of Negro preachers persuades their audiences — despite the moral weakness of some of them. The old-time Negro preacher is "a good man." Negroes stress this point: the preacher must not dance, play cards, or drink. Yet some preachers are "the biggest devils" in the church. Members of the church can name the "sweethearts" of such pastors. Occasionally, a "sister's" husband or lover takes a knife or a razor and "cuts up" the minister. Almost every Negro knows "dirty jokes" about the minister's lack of morals; it is common saying that preachers love three things: money, women and chicken.[b] Yet, the old-time Negro preacher is respected and honored. His being a "Man of God"[11] is not the full answer. Other elements of his character are important to an understanding of this paradoxical situation.

Perhaps, above all, the old-time Negro preacher is superior to his people in intelligence.[12] As James Weldon Johnson says:

> The old-time preacher was generally a man far above the average in intelligence; he was, not infrequently, a man of positive genius. The earliest of these preachers must have virtually committed many parts of the Bible to memory through hearing the scripture read or preached from. . . .[13]

Native intelligence gives him leadership, for the old-time preacher (even in Macon County today) lacks education to give him prestige. "The younger and better-trained Negro preachers" do not pastor these old-time churches.[14] It has been said that "poor leadership is better than no leadership";[15] educationally, that (poor leadership) is precisely what exists in this county: "Most of the preachers' education was completed at the one-teacher rural Negro schools."[16]

But the Negro preacher's small income explains this and introduces

---

[b] The author knows there are many upright and moral Negro ministers. His intention here is not to disparage such ministers or their profession.

other characteristics of these ministers. "Pastoring" three churches, the typical minister receives an average $546.60 a year.[17] He spends about one-sixth for traveling expenses. Even this small amount is not paid as salary. It is charity. The minister must "take-up collection." This explains two other characteristics of the preacher: first, why he is extremely money-conscious and, second, why he must please the audience. .Only a burning desire to be a leader could compensate for this situation.

This *desire to lead* is an important element in the preacher's character; it often accompanies natural leadership. Perhaps "leadership" is not the proper word, but certainly these old-time preachers tackle any problem. Dr. Johnson tells of an old Negro minister who opened his Bible one Sunday and read from a rather cryptic passage. He did not understand a word of it, but (always the leader) he removed his eye glasses, slammed the Bible shut, stared down as his respectful and expectant and congregation, and said: "Brothers and sisters, this morning— I intend to explain the unexplainable — find out the undefinable — ponder over the imponderable — and unscrew the inscrutable.[18]

Intelligence, leadership ability, and the "Man of God" conception serve the Macon County preacher, as the following discussion of each minister indicates.

THE AUTHOR OF SERMON I

THE YOUNG lady interviewer was unable to obtain his age, but he had been married for 29 years, had been a school teacher for 33 years, and a preacher for 22 years.

The Macon County preacher of some education often supplements his meager income by teaching; likewise, the poorly paid teacher sometimes increases his income by preaching. Reverend ——, a teacher, felt the urge and the need to preach. As a teacher, he was already a leader in the community; that made easier the step to the position of preacher. He had attended high school at Paine College, Augusta, and had attended summer school at Fort Valley State College.

His appearance is that of a "leader." Serious-looking in his semi-baldness, he creates the appearance of a man set apart, despite his almost short stature. But his is not the true old-time "Man of God" appearance. He is a transitional product — a mixture of the old-time preacher and the new, more-educated Negro preacher. He is definitely "on the fence:" (1) part of him says, "Make 'em shout and serve the Lord in the way that they should, and they'll like you and give you more money and perhaps make you their pastor";[19] (2) another part of him says, "You have been to school; you know that you should try to reason with the audience; teach them; that's it: teach them; you're a teacher, you know." This dual personality make him a pathetic figure to the outsider, but to his congregation, it makes him persuasive. They diagnose this hesitancy and indecision as piety and wisdom. A sufficient amount of the old-time preaching remains alive in him to satisfy the old-time Christians, and he also satisfies those members who want to be instructed.

His voice is ringing and "good." Although he speaks hesitatingly, his long pauses are effective. The audience feels he is either thinking profoundly or deeply moved by the Spirit.

Quotations from his sermon are illustrative. The intellectual urge in the teacher-preacher prompts this un-emotional declaration:

"This is the most changeable stage in man's history."

But it was the old-time preacher in him which declares emotionally that he is, despite his schooling, a Chilld of God:

"See that I can take a stand for myself, relying upon God in all things. Let my family life be high or let it be low; let it be elevated as it will, I still rely upon God. . . ."

He has character persuasion: his appearance, his learning, his earnestness, and his reputation as a good and moral man.

THE AUTHOR OF SERMON II

HE IS 36 and has two children; he was reluctant to speak of his wife. He attended the public schools of Georgia and spent one summer, 1941, at Georgia Baptist College of Central City. He has "pastored" Mt. Zion Baptist Church (where his sermon was recorded) for 8 years and, he said proudly, during his stay at Mt. Zion he has built a pool for baptizing and has remodeled the church inside and outside. He had "just been called" to the pastorate of a large church in Atlanta. His proudest expression was, "I was called by God to preach the Gospel in my childhood."

He is probably the best example of a relatively young man who is a direct descendant of the original old-time Negro preacher.[20] He is an unusually large and impressive-looking man. His facial expression, carriage, dress, manner of speaking, gestures — all blend to make "The Man of God." His voice is a marvelous instrument.

His story is the usual one — poor, rural family, nothing but hard work. But they never forgot God. He was reared in the church and received the "call to preach" when he was a child. Since that time, he has thought of nothing else but preaching as a life-work. He soon learned that, with his large body and his serious ways (he had always been "different from other boys of his community"), he could "stir people up." He heeded the "call," "got ordained" and has been "preaching God's Word ever since."

He is the best example of today's young Negro preacher who reflects the characteristics of the original old-time preaching as well as the results of the struggle of these characteristics against the new preaching characteristics of freedom and education. Certainly he persuades his audience because of his character as a "Chosen Leader." He has little respect for "education." He believes, sincerely believes, in the old-time shouting religion. And he can "make 'em shout."

His sermon illustrates his use of ethical (character) persuasion. The old-time Negro preacher maintains an air of importance; the people must (and they like to) "look up" to him as their superior. It is, then, with a knowledge of the prestige such a statement gives him that the minister says:

"We are very happy to bring greetings from Atlanta."

But he is not only a *great* man, he is also a *good* man, one who believes in helping others:

"I don't give a dime . . . 'bout men talking what somebody said on dey dying bed. . . . I want to know, what did that person say or do while he live?"

He is a' *good* preacher, but "it is not right for people to boast of what they can do." He possesses humility:

"I don't think people ought to brag about . . . how he can preach."

And if it were possible for these excellent elements of his character not to persuade his audience, he informs them of their special place in his great heart. He does this by the repeated use of the words "my belove'."[21] He is typical of John Jasper's most illustrous young descendants. His future is bright, along the dark road which he is to travel.[22]

THE AUTHOR OF SERMONS III AND VIII

IF THE previous minister represents the typical youthful descendant of John Jasper, this pastor represents the mature descendant of the old-fash-

[98]

ioned preacher. He gave his age as 55; said he was married and the father of two children. American Institute, he said, was the school where he "got some schoolin'." He was emphatic about his being "called to preach," saying "there is no doubt about it!" His story resembles that of the author of Sermon II: hard times, religious home, and then the "call." He has been a preacher for 30 years. He "pastors" four churches,[23] having been at Holly Grove for 9 years. He said his aim in preaching is "to save souls."

Although not a large man, he undoubtedly has the appearance of "a feeder of the sheep" (VIII), a Gospel preacher. With an intelligent-looking face, his hair cut in a "distinguishing" manner, and with "good" clothes and a fan to complete the ensemble, he is perfect. That is, even *before* the people hear his voice. When he moves majestically about the pulpit and "thunders out" in that voice, there is but one thing to do, *shout!*

But this preacher shows some degree of insincerity in his work. Once he *was* entirely sincere, but 30 years of traveling from one church to another — always begging and pleading for dimes, nickels, pennies — have changed him. This experience has made him a calculating philosopher. Not a *cold* one; as the discussion of pathetic (emotional) appeal reveals, he arouses both his own and the audience's emotions. But the original sincerity and eagerness have faded. The desire (and need) for money has overshadowed his aim to win souls for Christ; but he can still satisfy his audience.

He satisfies the audience because he is intellectually superior to his listeners; they never dream that his primary aim is money and that "saving souls" is secondary. He is an old-time preacher, all right, but he has "been around"; he has heard the sermons of educated ministers—and he knows that their income exceeds his own.

Shrewdness, tact, and good sense enable him to persuade his listeners. The elements of his character which tend to persuade his audience are obvious in his sermons. He leads the audience to think that he is a good man:

> "Charter [a] truck from Albany; be at Richmond. . . . If you don't have nothin', I pay for it." (III)

Above all, he is the mouthpiece of God and the Bible:

> "I ain't talkin'. [I] come to advertise John [the Baptist]." (III)

And at the emotional climax the minister becomes not God's spokesman, but God himself:

> "It it makes you cry, I'll be with you, [Not quoting.] will not forsake you!" (III)

[99]

A *good* man, yes, and a *good preacher* too:

> "Ain't gon' worry yo' patience. I been here long enough for you to know whether I kin [*preach*] or can't." (VIII)

Name *that* self-confidence and *this* courage:

> "I'm preaching to everybody in here today. Sinner here, I'm preachin' to dem; Christian here, I'm preachin' to dem; hypocrite here, I'm preaching to him." (III)

He adroitly suggests his great reserve to preach when, after sweeping the audience with his rhythmical preaching, he changes his pace suddenly and says calmly:

> "I wish I had time ter arger dis thing." (III)

The audience is unaware of the unlimited time available to the minister; instead, they reason: "Just think, if he can preach like this when he is rushed, what might he not do if he had the time? What a preacher!" The minister also knows the persuasive power of being a man who is important, one who preaches in distant states. He says casually: "I leave for Alabama next week to preach" (VIII). Although not entirely sincere, he knows sincerity is an important element of persuasion. Therefore, he seeks to convince the audience that he is sincere:

> "Some of us speak jest 'cost us got physical livin', good voice, know a little somethin' 'bout the Bible; we say it over in our prayer some time jest to be huard by men. But a prayer is a sincere desire. A prayer come up outta the heart, wid a meaning into it." (VIII)

Yes, he knows all the persuasive elements of character. He knows a sense of humor is one of these elements. Speaking of the great number of people who had been killed in the war, he says:

> "Some us could be gone too. Some of us *mean* enough to be gone." [*Laughter.*] (VIII)

A few sentences later he says:

> "You know I ain't lazy — [*Aside.*] 'til I *get* lazy." [*Laughter.*] (VIII)

But his greatest persuasive element of character is his speaking with the voice of authority:

> "I know what I'm talkin' 'bout. . . ." (III)
> "I know what I'se telling you 'bout." (III)
> "I told yo' what fasting mean." (III)
> "And then I heard Him [*Jesus*] say . . . ." (III)
> "I heard him . . . [*John the Baptist*]." (III)

Add to the above elements (1) his native intelligence and wisdom:

> "I don't care how you do, what you do, you gwine err some time." (VIII)

and (2) his attitude as God's representative:

> "You are a flock. You are a flock of Christian people. . . . De preacher oughta feed yer." (VIII)

and you have the ethical (character) persuasion of a truly able descendant of the original old-time Negro preacher.

THE AUTHOR OF SERMON IV

THIS MINISTER, a bachelor, did not disclose his exact age, but he is about 33 years old. He said the "divine call to preach" came to him when he was 17. His early childhood experiences were typical of the "Black Belt" Negro with the exception that his parents were the type of Negro who believes education is the solution to the colored man's many problems. Although his parents were poor, they somehow helped their son through high school, and he even studied for a while at Simmons Theological Seminary, Louisville, and at Morehouse College, Atlanta. He now "pastors" four churches.

He is the most highly trained of the group of ministers studied in Macon County. He is intelligent, ambitious, large, and impressive-looking. His ethical persuasion stems from his composite air of the successful, educated and well-informed, serious-minded, and thoroughly religious man.

He and the teacher-minister (I) are very much alike. There is this difference: the minister in this profile is not undecided as to his mission and he is not timid; he has made his decision; he knows exactly what he wants to do. It is true that he also has that two-fold religious point-of-view to contend with — the shouting old-time religion and the new, more intellectual religion. But he has solved the problem, not by mixing the two types of preaching throughout his sermon as the teacher-minister does, but by having two distinct parts to his sermon: one part intellectual and the other part emotional. Accordingly, he is at the same time both the typical old-time Negro preacher and the modern, intellectual preacher. He knows the two types of preaching are necessary to satisfy the entire audience, and he wants to please everybody (to keep his job and to get their money). He is indeed two-in-one.

Such a man persuades with his character because he is simply sufficiently intelligent and histrionic (all these ministers are able thespians) to please everybody — some to the extent of making them shout and others to the point of making them think. In obtaining this success, he also owes much to imagination, a flare for words, natural leadership, a good voice, and a strong body (his "holler"[24] is convincing that a man with a weak body could never preach in this manner).

The closest approach to the new type of preacher stresses punctuality[25] in starting services:

> "Regret very much for your being somewhat late. . . . We shall work out of this gradually."

To give the impression of the well-read, the well-informed, the minister refers to Amelia Earhart, Captain John Smith,[26] and to other events of national and international importance. He seeks to impress further by the use of mouth-filling words and phrases:

> corresponding, bankrupt, consequence, pneumonia, predominates, heathenism, conscience, cannibals, and prosecution attorney; pathetic; calamities; Dr. L. K. Williams, the president of the National Baptist Convention of the United States of America, Incorporated; *Titanic,* Southampton, iceberg, hurge [*huge*].

Even when he turns toward his emotional side, he impresses the audience with his knowledge of the exact location of Biblical references:[27]

> "Solomon said in Proverbs, 2 — 29, 2. . . . [*29th chapter, 2nd verse. And he is right.*]
> "I can hear Paul saying one day in the Book of Hebrew. . . ."

But it is the other side of him, his old-time religion of emotional escape, that thundered rhythmically (causing shouts) of the Holy Spirit:

> "I tell you what It [*the Spirit*] will do for you: It'll make an old man feel like a young man. . . . It'll make you forget about your heavy crosses. . . ."

He owes much in his successful preaching to his ethical (character) appeal — both as the old-time preacher and as the more modern type of minister.

THE AUTHOR OF SERMON V[28]

THE MINISTER, about 50 years old, is married to his second wife. His formal education ended with the third grade. He was "called of the spirit" to preach and has been preaching for 28 years. He has the distinction of being the pastor of four churches.

His story is an interesting one. Born of poor but religious parents, struck totally blind at the end of the third grade (when he was 8 or 9 years old), he might have taken a tin cup, placed the word "blind" across his chest and joined the ranks of beggars. But there developed within him that feeling of the man who has a mission. He considered not how "his light was spent ere half his days . . . ," not how unfortunate was his lot, for "God moves in mysterious ways." He was a man with a mission. Cloistered in his darkness, he drank deep of his parents' religious instruction. They often read the Bible to him, and he learned of the trials of Job and Christ. He was led to church; the ministers made his blind soul tremble with their cry of a better day to come, a day when God would heal the afflicted and give sight to the blind. Then, the "call" came. Now he knew his mission: to preach the Word of God. And so he does.

His appearance is impressive. Unusually tall, handsome, well-poised, and so accustomed to his pulpit that he moves easily from one part of it to another, this man might easily be mistaken for a man who has sight.[29] His very blindness gives him persuasion; the audience respects the man who has the ability and the courage to overcome such a handicap; they recognize in him their superior. And he has an excellent preaching voice. Because of these qualities and his apparent goodness, genuine intelligence, and wisdom, [*"Yer know, I'm dis way. I believe in doing everything where it ought to be done."*] he perhaps possesses more ethical (character) persuasion than any one of the other ministers who were studied.

THE AUTHOR OF SERMON VI[30]

THE MINISTER does not "tell his age" anymore (he is about 65), but he has been preaching for 43 years. He has three "grown children" and married his "last wife" a year ago. Asked how he happened to start preaching, he replied: "Felt the Spirit in me; kept worrying me; wouldn't give me no rest. Spirit had to get out." Regarding education: "I never been in a classroom in my life."

If the author of Sermon II was the typical youthful descendant of the old-time Negro preacher, then the author of Sermon VI is the typical old descendant of this type of preacher — if he is not the old-time preacher himself. His parents were slaves who were genuine old-time religious worshipers. Freedom had not changed their conditions in Georgia; their old "shoutin' " meetings continued, and the minister soon found himself "right in the middle of it." He had a flare for speaking and singing; his tongue was sharp, and many a sinner had bowed beneath its lash even before the "Spirit" told him to go "into all the world and preach" the Gospel. He needed no education. Had not the Lord said, "Open your mouth and I'll speak through you"? His four churches attest to the fact that the Lord had "spoken through him."

He is representative of those genuine old-time Negro preachers like Black Harry and John Jasper.[31] He is jet black in color. Not a tall or a big man, yet his appearance is sufficiently "distinguishing" to give him great persuasive power over his superstitious and emotional listeners. With protruding ears, a long head, African features, unusually long arms for his height, long feet — in his native Africa he would be a chief or a witch-doctor. Indeed, he seems a strange creature even before one hears his whip-like voice and his running delivery. To his superstitious audience and to himself, this strangeness can mean but one thing: he is God's prophet!

One old-time Church-member said the minister is called "the best Negro preacher in the South." Negroes come from as far away as middle Florida to hear this Georgia preacher. When the writer, in his Fort Valley, Georgia, home (located in an old-time religious community) first played the minister's records, Negroes came running from many directions crying: "Ain't dat '——'? "Who's dat preachin' lak '——' ——?" "Man, dat's '——' ——, ain't it?"

Some of the minister's elements of ethical persuasion are reflected in his sermon. The minister discloses in the beginning that he possesses a reputation to help him:

> "Preachin' out of my 'rep'. . . . If I ain't made it now, 's too late now."

Then, after striking his rhythmical stride once lightly, he watches the effect ripple through his audience — like a master musician (knowing his power over his listeners) who teases his admirers with a note or two and then pauses to admire the tumultous effect — and says in a conversational voice:

> "I believe I git on this horse this evenin' soon."

He indicates his reputation by belittling himself:

> "I got to hurry on and *be out the way* now. [*"Take yo' time, Reverend" and "Ha! Ha!" from the audience.*]

His great persuasive stand is that the Bible is the Word of God and that he is His mouthpiece:

> "You can read Moody, Calvin . . . . If you want the true record of God and Christ, you gotta git the Bible."

"The Nigger handlin' it [*the Bible*] may be wrong, but the Record's right."

"I don't care what nobody say . . . , [*if*] the Spirit of God didn't move 'em, dey did poor work. . . . I can't go nowhere unless the Lord God lead me."

He has a genuineness, a frankness (and a sense of humor) in facing the truth even if at his own expense:

"Some uv 'em [*some people*] done come here lookin' for mistakes. Well dat feller ain't gwin be disappointed, 'cause I'se full uv dem." [*Laughter.*]

The audience response illustrates that he possesses a reputation as an excellent speaker:

[*In his stride now.*] " . . . And Elijah and the three lambs come on behind." [*Audience*: "*Talk! Talk!*"] "The lightning hadn't played a lengthy game across the face of the muddy cloud. . . ." [*Audience*: *Talk now!*"]

But, above all, he reveals to his audience that he is a Christian of the old order:

"I don't mind deep waters! I don't mind enemies talkin' 'bout me! The Lord can hold me. . . ."

Thus ethical (character) persuasion plays an important role in his speaking.

THE AUTHOR OF SERMON VII

THE MINISTER said that he was 20 years old. He has had no formal education, has been married for 4 years, was "called by God" to preach, has been preaching for 8 years, and "pastors" one church.

He is the youngest of the preachers whose sermons were recorded, the youngest disciple of old-time Negro preaching. He is "trying his wings" in the ministry, but "he is learning fast." His is the usual story of a home of poverty, hard work, and old-time religious influences.

He is of average height, has brown skin (a lighter complexion than any of the other ministers in this study), and is rather frail. His voice is immature and shows nervousness. All in all, he does not, in his obvious youthfulness, make as impressive an appearance (as a preacher) as any one of the other ministers. This is to be expected of a beginner in a type of preaching which is disappearing. Yet, he *does* use ethical (character) appeal. His great enthusiasm, sincerity, and ambition are his assests. Not the voice of experience, no great reputation; simply a boy who sincerely believes that God has called him to preach; a speaker who can maintain a flow of words (with the aid of his stock "filler," "my belove' "[32]).

His sermon illustrates that his ethical appeal depends primarily on his belief that God has called him to preach. A great part of his sermon is merely the story of his "call":

"I remember when I wuz called to preach. Dere wuz one crowd preachin' [that] He didn't rise. . . . Er, my belove', but one day, my belove', I come just to readin' in de Bible and. . . . I seed in the Bible whar it said. . . . And I got worried again. . . . I said, 'Now, whut is God?' I said, 'Now one man said to me. . . . And I sit right there. I comest doin' like Job. Jest like [us] folks will do. I sit on my little 'do nothin' ' and wait on time. . . . [Laughter.] Got me a three-legged stool and I sot right down, my belove' until God, my belove', visit me one night.

"And He came to me one night, my belov'. I seed a bright light, my belove'! Lit the whole room up. I seed a light shinin' all 'round me, my belove'. A little man speak ter me again and led me ter de church. . . . [He said,] 'Preach de Gospel; [have] great faith in God — Christ, preachin' de Word of God.' And I wuz wonderin' 'bout dat thing. When I knowed anything, my belove', God done placed me on de wall, done put somethin' down in me. I come's ter preachin' fer dese ole . . . folks. And I said, 'When de world wuz in grope darkness. . . .' [Shouting.] Every since dat day, I been stand-ing right here, my belove'. Ain't been sittin' on dat fence no mo', my belove'."

He also shows his good sense. He keeps referring to "dese ole . . . Folks," making them see that he was one of them, that God had sent him to preach to *them*. He shows this good sense in the analysis of his audi-ence in another way: if the audience idolized the previous preacher (the author of Sermon VI), and he certainly knew the audience did, they would respect him for also admiring the earlier speaker. Therefore, when his turn comes to preach, he says:

"De text we jest herd was whut yer call 'sund doctrin'. Dere wasn't no 'duced mixture' in at a-tall. That's whut yer call 'right straight from the shoulder. . . . Reverend ———— done put him [Baal, the false god] out of business. . . . Ef yer ain't got no eyes, yer can't see dat. . . . Reverend ———— knows."

In this manner, although young and inexperienced, nevertheless — through his enthusiasm, sincerity of purpose, and good sense — he did have ethical (character) persuasion in his preaching.

The persuasive elements of character of the ministers of Macon County, as a group, indicate intelligence;[33] a desire to lead (the feeling that God has "called" them to preach[34]); courage; imagination; impressiveness in appearance and bearing; a sense of humor; ability to speak; excellent, melodious voices (they are usually good singers); and enthusiasm. The minister tries to give the impression that he is an authority on his subject; he attempts to convey the idea that he is a man of honesty and good character; and he tries to obtain the good will of his listeners. This is ethical (character) persuasion. The Negro preacher (and his people) strains at the leash (second-class citizenship) that enslaves and frustrates him. Will America release him and thus make "the Man of God" a *man*?

CHART 2. DATA ON MACON COUNTY PREACHERS

AGE		YEARS SERVING PRESENT CHURCH		DISTANCE FROM CHURCH		TRAINING		INCOME PER YEAR PER CHURCH	
less than 20 years	0	1 year	6	at church	0	5th grade and less	4	less than $50	1
21-30 years	0	2-4 years	2	4 miles or less	5	6-7th grades	3	$51-$100	4
31-40 years	6	5-8 years	1	5-10 miles	0	8-11th grades	12	$101-$150	4
41-50 years	13	9-16 years	1	11-15 miles	6	regular college course	0	$151-$200	6
51-60 years	9	17 years or more	0	16-20 miles	2	special college course	1	$201-$300	2
61-70 years	3	not reported	23	21-30 miles	10	degrees	0	$301-$400	7
71 years or over	0			31-40 miles	2	not reported	13	not reported	9
not reported	2			41-70 miles	4			AVERAGE: $182.20	
				71 miles or more	3				
				not reported	1				

Cf. Raper, *op. cit.,* "Data on 50 Negro Churches in Macon County and Green County, Georgia (Table LXIII, pp. 365-66)

CHART 2. DATA ON MACON COUNTY PREACHERS (*continued*)

SERMON	AGE	SCHOOLING	YEARS PREACHING	YEARS PASTORING	NUMBER OF CHURCHES	MARITAL STATUS	CHILDREN	ANOTHER JOB	APPEARANCE	CALLED TO PREACH
I	55†	some college	22	0	0	married	‡	teaching	medium	‡
II	36	public school	‡	8	3	married	2	none	large	yes
III and VIII	55	public school	30	35	4	married	2	none	medium	yes
IV	33†	some college	17	‡	4	single	‡	none	large	yes
V	55†	3rd grade	28	‡	4	married	‡	none	tall, blind	yes
VI	65†	none	43	‡	4	married	3	none	short	yes
VII	24	none	8	‡	4	married	‡	farming	frail	yes

† approximate; did not give age

‡ no answer available

PATHETIC (EMOTIONAL) APPEAL[1] — People listen attentively to a speaker if they feel that his message vitally concerns them. Are the speaker's ideas worthy of their sincere consideration? If they are, the speaker may be assured of their interest and good will. The emotions and the basic beliefs — friendship, duty, honor, fear, shame, emulation, patriotism, compassion, etc. — are the stuff of which pathetic appeal is made. These are the elements of emotional proof.[2] Stripped of the unparalleled emphasis upon this appeal, old-time Negro preaching is not unique.[3] But, as Johnson declares, the old-time Negro preacher "had the power to sweep his hearers before him; and so himself was often swept away."[4] That was the original old-time Negro preacher. Do the original elements of pathetic proof appear in Macon County sermons? What is the nature of the new influence?

It is true that "the sermon which only exhorts is like a man who blows the wood and coal to which he had not first put a light,"[5] but if the wood and coal carried within themselves a light or spark, would not the blowing suffice? This question suggests the role of pathetic appeal with the old-time Negro audience. Negroes keep this emotional light burning within themselves constantly — in their moans, in their spirituals, and in their prayers; as they work the fields or walk the roads; as they shy down the streets of the country town or bow into some country store (always fearful of the Lords of the South and of Judge Lynch). They come to church with this emotional spark already within them; they only want the minister to fan it into a flame —to encourage them to let this light set them on fire with shouts and groans. This is their emotional escape from an impossible world; this action of shouting and moaning and laughing and crying relieves them.[6] Therefore, a consideration of pathetic appeal with such people resolves itself into a determination of the methods the Negro minister employs to fan these emotional sparks into flames. Certainly, working on such a definitely emotional mission, he remains on the emotional and not on the intellectual level. The audience's knowledge of the Bible (the chief source of information) equals that of the speaker; the congregation and the minister share the

---

[a] "Talk to me now. Them little black places dere ain't no good if you can just sit down. . . . Benches can't say 'Amen.' You all can hear, can't yer?" (III)

same religious ideas. Therefore, this is not an intellectual occasion; this is not a time for thinking. The problem becomes one of arousing the emotions, of helping the tired, subdued Negro to associate his trials, sorrows, and joys with those of Biblical characters.

The genuine old-time preacher knows that his mission in part is to fan emotions into flames. He accomplishes this by leading the audience to concentrate[7] upon "getting happy" by suggestion (directly and indirectly) — through action,[b] by the audience and by the minister (delivery). This initial action suggests the climactic emotional state which the audience and the minister seek.

The old-time Negro preacher, although a master hypnotist, follows in the footsteps of great orators when he appeals to his audience's basic beliefs — Biblical ideas which have been adjusted to fit the descendants of Africans and of American slaves. The conception of God is at the center of these beliefs; to the Negro, God is mysterious and all-powerful.[8] Observe how this Macon County preacher appeals to this basic belief:

> God "is past man's finding out. So high, can't go over; so deep, can't go under; so wide, can't go around." (II)

The Negro's attitude toward God makes the congregation susceptible to certain emotional appeals. This preacher appeals to his audience's great *admiration of* and *joy over* the power of God:

> "God worked on the soul and He changed 'im [*Joseph*] so, makes 'im look different. He makes a ugly person look pretty well. Can't He make you pretty, so to speak? . . . He changed his walk; He changed his condition; He changed his life." [*Preach it good now!*"] (VIII)

Revealing how vital to them was his subject another minister dwells on the audience's *love* for God and their *hope* for a new life to come:

> "Had not been [*for*] the influence of Calvery, man [*would have*] had no salvation; world woulda been lost." (II)

One minister's entire sermon treats the Negro's *love* of God. (I)

The *fear* of God is another emotion to which the old-time Negro preacher appeals:

---

[b] Action is important in stimulating the emotions. The emotion results from the action: a man sees a bear and runs; he is afraid—an emotional state—because of the action of running. Pretend that you are angry; concentrate on this and act angry. You will experience the genuine emotion of anger. (See Boleslavsky's *Six Lessons in Acting* and Stanislavsky's *An Actor Prepares*.) When the Negro sings, moans, pats his foot, claps his hands, and says "Amen!" he tends to stimulate his emotions because of those very actions. Not an *intelligible* word need be spoken, but words hasten the arrival of the desired emotional state.

"My Lord! God got His eyes on you! See all you do."
"Have mercy now; oh Jesus, have mercy now." (III)

Fear has constantly dogged the footsteps of the Negro — as an African, as an American slave, and now as a second-class citizen.[9] Observe how a minister produces shouting by appealing to the *fear* of God:

"Yonder He come. . . . God Almighty. . . . Thunder, your conscience; lightning in Your hand. . . . Everybody is gwine ter pray now!" [*Audience shouts wildly.*] (VI)

There is suggestion too in the last statement:

"You may be too proud [*Suggests the preacher.*] to pray now; too proud to shout now, but you *will* shout and pray when God comes, so why not now?"

The people agree, and they do shout and pray. The audience's *fear* of God often approaches *awe* under the spell of the preacher's description of God's work.

[*In rhythmical stride.*] "It thundered and no one hadn't heard! The lightning hadn't played a lengthy game across the face of the muddy cloud! Heaven hadn't been burned or hell even warmed up, or even organized. . . . [*Talk now!*" "*Ride it,*" etc.] Go on — on this thing now [*He means that he is, emotionally and rhythmically, "in the groove;" he is at that emotional state toward which he and the audience have been working; the embers have been blown to the flaming point. A woman laughs in a high, hysterical voice; everyone (the preacher too) seems literally happy; this is escape through laughter; no tears here.*] Heaven!" [*From this point until the end of the sermon, clarity of words and of thought is entirely lost in a whirlpool of emotional ejaculations.*] (VI)

But unadulterated *fear* of *death* is the emotion to which this minister appeals:

". . . Men talking what somebody said on dey *dying* bed, when dey were *dying*." (II)

"I could hear Job saying one day, 'There's no way to escape *death*, because your bounds been struck and you can't go 'round.' Oh-h-h-h Glory! '. . . It's so high, you can't get over; so wide, you can't go around; then it's so deep down [*melody in voice*] you just can't turn under it; no way around it'." (IV)[10]

The minister, even when not striking directly at fear-producing descriptions of death, likes to talk about things with which *death* has some connection. Any mention of the grave or of death serves the purpose — to produce shouting. Jesus' triumph over the great mystery, *death,* is most effective:

"When God Almighty's Son got ready to come out of the grave, He busted the grave and blinded dem men and put 'em to death, God bless yo' souls, and come on out." (VII)

He appeals also to their *admiration* of and *respect* for the power of God (through His Son):

"He [*God*] knows your days; He knows how long you is come; He knows how long — when to pick you up." (VI)

The Biblical story of the strange death of Almighty God's Son is used frequently:

Christ "kept on dying [*on the cross*]. He never stopped dying." (II)

The old-time Negro minister is indeed a master of this art of emotional appeal. Even the order of services builds toward the desired emotional climax of shouting. Observe the order of services for the sermon, "Thou Shalt Love the Lord Thy God" (I):

1. *Song*: "My Faith Looks Up to Thee."
2. *Prayer*: A deacon thanks the Lord for having permitted *death* to leave them in the world "a little longer." [*The minister did not ordain the use of these exact words, but he knows the content of the average Negro old-time prayer.*]
3. *Song*: "I Love Jesus." [*A perfect selection.*]
4. *Song*: "Come, Thou Fount of Every Blessing."
5. *Hymn*: "Father, I Stretch my Hands to Thee."
6. *Responsive Reading from the Bible.*
7. *Song*: More of "Father, I Stretch my Hands to Thee."
8. *Prayer*: A preacher thanks the Lord for sparing them. The goodness of God is stressed.
9. *Song*: "Where He Leads Me I Will Follow."
10. *Scripture Reading*: "Thou Shalt Love the Lord Thy God."[11]

In the order of services a prominent place is given to the prayer. Much can be said of the importance of prayer in emotional appeal. The prayer (or prayers) precedes the sermon and, using many of the same appeals to the emotions that are to be found in the sermons, serves to prepare the way, to set the mood, for the ultimate emotional frenzy caused by the sermon. The following prayers reveal the importance of the prayer for pathetic appeal:

[*The congregation, bowed, hums the last verse of "My Faith Looks up to Thee" as the deacon moves searchingly and rhythmically into his prayer.*] "Dear Lawd, we come befo' Thee and ask Thee ter stand by us. Thank Thee for ev'ry thing Thou's did for us. Christ, essemble between these four walls; git in the hearts uv men and women, boys and girls, Thou art God an' God alone.

"Since the last time we's bowed, we's done things what we ought not uv done, an' we's left things undone what we ought uv done. Rule over Heav'n and earth; rule over these people down here, the sick an' afflicted and weary. And bind us one to another.

"Now, Lawd, when it come our time to *die*, pray You receive us into Thy kingdom an' give our souls a resting place. Amen."(1)

The following prayer was given by a minister (not the one who delivered the sermon) from the pulpit:

"We thank Thee this morning for the opportunity extended towards us. Thank Thee that Thou hast saw fit to have us continue here in Thy vineyard to work out our soul salvation. Thank Thee that Thou hast left a written record, guide, and assurance that we have at Thy right-hand-side a friend, a friend-in-deed; at Thy right-hand-side a scarred Savior; at Thy right-hand-side a mediator and redeemer—but standing to receive our souls.

"Thou have widen the way for us. We're knowed by our acts as did the disciples. They knowed Him by breaking of bread, giving livin' circumstance; to those we does meet, may we realize by our acts (by being born again) become living witness of Him.

"Paul said to the Corinthi'ns. brothern, that—that 'He came at Peenakost; and last of all, I saw Him myself.' May we see 'im in our conversion and may we see 'im as we go about our daily occupation.

"Now we pray Thee, bless the man of the hour. The Man of God. The one that Thou hast at present in this foreign part of the vineyard. When we are called from here to another world, Jesus did promise to sinner on cross, may we kneel at Thy feet and cry, 'Redeemer!' Amen." (1)

These prayers reveal the effectiveness of prayer in emotional appeal: They "warm up" the emotions of the audience for the sermon. The Negro's old-time religious prayer is not confined to the church. Outside the church, it keeps the emotional flame alive. It replaces the sermon at home, at the sick-bed, and at "wakes."[12] The prayer given at a "wake" in the "Black Belt" is not unusual—and demonstrates too the new influences, which fight against the prayer's old-time emotional appeal:

" 'Oh, Gawd, we come this evenin' beared down wid the sorrows of this worl.' We come as paupers to Thy th'one o' grace. We been down in the valley o' the shadder, an' our hearts is heavy this evenin,' Lord. Thou's done thundered fo'th Thy will. Thou's done took from out our mist one o' Yo' lambs. Thou's done took a good brother who's done lived his 'lotted time an' died, Gawd, like we all mus' die. Ummmmmmmmmmmmm. Thou's done come into this house o' sons an' wid Yo' own han', Yo' own grat han', Gawd—Ummmmmmmmmmmmmm—Thou's done dashed down the vessel outa what Yo' po'ed life into them. Thou's done took a father an' a gran'-father. Thou's done beared down hearts. Thou's done put burdens on 'em. Thou's done whupped 'em wid stripes. 'Member dese hearts, great Gawd. Relieve 'em. You know when t' suns's been a-shinin' too long an' the earth's all parched an' barren, You sen's Yo' rain, Lord. You relieve the earth. When wars rage, like the one ragin' now, an' mens dies an' makes widders an' orfins, den, in Yo' own good time, Gawd—Yo' precious time Ummmmmmm —You sen's peace. You takes the burden off'n the hearts o' nations. An' You promise', Father, by the sweetflowin' blood o' Jesus, to rescue the perishin', suckle the needy, give health to the ailin'. . . . ' He did not pause at a piercing scream from Jamie. [*She is shouting.*] His extended fingers worked spasmodically, as if each had a life, independent of him. '. . . An' sen' balm to the hearts o' sufferin'. Sen' it now, Lord. Let it flow like the healin' waters o' Gilead, an' ease the burden o' dese hearts broken by the fulfillin' o' Yo' almighty will. Amen.'

"The preacher opened his eyes and looked around as he lowered his arms, shooting his cuffs as he did so. The three brothers stared at spots about six inches beyond their toes. One corner of his thick mouth drawn in a hard snarl, Paul lifted the pitcher [*of whisky*] from the table and drank. In the other room there was a general snuffling and loosening of throats. Walter was the first to recover.

" 'That was a fine prayer, Rev'ren',' he said. 'Mighty fine.'

" 'Thank you, brother. I s'pose the arrangement's ain't been changed none sence I talked wid y'all?'

" 'No they ain't, Rev'ren. Not's I knows of,' Walter said, looking at Neely.

" 'Ain't been nothin' changed,' Neely said.

" 'That's fine. That's jus' fine,' the preacher said pompously. 'Uncle Henry's [*Refers to the dead man.*] goin, a smile up there wid Gawd tomorrer. I'm aimin' to do him proud.'

"With that, he went back into the other room. Neely closed the door.

" 'He can lay a pow'ful prayer,' Henry said.

" 'Yeah,' said Paul. 'He comes on like Gang Busters.' "[13]

The prayer, like the sermon, appeals to the emotions of gratitude to God, compassion, fear of death, fear of God, sorrow, shame; it, too, employs suggestion.

Like the prayer, the singing is important in stimulating the emotions. The hymn (like the spiritual) is really a blending of emotions. The words themselves are unintelligible unless they are "lined." That is, someone states a line or two before the audience sings them; the audience sings and pauses while additional lines are stated; the singing continues in this manner until the end; the audience is seated part of the time and stands part of the time. Even after the song is "lined," the words are so run together in the long-meter fashion that they are not distinguishable. Such singing is an emotional experience, like an instrumental rendition. Spirituals carry the same emotional charge. The singing[14] is so important in setting the stage emotionally that the sermon is almost inconceivable without it.

The old-time Negro preacher appeals to the audience's *sympathy* for him. A minister often begins a sermon in this manner:

> "Not feeling good; got headache," (III)

Or:

> "I haven't felt good all day. Gonna 'make it' all right." (VI)

Second in importance, perhaps, to the appeal to the emotion of fear is the minister's appeal to *hope*, the basis of escape from this world. It enables the Negro to endure the trials of this life in expectation of the joys of a new life after death:

> "If we [*want to*] get to Heaven, we must learn to bear one another's burden." (II)
> "Heaven! I feel like it's a very splendid place." (III)
> "The sweetness of His disposition in the hearts of many have caused us to have hope." (v)
> [*God's going to*] "take you in Kingdom; see after you. No rain; [*The audience intones each of the statements.*] no bad weather; no trouble; no sorrow; no crying; Lord. . . !" (III)

The Negro minister appeals to the audience's *common sense*:

> "You know, sometimes a feller take things off people he wouldn't do it, but it's conditions." (III)
> "Yo' own kin folks sometimes kin be your worst worry. Yo' own kin folks do you mo' harm den anybody else." [*"It's de truf!"*] (VIII)

Referring to having helped another minister in the latter's revival, one minister appeals to the listeners' *pride*:

> They "gave me swell time down there. Only one thing. . . : didn't have the spirit you got." (III)

This statement demonstrates the effective use of flattery; it also indicates that Negro ministers, in their "play" upon the emotions of the audience, encourage the listeners to speak out with "amens," to sing, moan, and use other actions associated with the climactic emotional state. The following are not *suggestions;* they are *requests:*

"I ain't expectin' dumb people to sing, but even dey got ways to make signs." (VIII)

"Want yer to follow me pretty close. . . . Don't lack what I'm saying, go on and talk anyhow.[15] ["*Amens,*" *etc.*] Help me out some . . . . Don't look at me; open your mouth! . . . Now, John, I want you ter help me out. . . ." (VI)

"You'll do. Talk to me now. Then little black places dere ain't no good if you can just sit down. . . . *Benches can't say Amen.* You all can hear, can't yer?" (III)

The following are closer to suggestions:

"Whatever fer you all this evening, [*In the way of getting "happy."*] just hold yer cups. . . , yer git it. . . . So jest keep everything waiting and we'll see what's gwine to come ter you." (V)

"Ain't you never got happy? By yourself?" (III)

"Yer know, when us git hooked up here together, it's like a city and a town, ain't it? When you turn on the light. . . . It shine everwhar." (V)

As the audience becomes emotionally aroused, the hypnotist-like minister uses suggestion more frequently; the members of the audience are under his spell now to a greater degree; they take his suggestions more easily:

"Preach it out there with me. I know what I'm talkin' 'bout. You too!" (III)

"Oh Lord! Let's call on Him this evening" (II)

"We live it [*the Christian life*]. . . in your songs, your moans, and your groans."

"I heard Your [*God's*] influence in town—talk, Children of God!" (III)

"One reason why . . . we can't all cry the same cry [*Audience moans.*] is we neglect our spirit [*Moan.*] and we get luke-warm. . . . The spirit can't find its way into our soul. I tell you, if you let the spirit find its way into your heart, it'll move in your heart and it'll make you move. Ahhhhhhhhhh, Glory! Jeremiah said, 'It's like fire shut up in my bones' and, 'It's like a mighty hammer.' Oh, Glory! But I'll tell you what it'll do for you. . . . It'll make you forget about your trials. And then you'll say, 'Whatever it takes, [*Loud accent by striking the speaker's stand rhythmically.*] I'm going on. . . .' " (IV)

[117]

"On bended knees, won't He tell yer whut ter do? [*"Preach, sir!" etc.*] My belove', yer know, something have to happen. . . . God have ter let somethin' happen! [*Tear it up!" screams a woman, etc.*] My belove'. . . . And ole Paul said he had a great God. . . . [*"Hold yer horse, boy!" "Talk, hon'," says a woman; "Pull 'em down!" etc.*] The whole world. . . . " [*Words lost in audience reaction.*] (VII)

This preacher stimulates the emotions of his audience by telling of his "call" to preach. In all instances, when the members of the audience are excited and open to the mildest suggestion, they are thinking of their own trials, joys, and sorrows, and their emotional condition is heightened by the rhythmical delivery and their own actions. With their strong imaginations, they are ready to explode emotionally at any word which vaguely suggests their trials or joys. Every such word is now charged. Often the relationship between the word suggesting the sorrow or joy (which results in shouting) and the sorrow or joy is so vague to the outsider that the preaching appears incoherent° and the shouting, inexplainable. For example, when the minister, after telling the Biblical story of Joseph the Dreamer, says:

"I seed Him. . . . , a shield over here one Sunday mornin'. He was takin' on board. . . . And I *dream, chillun*," [*Sings the last two words; the audience joins in. Shouting.*] (III)

he unlocks the door of his audience's world with the words *"dream, chillun."* They too had trials and problems (like Joseph); they too were *dreaming* and hoping for a better day to come. When the preacher says "dream, chillun," he stimulates thoughts and emotions within the audience which lie too deep for words. The people understand; they shout. "How long" is the unlocking key to the door of frustration when a minister moans:

"How long? How long must I work in the vineyard?"

The words "how long" suggest to the Negro his apparently endless chain of trials. How often he has wondered *how long* the Lord would permit his chosen servant to be mistreated in this world below. *"How long."* Pent up emotions overflow. Shouting. Another minister stimulates an audience to the brink of shouting madness with the word *pray*:

"When you feeling lonely, *pray* right on! Lord! . . . Can't do nothn' unless you a prayin' person. *Pray! Pray!.*" [*One woman screams and shouts. Another cries, "Preach it ter us!"*] (VIII)

° "Speaking in tongues" is the description sometimes used.

When the preacher uses the word "pray," the Negroes think of the many mistreatments heaped upon them; they must bear their misfortune, being able only to pray to God about those who misuse them. The minister knows, and they know too, that prayer is a weapon which the "Lords of the Land" cannot take away from them. "Pray!" They shout. The same type of suggestion in the word *looking* causes shouting. The minister merely moans:

> "When you ask God for a blessing, don't you *look* for it? Looking!." [*Shouts.*] (VIII)

Looking strikes the emotion of hope; they are all hoping and looking for a better day. The minister goes even further than the remote connections of the words and the ideas. He plays directly upon the emotion of *sorrow*—the following thought is thrown in and has absolutely no apparent thought connection with that which preceded or followed it:

> "Ehhhhhhhh, Lord! [*Intoned.*] I jest feel lack saying sometime, 'I lost both of my hands, both of my hands; let me git my hand.' [*Intoned.*] Need to look for 'em!" (VIII)

But there is emotional connection. The minister wants the audience to experience the emotion of *sadness* and *sorrow*. He gives them an image, but it is not the loss of their hands which causes them to shout; they still have their hands. But with their strong imagination, and by concentration, they easily make the association, and find the door to the *sorrow of their lowly condition;* this sorrow is within them, a smouldering ember which they have brought to church.[17] That is the ultimate in the power of old-time Negro preaching to arouse the emotions of the audience through suggestion.[18]

The Macon County sermons reveal pathetic appeal which is not characteristic of original old-time Negro preaching. One minister, for example, appeals to the *desire for success* "in this life" in a coldly intellectual manner:

> "We must love God if we want to be successful in this life." (I)

Then, reverting to the old-time religion, he adds: "If you want to be saved, [*That is the original note.*] must love God. . . ." (I). He builds the entire intellectual part of his sermon on an appeal to the audience's *desire for security and success in this life.* His theme is "It's Dangerous to Neglect." (IV). In the old-time religious aspect of this sermon, however, the minister stresses the belief that a neglect of salvation in this life might deprive one of the future life. But these notes of the new influence are off-key in Macon County preaching.

Basically, Macon County preaching still employs original old-time Negro preaching pathetic appeal. Ministers appeal most frequently to *fear* and to *hope*, but there are also appeals to *common sense, pride, shame, gratitude, compassion, duty, joy, sorrow, pain, affection, hatred, love, desire for happiness, etc.* Basic, however, is the Negro's subconscious (and conscious) desire and need to escape from "an impossible world"; the emotional outbursts of shouting, laughing, and crying serve this purpose psychologically. Pathetic appeal is as important in the persuasion of Macon County sermons as it was in the original old-time Negro preaching.

LOGICAL ARGUMENT[19]—One observer of old-time Negro preaching says the preacher only assumes an appearance of being logical. Certainly these ministers are entirely unaware of the classical works on logic. But logical argument does appear in the Macon County sermons. What are these aspects? Are there enthymemes? Are there arguments from examples, from authority, from analogy, from cause to effect, from effect to cause, from effect to effect? By inference, by explication? Are there negative arguments, confutational arguments? Is there reasoning by contrast and comparison? Which are most frequently used? What is the nature of the new influence of old-time preaching, if there are any indications?

The most frequent type of logical argument in the Macon County sermons is argument from authority. The usual authority or source (Sermon IV excepted) is the Bible. The Bible is the basis for practically all proofs; it is the source of examples and evidence. The Bible is the great storehouse of information and material for these Macon County preachers, as it was for the original old-time Negro preacher. The dominant type of the logical argument, then, in Macon County preaching is the use of evidence and authority from the Bible.

Four types of argument from Biblical authority appear: (1) argument presented with the Bible as the direct authority; (2) argument which is a generalization based upon examples which are cited on authority of the Bible; (3) argument presented with no direct reference, but which implies the authority of the Bible; and (4) argument based upon one Biblical reference or example.

Because the information of the "Black Belt" Negro preacher is Biblical in the main, his arguments often have only the Bible as the direct authority. The following illustrates the manner in which these preachers, using no other process of reasoning to establish a contention, use the Bible as the great authority:

"The Bible tells, 'We shall know them by their fruits.'" (II)

The minister needs no other proof or authority that men are to be known by their "fruits" what they do in life). Who would dare question the authority of the Bible?

Argument reached by a generalization based upon examples cited on the authority of the Bible are not frequent, because these ministers and their hearers accept the word of the Bible; one Biblical reference is satisfactory. In Sermon I, the minister (showing some influence of education on old-time preaching) does establish a number of examples (*he calls them "facts"*) by Biblical authority and then by inductive reasoning comes to the conclusion:

> "Since these are the facts, we come to the conclusion: as we go forward in life, we should go forward toiling for the Master, using all our knowledge, all our wisdom. . . , a living influence to lead the wanderer to the fold of Christ." (I)

One might expect uneducated Negro ministers to present argument which implies the authority of the Bible. Although the preachers are filled with the ideas of the Bible, they do not always know the exact quotation or its location in the Bible; they only know that "somebody said it somewhere in the Bible." Jesus is often quoted in this manner. For example:

> "I don't care how humble, how submissive you are, you gwine make a mistake sometime, because Jesus said, [*He does not say where in the Bible.*] 'There's no perfect person on earth.'" (VIII)
> "If you never do wrong, you don't have no right to pray. He left His word, 'He that's already clean don't need to be made clean.' [*Certainly those exact words are not to be found in the Bible. He goes on, using an example, to clarify his idea.*] Not a woman tomorrow gwine take what de wash—gwine take—ain't gwine git dem clean garments and wash em. Huh? No, no, honey. . . . I ain't foolin' yer. I'm puttin it just as plain as you got eyes to see." (VIII)
> "Jesus said, 'Lift Me up from the earth and I draw all men unto me.' In the life you live. . . . , lift Him up. . . , in your songs, your moans, and your groans. Lift Him up." (III)
> "As the Sunday School lesson [*Biblical verses.*] bears witness, it's ours to spread, to make greater, more important and more impressive th' knowledge of our Christ." (I)

The most characteristic element of the logical argument of the sermons is argument based on one Biblical reference or example:

> "I think the more the Lord bless us the more humble we

ought to be. . . . The Master said on one occasion. . . , 'He that humble himself shall be exalted and he that exalt himself shall be abased.' . . . I don't think people ought to brag about praying, brag about how he can sing, or brag about how he can preach. . . ." (II)

After the minister has reached his generalization (people should not "brag"), he seems to reason deductively from this generalization to prove that each member of the audience should not "brag" about his ability to pray and to preach.

Observe another minister's generalization from a Biblical reference:

"It's a fine thing to be a peace-maker. . . . The Bible tell us, 'We shall know them by their fruits.' " (II)

Argument from Biblical authority often is of mixed types of reasoning. One minister quotes a passage from the Bible:

"Thou shalt love the Lord. . . , "

and, reasoning inductively from the authority of this direct Biblical reference, draws his conclusion. Then he proceeds to explain the passage, deductively (by explication)[d]:

"Your whole heart, your whole soul, and your whole mind, and your whole strength! Forceful words of the Savior. The word 'whole' itself carries a strong meaning. . . . " (I)

Implication is used with the argument from the Bible as the authority:

"Love alone is not enough. In the 13th Chapter of 1st Corinthians there is no praise given to love alone." (I)

He infers that (since no mention is made in the 13th Chapter of 1st Corinthians that love alone is sufficient) the implication of the Bible is that love alone *is not* sufficient. This, then, becomes the authority for his generalization that love is not sufficient.

Occasionally the minister presents evidence from the Bible and draws a conclusion somewhat contrary to logical reasoning (the audience accepts it, however, because they respect him as a Man of God) :

"If we [*are to*] get to Heaven, [*Effect.*] we must learn to bear one another's burden. [*Cause.*] Jesus said, 'Take your burden to the Lord and leave it there.' " (II)

---

[d] This is a straightforward explanation of a proposition, but such an argument is in reality a series of enthymemes which the audience accepts. It is the type of reasoning used, for example, by the school teacher—by those who speak from the vantage point of superior knowledge.

One observes the reasoning from causal relation (argument from effect to cause) and also sees that the minister's Biblical authority does not necessarily lead to his generalization: bearing "one another's burden"; the logical conclusion might be: do not bear "one another's burden" but "take your burden to the Lord."

Then there is the negative argument: showing what a thing *is* by showing what *it is not*. One minister who would convince his audience that they should "grow closer" to God, reasons in this manner:

> "Seems very common that we often see people grow in knowledge and wisdom and understanding and grow *away* from God. . . . " (I)

Another minister, using contrast as a method of reasoning, first shows what prayer should *not* be and then tells what is *should* be:

> "Some uv us speak just cost us got physical living, good voice, know a little somethin' 'bout the Bible; we say it over in our prayer sometime just to be huard by men. But a prayer is a sincere desire. A prayer come up outta the heart, wid a meaning into it." [*The authority of the Bible is implied.*] (VIII)

And this minister, using argument by explication and elimination, tells what the Word of God *is not* before telling what the Word of God *is*:

> "One Word! Not the word of Greek, Latin, grammar, Moody; not a word of source from anybody but God. The Word of God is food. The Word of God is shelter. The Word of God is water. The Word of God is protection." (III)

Old-time religion offers the Negro a means of escape from "an impossible world." This process includes a comparison of the Negro's condition with that of the characters of the Bible. Accordingly, it is not surprising to find that argument by analogy plays an important role in Macon County preaching. For example, after describing the uselessness of Baal, the idol god mentioned in the Bible, a minister says:

> "When you worshipin' up a man, ain' nothin' but Baal. . . . When you worshipin' up that fine car you got, ain't nothin' but Baal." (VI)

The following analogies need no comment:

> "The same gallows that Haemon built for Modekiah, he got hung on it himself. And when he hung old man Haemon he had ten sons and they hung dem. It's a bad thing to bother with a Child of God." (VI)

"Whatever fer you all this evening, just hold yer cups, and whatever fer yer all, yer git it. Kinda like a mail-carrier or post office: give yer whatever fer yer."ᵉ (v)

"Yer know, when [*Referring to a previous speaker.*] wuz talkin' showing ya!l somethin' happen in de days of old. . . . ; dem days was, de days of old, just like de is now." (vii)

" 'Ah, Jerusalem, repent!' [*cried John.*] Jews was in Jerusalem; Pharisees, Sadduces, all of them her [*there*]. Preach! I'm preachin' to everybody in here today. Sinner here, I'm preachin' to dem; Christian here, I'm preachin' to dem; hypocrite here, [*Probably directed at the author.*] I'm preaching to him." (iii)

John "preached only one text. I'm got to git 'nother text every time I come here." (iii)

After showing how his brothers eventually had to bow down to Joseph, the preacher says:

"The very one you hate in this world, the very one you walk around, the one you gwine scorn, chillun, is the very one gwine fan the flies outta yo' face. That feller you got ter order into yer home, he's gwine walk pass yo' door, because he couldn't pass another way. Dey ain't had no idea dat dey'd have to come to bow to Joseph." (viii)

This story of Joseph and his jealous brothers offered the minister a good opportunity to compare conditions today with those of Joseph's day and to show that jealousy is undesirable (as well as to enable the minister to indulge in humor):

"Jealousy is a bad thing. . . . Some men can't work 'cause de [*they*] so jealous. . . . When you working, you jest worried in mind. Can't wait tell he git home. . . . You can tell 'im dat Old Buck ain't been here, but he don't believe you." (viii)

There were not many people in the audience (they came later), but the preacher reasoned that he should not let that worry him:

"John was a preacher and he went down there by himself. . . . Wasn't no crowd down there when he got dere." (iii)

Often there is genuine wisdom in the analogy:

"When the Tempter [*the Devil*] came to him, [*he said to Jesus,*] 'If thou the Son of Man, turn these rocks to bread.' . . . Testing Jesus. . . .If He done got hungry, 'then make bread otta these stones. . . . ' They say to Him, 'If Thou be the Son of God command that these stones be made bread.' . . . They thought that

---

ᵉ Not based directly on the Bible; such an analogy is rare.

a fast change Him and carry Him their way. Some folks, if dey carry you their way, it's all right; ain't got nothin' to do for you if dey can't." (III)

" 'He [*Christ, before the Tempter, who has ordered Him to make bread out of rocks.*] hungry; got nothin' to eat and got no money, and quite natural He'll yield to it.' You know, sometimes a feller take things off people he wouldn't do, but it's conditions. Conditions make you do things that you wouldn't do. If conditions didn't have us so 'tight,' [*Cause.*] don't you know you wouldn't work all day and all night Saturday? [*Effect.*] Our Conditions." (III)

Sometimes the completion of the analogy is left to the audience:

"I been had hold Him [*Jesus*] a long time. He ain't never let me down. . . . Won't He take care of you, chillun? I done tried! I know He do take care of you. . . . [*Therefore, He'll take care of you, sinner.*] Gwine open de doors of the church." (III)

In the following, the minister uses generalization based on a specific example (not from the Bible, but implying the authority of the Bible) and also infers or suggests an analogy:

"We come to this house [*the church*] for the purpose of singing and praying. . . . I believe in doing everything where it ought to be done at. I believe when you have a car, don't put no gas in no radiator; it don't belong dere. Put de water in de radiator and the gas in the tank whar it belong and it'll do good." (V)

From the speaker's delivery and the situation at the time, everyone knew the suggested analogy was that the church was not the place for making recordings.

This minister uses inference purely and simply:[f]

"The famed John had a raiment with camel hair on it, brother. John advertised." (III)

Thus far, the Macon County preacher's inductive argument has been analyzed (1) from specific instances; (2) from analogy; and (3) from authority (usually the Bible). There is also the inductive argument from causal relation. Following are examples of reasoning from cause to effect:

"Some folks say, 'I'm a straight man myself; I'm a straight woman. . . . [*Cause.*] You just go her way; you'll find out whether she's straight or not." [*Effect.*] (III)

---

[f] He is incorrect in believing that John's coat was like the expensive camel hair coats of today.

"A parent's whole heart must be fixed on Christ, [*Cause.*] so that she can dictate the right policies for the correct guidance of th' child." [*Effect.*] (I)

"We must love God supremely [*Cause.*] if we desire to be successful in this life [*Effect.*]." (I)

"If people [*would*] think about [*the*] responsibility Jesus take, [*Cause.*] the world would be better." [*Effect.*] (II)

There is reasoning from effect to cause:

You "can't make a good deacon [*Effect.*] undoubt yer a prayin' man; [*Cause.*] can't make a good Mother of the Church [*Effect.*] undoubt yer a prayin' woman." [*Cause.*] (VIII)

"A child's a man at twelve years old. [*Effect.*] But us ruin our little chillun. . . : 'Mamma's little man'; 'Mamma's little woman'." [*Cause.*] (VIII)

"It gives you a better understanding of our Master [*Effect.*] when we can bend to the will, comply to the behest of our Master." [*Cause.*] (I)

Mention has been made of the deductive argument of explication, the teacher-like explanation (from a position of superior knowledge) which is really a series of enthymemes the audience also believes. The "Man of God," as is expected, uses this type of argument often:

"The reason we come together is to sing, pray and talk about God." (V)

"When God wakes you up, you don't have to think." (VI)

"This here [*the Bible*] the only book to give you a true record of God's Word." (VI)

"Yer hear His Word: His Word is good." (V)

"I know what I's telling you 'bout. . . . Heaven! I feel like it's a very splendid place. . . . I feel like it's the best place ever I had known." (III)

"Truth breaks down things." (III)

"All we know, all we grasp, all we get control of should render us nearer to the Master." (I)

Argument by explication is often mixed with another type of argument. Inference is used with explication:

"There have never been a man. . . gwine to school to git his diploma on God." (II)

Speaking as an authority, he says man has never "gone to school to get a diploma on God;" then he infers from this "evidence" that God must be above man's understanding. The preacher says again:

[126]

"Had not been for the influence of Calvary [*Cause.*], man would have had no Salvation." [*Effect.*] (II)

With a suggestion of an analogy, the preacher explains the audience into the understanding that they should love God more:

"We should grow in intelligence, grow in intellect, grow in mind, grow in understanding, and grow in the love of God." (I)

Contrast seems to be a part of the following argument by explication:

"The Nigger handlin' it [*the Bible*] may be wrong, but the Record is right." (VI)

These sermons from Macon County also show many instances of refutation. One minister, for example, clears himself of the blame for mistakes that might be made in his sermon by making the Lord responsible:

"Dere's people done come for one thing and some come for another. Some uv 'em done come here looking for mistakes. [*He refers to the recorder.*] Well now, I know dat feller ain't gwine be disappointed, 'cause I'se full uv dem. . . . I can't go nowhere unless the Lord lead me. . . . " (VI)

Another minister becomes involved in a grammatical refutation:

"Heard a feller say in Atlanta the other day, [*Talking voice now.*] Sunday School. . . . , that that word 'shalt thou' and 'shall thou' much difference; that he doubt that the thief was on the right side of the Savior. . . . 'Thou *shalt*' short. Don't let nobody fool you; He told the thief, 'You *will be* with me; where I go, you also.' " (II)

Not good refutation? It convinced his audience, apparently. But the common type of refutation is with the authority of the Word of God:

"There is a little song that says something like this: 'Time change. . . . Do whatever you please; there is no harm.'
"But you can't find a way around the Savior's strong answer and still be followers of Christ. The Savior say that the time and condition doesn't change the law: 'Thou shalt love the Lord thy God with all thy heart, with all thy soul, and with all thy mind.' " (I)

A common device of refutation (in debate) is to accept the opposition's arguments, but show that these arguments lead to a different conclusion, a conclusion that helps one's own contention. For example, one minister proceeds as follows to refute "education's stand" against loving God more:

"Of course we can have intelligent homes. . . . God doesn't disapprove of our culture. . . . Certainly not! He placed things here for us. . . . But, my brothers and sisters and friends, when we drift away from Him, when we after He has given us all these opportunities. . . ; we should not forget that with all this we should love Him. . . . " (I)

After another minister had criticized his audience severely for not "bringing up their children right," he strikes at any opposition to his approach:

"Yall don't lack dis argerment, but it's good! It's good!" (VIII)

Even ridicule (*reductio ad absurdum*) is not overlooked:

"Feller say, 'Son, go to Heaven; sweetmilk and honey dere.' Son replies, 'Don't lack 'em. So I will have nothin' ter eat.' Nigger ought be knocked in head—'Don't lack 'em'!" (III)

These illustrations of logical argument are not typical of *all* parts of Macon County sermons. In every instance there is little or no logical appeal at the highest emotional point of the sermon. For example, this minister is "arguing" throughout his sermon that God is mysterious, and now, in his rhythmical stride, he is at the "Mount Calvery argerment" (the audience is excited emotionally):

"Last thought and last outline—Mount Calvery. . . . Ah, the world swolled up 'gainst man; the seven seas swolled up 'gainst man. Lawd! Telephone wire done come off the post—torn down. Lawd! Gonna make one day—it— Last mountain, Mount Calvery. Man had no salvation. I kin see 'im goin', 'I must go to Calvery.' Ah, Lord! 'Captain's been waiting for me; Captain been looking for me; Captain have been waiting for me—four thousand years ago.' Ohhhhhhh, Glory! Going to Calvery, upon the mountain. Last thought, Mount Calvery. Look at Him this morning on Calvery! Two thieves hang beside Him; tried to make His death disgraceful. Thief beside Man of Calvery. Of God's mysteries on Mountains. Tried to make Him a bad man. Ohhhhhhhhh, Lawd! On Calvery dying. Great mystery on the mountain. Look at Him dying on Calvery. . . . " (II)

The preacher is appealing to his audience. But not mainly by logical argument. He uses description, delivery (rhythm, gestures, and voice modulation) to appeal to their emotions (pathetic appeal). Logical argument is reserved for calmer moments, which form the greater part of most of these sermons. The point of high emotional excitement lasts but a short time; however, the sermons are relatively long. Even when the climax has been reached, the minister often changes his pace suddenly to use logical argument, and then moves on to another emotional climax.

The new influence is apparent when a minister sustains logical argument throughout the greater part of his sermon. This was true in Sermon I and in Sermon IV. The logical argument of a part of the latter follows a method which seems to be a complete exhaustion of the subject by inductive reasoning. The conclusion, or theme, for the entire sermon is: "It's Dangerous to Neglect."

This theme is inferred from the Bible:

> " 'I went by the field of the slothful, and by the vineyard of the man void of understanding; And, lo, it was all grown over with thorns, and nettles had covered the face thereof, and the stone wall thereof was broken down. Then I saw, and considered it well; I looked upon it, and received instruction. Yet a little sleep, a little slumber, a little folding of the hands to sleep: So shall thy poverty come as one that travelleth; and thy want as an armed man.' " (IV)

Then the minister says:

> "This is our text, *Proverbs* the 24th Chapter, beginning with the 30th through the 34th verse. From these verses the theme *suggest* itself to our minds is this: The Danger of Neglect."

Following is a consideration of his argument:

FIRST SUPPORTING ARGUMENT: "Most calamities and accidents are caused by neglect."

Specific instances to prove this argument:

1. The misfortune of Amelia Earhart.
2. The death of Dr. L. K. Williams in an airplane.
3. The railway wreck on the Little Southern Railway.
4. The sinking of the *Titanic*.
5. A negligent merchant. (Reasons from cause to effect.)
6. A negligent gardener. (Reasons from cause to effect.)
7. Negligence of proper food and clothing. (Reasons from cause to effect.)

[These instances have as proof his word (by explication) and reasoning from cause to effect.]

SECOND SUPPORTING ARGUMENT: "Where ignorance predominates, there is always a great loss."

[This is the manner in which he supports this argument: "For

[129]

the mind, to be neglected, there will be no education. And *where ignorance predominates, there is always a great loss.* Solomon said in *Proverbs*, 29, 2, 'When the wicked beareth rule, the people mourn.' So, then, it produces a great loss" (VI). Everything centers around the meaning of the word "wicked." But, first, by means of reasoning from *cause* (neglect of the mind) to *effect* (no education), he makes (by explication) "lack of education" mean "ignorance." Then, using a single quotation from Solomon (argument from the authority of the Bible, one specific reference), he proves that ignorance causes a loss (if one accepts his reasoning by explication that "wicked" means "ignorance").]

THIRD SUPPORTING ARGUMENT: "Where conscience is neglected, there will be heathenism, cannibals and prisons."

[Substantiated by explication only.]

FOURTH SUPPORTING ARGUMENT: "The soul, neglected, becomes dwarfed and die."

[He uses an analogy for support: "Maybe with this illustration you see the condition of a soul that has been neglected. When the basket-maker works his white oak around in the yard, under the shade tree, once in a while he'll leave a piece of it laying out in the sunshine and the sunshine will so twist and so dry that piece of all until it's impossible to put it back in any kind of shape. It was neglected; it wasn't put in the shade or in the water, but it was left out in the sunshine. And that's the way it is with a soul that's been neglected. It loses its shape and it soon dies."]

FIFTH SUPPORTING ARGUMENT: "Neglect weakens the power to decide."

[He supports this by giving one specific instance, not from the Bible.]

SIXTH SUPPORTING ARGUMENT: "Neglect produces a loss of sensitiveness."

[He gives two examples, neither from the Bible.]

SEVENTH SUPPORTING ARGUMENT: "Neglect destroys interest . . . in school . . . , music . . . , social affairs . . . , in the soul of man."

[He gives general reference to the Word of God as the authority; mostly argument by explication.]

EIGHTH SUPPORTING ARGUMENT: "Neglect in any way cause a great danger."

[He lists specific instances:

1. The man who, neglecting to remove a living snake from his bosom, was bitten; he died.

2. A huntsman who, neglecting to unload his gun, shot his daughter; she died.
3. A man who, neglecting to learn to swim, saw his only child sinking into the water; she died.]

NINTH SUPPORTING ARGUMENT: "Dangerous to neglect salvation."
   [He supports this by:
1. Biblical authority: Paul, Book of Hebrew, Job.
2. Analogy and implied Biblical authority: "I looked one day, I tried to figure a way 'round Him; tried to neglect salvation. But I just kept on reading where He said to Nicodemus, 'You must be born again.' "
3. Contrast and authority: "I said, 'Well, now, men escape from the county chain gang; then,' I said, 'men escape sometimes from the jail house; they escape from their state prisons sometimes and then every once in a while, somebody escape from the federal prison.' . . . But I could hear the Word of my God ringing in my heart, good news and glad tidings, saying, 'It ain't no way around salvation.' "]

CONCLUSION: "It's dangerous to neglect." (IV)

Logical argument as a whole in the sermons offers evidence of both inductive and deductive reasoning: argument from specific in-

CHART 3. METHODS OF PROOF IN MACON COUNTY SERMONS

SERMON	ETHOS†	PATHOS‡	LOGICAL ARGUMENT
I	b	a	a
II	a	a	c
III	a	a	b
IV	a	a	a
V	a	a	b
VI	a	a	c
VII	a	a	c
VIII	a	a	b

† persuasion through the character of the speaker
‡ persuasion through the emotion

   KEY: a—primary
        b—secondary
        c—little or none

stances, argument from causal relation, argument from the authority of the Bible (by far the most characteristic type of logical argument), argument from analogy, by inference, by explication, negative argument, and reasoning from contrast and comparison. Much of this is the new influence in preaching, but much of it seems to be a part of old-time Negro preaching. Little appears during the emotional climax of the sermons. Much of the argument merely *appears* to be logic, but it apparently convinces the audience. Chart 3 indicates the methods of proof in the preaching.

SUMMARY OF MODES OF PERSUASION — Old-time Negro preaching, as reflected in the sermons recorded in Macon County, uses all three modes of persuasion: ethos, pathos, and logical argument. Pathetic appeal is easily the appeal used most often by the old-time Negro preacher, but ethical persuasion follows close behind in importance. Logical argument is emphasized more in the new, more-educated type of preaching than in the old-time Negro preaching. But logical argument does play a part in old-time Negro preaching; it is often used during calmer moments.

INVENTION—In the matter of *Invention,* then, Macon County preaching shows both the influence of original old-time Negro preaching and the new influence of education and greater freedom. The purposes of the preaching (aside from the religious motive) are primarily to arouse the emotions (and to "raise" money) ; logical discussion and instruction are seldom the primary purposes now. For topics or ideas, the Bible is still the great source from which the ideas of God, Heaven, and sin tend to formulate the Negro's basis of emotional, religious escape from the world of reality; but ideas do come from sources other than the Bible, and this is evidence of the new influence. For modes of persuasion, these sermons indicate that some consideration should be given to logical argument, for there is evidence of both inductive and deductive reasoning in this preaching. However, logical argument occurs only at the less emotional points in the sermons, and it is emphasized more by the new type of preaching than by old-time Negro preaching. Ethical appeal (the man of God) runs a close second to the most important method of persuasion in Macon County preaching: pathetic (emotional) appeal. The preacher demands and receives emotional response from his people, for "benches can't say, 'amen.' "

This chapter illustrates another aspect of the lowly condition in which second-class citizenship keeps the Negro in the United States.

VII. Gwine Fan the Flies Outta Yo' Face[a]

"IT IS not enough to know *what* to say — one must also know *how* to say it.[1] The right way of doing this contributes much to the right impression of a speech."[2] This study of Macon County preaching has considered the *"what"* of the recorded sermons, "the facts themselves as a source of persuasion. But next comes the question, how to state these facts in language."[3] What is the nature of the language of the sermons? Is it the language of the audience? Are there apt and exact analogies and comparisons? Are they expressed in a manner which appeals to the unlearned audience? Is the language of the ministers flavored with the Bible? Does the presence of Negro dialect play an important role in these sermons? Does the style of the sermons seem to be appropriate for the speaking situation? What is the nature of the new influence on the style of old-time Negro preaching? These are questions which the treatment of *style* should answer.

A consideration of the language of Macon County preaching immediately involves the Negro dialect.[4] But Negro dialect has little rhetorical significance in the Negro sermons because the language of both the preachers and the audiences is in Negro dialect. (It is indeed significant that the ministers are speaking on the language level of their audiences). Only for the outsider does dialect color old-time Negro preaching. When Hatcher heard the original old-time preacher, John Jasper, he was moved to express himself:

> Shades of our Anglo-Saxon Father! Did mortal lips ever gush with such torrents of horrible English. Hardly a word came out clothed in its right mind.[5]

To Hatcher, who considered the language subjectively and as a student of language, Negro dialect *was* horrible; but to the audience of Negroes, the language created no distraction. Jasper's language was adjusted to his audience; it, therefore, was appropriate.[6] If Hatcher had addressed that same audience, his correct English would have appeared "horrible" to the Negroes. Suffice it to say, then, of Negro dialect in the Macon County preaching, that dialect was appropriate for the speech occasions.

---

[a] "The very one you hate in this world. . . , the one you gwine scorn, chillun, is the one gwine fan the flies outta yo' face." (VII)

James Weldon Johnson thinks the preacher's Negro dialect is often misrepresented. He believes the old-time Negro preacher's language is unique:

> The old-time Negro preachers, though they actually used dialect in their ordinary intercourse, stepped out from its narrow confines when they preached. They were all saturated with the sublime phraseology of the Hebrew prophets and steeped in the idioms of King James English, so when they preached and warmed to their work they spoke another language, a language far removed from traditional Negro dialect. It was really a fusion of Negro idioms with Bible English; and in this there may have been, after all, some kinship with the innate grandiloquence of their old African tongues. To place in the mouths of the talented old-time Negro preachers a language that is a literary imitation of Mississippi, cotton-field dialect is sheer burlesque.[7]

That was the original old-time Negro preacher; his language was Biblical. We shall see how this conception compares with the language of Macon County preaching today.

The style of the sermons indicates the influence of the Bible in the use of words and phrases. Like the 1641 edition of the King James version of the Bible, the language of these sermons reveals a preponderance of plain, familiar, short, and simple words. A study of the length of the words in these sermons (*see* Chart 4) reveals that more than 75% of the words have from two to five letters; 20.8% of the words are 2-letter words; and the average number of letters per word for all the sermons is 3.73 letters. These figures indicate the use of short words, which secure clearness because they are "name-words and verbs that are current terms."[8]

Not all the words are short and simple. Occasionally, the minister uses a big word. Johnson has an explanation:

> Gross exaggeration of the use of big words by these preachers, in fact by Negroes in general, has been commonly made; the laugh being at the exhibition of ignorance involved. What is the basis of this fondness for big words? Is the predilection due, as is supposed, to ignorance desiring to parade itself as knowledge? Not at all. The old-time Negro preacher loved the sonorous, mouth-filling, ear-filling phrase because it gratified a highly developed sense of sound and rhythm in himself and his hearers.[9]

Macon County sermons suggest the preacher's love for a large word occasionally.

In John Jasper, the typical old-time Negro preacher, the style of

CHART 4. LENGTH OF WORDS IN MACON COUNTY SERMONS*

(stated in percentages)

SERMON	TWO-LETTER WORDS	THREE-LETTER WORDS	FOUR-LETTER WORDS	FIVE-LETTER WORDS	TOTAL	AVERAGE NUMBER OF LETTERS PER WORD†
I	25	20	21	11	77	4.08‡
II	20	23	22	14	79	3.22
III and VIII	17	29	25	13	84	3.81
IV	18	19	18	6	61	4.40‡
V	31	25	14	9	79	3.92
VI	20	33	24	10	87	3.48
VII	15	27	17	10	69	3.24
AVERAGE	20.8	25.1	20.1	10.4	76.5	3.73

* based on a 100-word passage from each sermon
† total number of letters in the passage, divided by the number of words
‡ sermon of a more educated minister

old-time preaching showed: (1) the use of Biblical English; short and simple words (a large, mouth-filling word occurred at times and gave variety to the style); and (2) the use of language which was familiar to the audience — a language of common *things* rather than of *ideas* (with the exception of Biblical ideas, which *were* used often). This is true of Macon County preaching, but new stylistic influences have entered.

The following series of descriptive symbols characterize the sermon quotations to which they apply:

1. Long, sonorous word.
2. Slang expression.
3. Biblical word (like "doth") or word showing Biblical influence.
4. Unfamiliar, strange word or phrase (dialect excepted).
5. Vivid word.
6. Original word (dialect excepted).
7. Word repeated (small vocabulary).
8. Synonym (large vocabulary).
9. Word or phrase familiar to audience, drawn from the experiences of the audience.
10. Biblical passage; might be mistaken for verbatim passage from Bible (not considering dialect).
11. Repetition of phrase (small vocabulary or lack of fluency).
12. Influence of education; proper tense of verb, etc.
13. Repetition for emphasis (influence of education).
14. Parallel construction (influence of education).

SERMON I

"Service (9) of power; service of knowledge (1); service (13, 14) of ability (1). Use to uplift (3) Him and spread th' kingdom (1) of Christ and His accomplishment (1). As the Sunday School (9) lesson bears witness (3), it's ours to spread (9), to make (9) greater, more important (1), and more impressive (1, 14) th' knowledge (1) of our Christ (9)."

SERMON II

"Quickly (5) they built (9) the altar (9) on the mountain (1) . . . and built (7) a . . . around the wall; you know about it. And they began (12) to cry (3, 5) to God (9). Called (8) Baal (9) all day and Baal (7) — from morning (9) until high twelve (4, 12) — (9) told them, 'I want you to tear down (9) your altar. . . .'"

SERMON III

"After he'd taken Him on the pinnacle (1) of dat temple, then He got hungry (9). He got — let me tell you (2) — He don't eat (9), don't drink (9). After that, at a certain time, He got hungry, see (2)? He got hungry (7). Then he [*Satan*] say that 'this is my time.' (*We are on our way.*) (2)."

SERMON IV

"And then I think of the *Titanic* (1), that great ship that started out from Southampton (1), that (14) ship (7) that had Captain (1) John Smith (12) as its captain (7) and had (7) all of the luxuries (1, 4, 8) the heart could desire. Had (7) everything for their pleasure (1) and their comfort thereon (3). They were well-warned as they left Southampton of the icebergs (1) that were way out there in the ocean."

SERMON VI

"Baal (9), Baal (7) is the god (9) — and I said the God (9) of Heaven (9), and ain't but one of them. . . . Gwine wake up (9) in the morning (9). . . . Get yourself together (2). I'm thinking right now — Sodom (1, 9) — of . . . . Ain't dat right, brethern (3, 11)? Ain't too many to try (2) yo' God."

SERMON VII

"My belove', ole, ole (11) man (2) Elijah (9) said, my belove' (11), when he got worried (9), my belove', [that he] went (9) out and set on the fence (9), my belove'. . . . Ain't it so, my belove' (11)? And . . . promised him and said (7), 'Oh, Lord (9), dey've done kill (9) all our God's folk (9). . . .' Ain't it so, my belove' (11)?"

These quotations indicate that the words and phrases of the Macon County sermons still have a Biblical flavor. But this flavor is often very weak; even the use of Biblical words like "hath" and "doth" is infrequent, but there *are* words which show the influence of the Bible. The use of short, concrete words that are within the experiences of the audience is apparent. The "Man of God" also speaks frequently in the first person singular (I); he still loves to use a mouth-filling word (often Biblical) occasionally. These uneducated speakers use repetition instead of synonyms because of their small vocabularies; the more educated preachers use parallel construction and repetition for clarity and emphasis.

The above passages also illustrate the effect of the new influence on the style of old-time Negro preaching. Macon County preaching shows a shifting away from the Biblical language which James Weldon Johnson says "was not prose but poetry."[9] The following fluent, descriptive passages *are* poetic:

"The wind hadn't blown. It thundered and no one hadn't heard!

[137]

The lightning hadn't played a lengthy game across the face of
the muddy cloud! Heaven hadn't been burned or hell even warmed
up." ["*Talk now!*"] (VI)

"The sweetness of His [*Jesus'*] disposition in the hearts of many
have caused us to have hope." (V)

"God had sent a famine on the land and in the land and had
dried up the rivers, and the grass had withered down, and the wells
had gone dry." (II)

"Lily of the valley. . . . Sundown; pinnacle of temple; Lily
of the Valley; beautiful things. . . ." (III)

But the use of such "poetic" words is restricted to the most rhythmical
and emotional climaxes — which are short and few in number.

Unlike the four quoted passages, the average passage in the sermons
is not poetic. The reason is probably the influence of education and freedom. Preachers now know of books other than the Bible; even a few
years in school have opened a new world of ideas to many of the ministers; and the preachers have heard educated ministers at conferences and
conventions. The result of these new influences is that the style of the
sermons is beginning to show signs of the use of words not based entirely
on the Bible, and the ministers are attempting such devices as periodic
construction and parallel construction to obtain emphasis rather than
beauty of expression. This is particularly true of Sermons I and IV.

Despite the new influences, however, an old-time characteristic of
the words and phrases of Macon County preaching is still the general
tendency to use down-to-earth words that are within the experiences of
the hearers. The use of slang expressions shows this tendency:

"I been 'gwine to it.' " (III) [*I have been workin' hard.*]

"I am gonna 'make it' all right." (VI) [*I am goin' to succeed
at what I am doin', but with difficulty.*]

"You got me 'in a tight.' " (VI) [*You have me in a difficult
situation.*]

"I sit on my little 'do nothin' ' and wait on time." (VII) [*I sat
on my buttock and waited.*]

"Dere wasn't no ' 'duced misute' in it." (VII) [*The sermon
was the pure, undiluted Gospel of the Bible.*]

The audence often answer with slang expressions. For example:

"Hold yer horse, boy!" [*Continue your rhythmical stride in
preaching!*]

Such slang expressions make the preacher's language vivid for the audience because these are expressions they use every day.

Almost every word, every phrase, in the Macon County sermons is charged with suggestion. Often these expressions are so much a part of the listeners that a single word or phrase suggests meaning whose full explanation would require sentences or even paragraphs.[b] These words and phrases are meant to be heard (not read) by the Negro audiences of Macon County. The use of words and phrases within the experiences of the audiences, then, is one of the most vital elements of the style of the old-time Negro preaching.

Following a discussion of words and phrases, clauses and sentences should be considered. But, because (1) the sermons under consideration were not written and (2) the preachers, in their rhythmical delivery, connected practically all their thoughts by means of coordinating conjunctions, it is difficult, if not impossible, to conclude with finality that the preacher meant *this* or *that* to be a clause or a sentence, a compound sentence or two simple sentences. (As a matter of fact, the uneducated minister has none of these grammatical ideas in mind.) It does seem, however, that the tendency is toward the use of the short, simple, declarative sentence (with the subject or verb, or both, often elliptical). This usage is not evident on first glance at the transcriptions of these sermons because of the presence of the coordinating conjunctions. However, these conjunctions are undoubtedly, in many cases, merely "jogs" between simple sentences, enabling the minister to maintain his rhythmical flow of words in delivery. Even the appearance of the interrogative sentence is often a "filler." The minister, while he is searching for his next word, often maintains the flow of rhythm by saying, for example: "Ain't dat right, brethern?" Hence, it seems the sentence structure of these sermons is (as might be expected of the language of the uneducated) of the primer-sentence type; or, because of the conjunctions, they may be labeled "and-and sentences" or "run-together sentences." From a literary point of view, this is an undesirable style, but for the down-to-earth, talking style of the Macon County preachers it is appropriate; it makes the ideas clear[10] to the audience.

Using this talking style, the Negro preacher achieves his greatest stylistic success by the use of imagery[11] or figurative language.[12] However, the minister paints his pictures with expressions that are simple, familiar, and within the experience of his listeners. Biblical truths are compared with familiar experiences in the lives of the audience, but the comparisons and analogies are always expressed in words which even the most uneducated member of the audience is able to understand. The result is that the images are vivid and clear.[13] In this manner, the Macon

---

[b] For this reason, the words and phrases of the emotional climax of an old-time Negro sermon (standing alone without subjects or predicates) seem to be incoherent to the outsider. On paper, such expressions appear senseless.

County preachers stimulate the imaginations of their listeners with image after image — taken both from the Bible and from everyday experiences.

Quotations illustrate the Macon County preachers' use of imagery—metaphors for the most part (*see* Chart 5). They reveal the secret of the ministers' ability to open the doors of the listeners' minds[c] by dwelling on words which are familiar to the audience.

Indeed, the Macon County sermons are veritable feasts of images. Even the audience is moved to speak with images, with figurative language:

> "Hold yer horse, boy!" (VII)[20]
>
> "Tear it up! . . . Talk, hon'; pull 'em down!" (VII)[21]

CHART 5. MACON COUNTY PREACHERS' USE OF IMAGERY'

FAMILIAR WORD	QUOTATION CONTAINING THE RELATED IMAGE-WORD (*italicized*)	SYMBOL DESIGNATING THE TYPE OF IMAGERY *
car	"When you worshipin' up that fine *car* you got, ain't nothin' but Baal." (VI)[14]	*v*
birth	"I know I been *born again*." (III) [15]	*v*
bristles	"Goin' ter take my time. Ef I don't raise no *bristles*, it's all right wid me." (VIII)[16]	*t, v*
crawling	"Have trouble and tribulation; sometimes afflicted; have to *crawl* into your home." (III) [17]	*m, v*
dog	"You women — same *dog* jealousy bit you." (VIII) [18]	*v; t*
flies	"The very one you hate in this world. . ., the one you gwine *scorn*, chillun, is the one gwine *fan* the *flies* outta yo' face." (VIII) [19]	*v, m; m, v, th; v, m, t*

* *v* (visual, eye); *a* (auditory, ear); *m* (motor, action); *t* (tactile, touch); *o* (olfactory, smell); *g* (gustatory, taste); *th* (thermic, temperature)

---

[c] The seven principal kinds of imagery have been called "The Seven Doors to the Mind" (V. A. Ketcham, in Sanford and Yeager, *Business Speeches by Business Men*, McGraw-Hill, New York, N. Y., 1930, pp. 405-416). They include: (1) the visual (through the eye); (2) the auditory (through the ears); (3) the motor (through action); (4) the tactile (through touch); (5) the olfactory (through smell); (6) the gustatory (through taste); and (7) the thermic (through temperature).

The images used by the preachers and by the audiences are vivid because they are based on the common, recent, and intense experiences of the audiences and the ministers.[22] Every Negro in the audience knows the meaning of "car," "birth," "bristles," "dog," "flies," "crawling." The use of imagery in this manner is easily the most significant characteristic of the style of old-time Negro preaching of Macon County.

Other scattered stylistic devices appear in these sermons: alliteration, personification, humor, irony, sarcasm, hyperbole, euphemism, negation, repetition, parallelism, dramatization (dialogue), and quotations (often incorrectly quoted) from the Bible. But these characteristics appear to be entirely subordinate to the usage of images based on the Biblical ideas and the everyday experiences of the audiences. The style, therefore, is Biblical, familiar. It is the talking style; it is a style; it is a narrative style. As Raper summarizes the direct style of the old-time preacher in Macon County:

> He talks to his congregation about Moses and Daniel at mid-day as though he had eaten breakfast with them. Incidents which the more learned preacher spends time explaining, he merely relates and presently, the 'arousements' are in evidence.[23]

A combination of this ability to speak informally in images and a natural sense of rhythm and fluency in the Negro minister prompts Woodson to say of the old-time Negro preacher's style:

> Crude sometimes though the language might be, these self-made philosophers are original, and few can hear them preach without wondering how men of such limited opportunity can speak with such fluency and wisdom.[24]

SUMMARY — The language of Macon County sermons is basically simple: short words (with a long word thrown in occasionally for effect); simple, elliptical sentences (which, however, are joined by conjunctions to help maintain the rhythmical flow of words in delivery); and slang and Negro dialect (the language of the audience). The language, like that of the Bible, is particularly methaphorical; it consists of images which open all the "doors of the mind" because they are based on the common, intense, and recent experiences of the audience (experiences which include almost any reference to or quotation from the Bible).

The style is simple and narrative. It is the style of speeches which are to be heard rather than read. It demonstrates a small vocabulary; there are patches of poetic prose, but these are few. These characteristics are definitely in the vein of the original old-time Negro preaching. However, education *has* introduced new words; two ministers who were more educated than the others tend to use longer words than the other ministers; they attempt to use words which are unfamiliar to both the audiences and to themselves, but even these two ministers seem to prefer the simple, narrative style of the original old-time preacher. Basically, little change has occurred in the style of old-time Negro preaching in Macon County. It is still so similar to the style of the Negro preaching of the days of John Jasper and Black Harry that one of these original old-time preachers might have said, "The one you gwine scorn, chillun, is the one gwine fan the flies outta yo' face." (VIII)

The English usage found in this old-time preaching declares the Negro's prolonged period of second-class citizenship in "the land of the free:" after 332 years in America, the average Negro's language is the speech of a frustrated, semi-illiterate people. When will this country "fan the flies outta" her face?

VIII.   You Don't Have to Think[a]

DISPOSITION[1] — The purpose of disposition is "to arrange what you have invented."[2] Previously in this work *the ideas* (*Invention*) of Macon County sermons are discussed. But what of the minister's arrangement of his ideas for a sermon?

The old-time Negro preacher makes little preparation for a sermon; he believes the Lord will supply the necessary words for the occasion. The old-time Negro preacher's speaking is impromptu;[3] he arranges his sermon while he is speaking.[4] Despite this "spur of the moment" arrangement, the sermons of the old-time Negro preachers do not lack uniformity in this constituent of rhetoric. What is responsible for this uniformity in arrangement? What is the nature of this arrangement? Does it conform with the four parts of a well-organized speech: (1) introduction; (2) thesis or principal idea; (3) discussion; (4) and conclusion? What is the effect of the new influences of education on the old-time arrangement of Negro sermons?

Old-time Negro sermons have practically the same organization. These sermons are all designed in part to arouse the audience to shouting and general frenzy. The plan of the sermon must conform to this overall requirement; it must do its share in the changing of a tired, subdued, calm, and quiet Negro audience into a happy, shouting, and emotional group of people. Every old-time Negro preacher is aware of this requirement, and it is this fact that accounts for a common type of arrangement in old-time Negro sermons. The arrangement consists essentially of progressive steps in the development of emotional excitement.

An analysis of the four parts of a speech, as they are reflected in the Macon County sermons, is presented below:

I. INTRODUCTION[5]

A. PURPOSE

1. To establish a common ground of religious feeling which will lead to the "arousements" (Each preacher reads a passage from the Bible):

---

[a] "When God wake you up, you don't have to think. Only one thing—to preach!" (VI)

[143]

"I'm glad we could come together again to pray and thank God, observing His will." (v)

2. To secure sympathy, confidence, and respect for the speaker:

"We had great service over there [*in Atlanta*] for twelve nights. You know about it. I'm tired." (II)

"Got me kinda run up. Communion [*to be held*] this afternoon at Red Chapel. [*I am*] to preach Anniversary Sermon. Not feeling good; been on road, two weeks of service. Journeyed all night to get home. Don't feel good; got headache." (III)

"I don't — I haven't felt good all day." (VI)

"The Lord be good ter us." (VII)

3. To make announcements:

"Revival meeting about here." (III)

B. REFERENCE
1. To the particular occasion:

"We very glad to have our visitors out with us from the Fort Valley High School. . . . We told they're taking the sermons from different churches." (II)

"I am glad to be present; happy also to see you present, your presence. Regret very much for being somewhat late; however, we hope to work out of this gradually." (IV)

2. To surroundings, to the familiar:

"You all peach-struck; you all tired; been gwine to it." (III)

II. STATEMENT OF THE TEXT

Invariably the text was taken from or based on the Bible. However, "the text seemed mainly a starting point and often had no relation to the development of the sermon" (Johnson, *op. cit.*, pp. 405). The Macon County preachers repeat the text throughout the sermon, giving the appearance of organization:

"We find our text, let me repeat: 'Sun, stand thou still upon Gittia and thou, moon, go in the valley. . . .'[6] The subject: God's Mysteries upon the Mountains." (II)

III. BODY OF THE SERMON

There is, as a rule, no logical organization of the ideas in this part of the sermon (discussion). The text is repeated again and again; illustrations from the Bible and from everyday experience are presented; — all working toward an emotional climax. The distinct divisions in the body of the sermon are the gradual steps in emotional excitement leading to the climax[7] and then to a calmer state and then back again to another emotional climax; this movement from the calm state to the shouting and back to the calm may continue as long as the minister desires to preach or, if he is "good" enough, until the shouting drowns out his preaching. (The author has seen shouting women in their excitement chase the minister from the pulpit.) There is no logical organization of ideas as such; the body of Sermon IV does have logical organization but this shows the new influence of education rather than an element of old-time Negro preaching. Most of the Macon County preachers use the text as a refrain; this gives the body of the sermon an appearance of organization, but the body of the sermon is really a collection of digressions (from the point of view of the logical argument of the stated text); these digressions, however, lead to the purpose of the sermon: emotional excitement.

IV. CONCLUSION

A. PURPOSE

1. To create the final impression: to cause "sinners" to join the church:

"Don't you feel lonely sometime in world by yourself? Give me your hand. . . . Won't He take care of you, chillun? . . . Gwine to sing and open de doors of the church." (III)

[*This minister's thesis had been, Love God*:] "See that I can take a stand for myself, relying upon God in all things. Let my, let my family life be high or let it be low; let it be elevated as it will, I'll still rely upon God, and have them to know I trust in Him. May the Lord bless us and may He bring us safely to Him." (I)

2. To return the audience and the preacher to emotional normalcy:[8]

"Now my spiritual strength renewed; then I am going to remember that Salvation is free for all." (IV)

3. Characteristics
   a. Never humorous.
   b. "Happiness;" talking about the goodness of being a "Child of God":

"Get happy, you'll pray in town! If you in jail jest keep prayin'! Paul and Silas kept prayin'! Pray!" (VIII)

   c. Personal (speaker-audience):

"May the Lord bless us; may He help us, and may He save us when it comes our time to die. Amen." (IV)

[145]

(Some of these sermons have no conclusion. At the highest point of emotional frenzy, the minister and audience become inarticulate in their excitement, and the minister either cannot be heard or he deliberately pauses suddenly — to leave everything in turmoil; examples are Sermons VI and VII.)

Two sermons are outlined below to illustrate in detail the arrangement of the Macon County sermons. The first outline represents the arrangement of the less-educated minister's sermon; the other outline represents the arrangement of the more-educated minister's sermon:

OUTLINE 1: *"God's Mysteries Upon the Mountains"* (II)

    I. INTRODUCTION
- a. Refers to his preaching at another meeting, which has tired him.
- b. Welcomes the visitors.
- c. Reads a verse from the Bible.

    II. STATEMENT OF THE THESIS
"The Subject: God's Mysteries Upon the Mountains."

    III. THE DISCUSSION
- a. Many great men have been unable to "dig out all the mysteries of God.
- b. God's mysteries are unknowable. Illustration — a river.
- c. The First Mountain: Christ's Sermon on the Mountain. Discusses the "Be Attitudes" (digresses).[b]
- d. Elijah and Ahab on the Mountain. Relates the Biblical story (digresses).
- e. Moses on the "Mountain Mebo. Relates the Biblical story (digresses).
- f. The Mountain of Transfiguration. Relates the Biblical story (digresses).
- g. Mount Calvary. Relates the story (digresses; climax; shouting).

    IV. CONCLUSION
- a. Discusses Mount Calvary calmly, allowing his emotions and those of the audience to return to normalcy.
- b. Repeats the text.

OUTLINE 2: *"It's Dangerous to Neglect"* (IV)

    I. INTRODUCTION
- a. Greets the audience and regrets that the meeting is starting late. Reads a passage from the Bible.

    II. STATEMENT OF THE THESIS
"From these verses (PROVERBS, 24:30) the theme suggest itself to our minds is this: The Danger of Neglect."

[b] Probably the digression is his "proof."

III. DISCUSSION
  a. "Most calamities and accidents are caused by neglect."
  b. "Where ignorance predominates, there is always a great loss." Proof.
  c. "Where conscience is neglected, there will be heathenism, cannibals, and prisons." Proof.
  d. "The soul, neglected, becomes dwarfed and die." Proof.
  e. "Neglect weakens the power to decide." Proof.
  f. "Neglect produces a loss of sensitiveness." Proof.
  g. "Neglect destroys interest . . . in school, music . . . social affairs . . . , and in the soul of man." (Until now the sermon has been intellectual; here it becomes emotional; the emotion part of the sermon is soon to come.) Proof.
  h. "Neglect in any way causes a great danger." Proof.
  i. "Dangerous to neglect Salvation." (This is the old-time emotional part; causes shouting; the climax.) Proof.

IV. CONCLUSION
  a. Repeats the subject calmly.

The above quotations and the two outlines indicate that the arrangement of the old-time preacher's sermon observes somewhat the traditional divisions of a speech into introduction, statement, discussion, and conclusion. But the organization of these parts is not always logical. Each main division of the sermon builds toward the emotional climax. Therefore, (1) the introduction sets the stage emotionally, by the preacher's use of Biblical reading and his references to the purpose of the occasion; (2) the statement is always Biblical; (3) the discussion, although having the appearance of logical order, is not always logical, with the exception of the consistent use of illustrations from the Bible or from everyday experience, to arouse the emotions of the audience; transitional words and sentences are rare; (4) the conclusion (unless omitted entirely) emphasizes the thesis and allows the emotions of the audience and the preacher to return to normalcy.

Outline 1 illustrates this type of disposition, which is typical of the old-time Macon County Negro sermon. Outline 2 illustrates the more-educated minister's tendency to organize the discussion of his sermon more logically; but he is still an old-time preacher at heart, as the latter part indicates.ᵉ

ᵉ The minister's discussion has two parts: (1) the intellectual; and (2) the emotional. The minister who delivered Sermon I attempts to combine the intellectual (the modern) and the emotional (the old-time) types of preaching. The result was that he did neither very well. The use of two distinct parts in the discussion seems to be the young, educated Negro minister's solution to the problem of having in his audience both the type who wants to shout (the old-time Christian) and the type who wants to think (the modern, more-educated Christian).

As a whole, then, the arrangement of the Macon County sermons is poor according to some standards; but, according to the main purpose of the sermons, these sermons could hardly be arranged in a better manner.

DELIVERY[9]

THE SUCCESS of the old-time Negro sermon does not depend entirely on the logical ideas it contains. It is the *manner* in which the sermon is delivered that determines the success or failure of the old-time Negro sermon. Therefore, the preacher places more emphasis on the techniques and devices of his delivery than he does on the ideas of his sermon. He knows that one of his purposes is to arouse the emotions of his audience and that *action* instead of *thought* is his most effective tool. How does the old-time Macon County preacher arouse the emotions of his hearers with his delivery? What is the nature of the influence of education on the techniques of the minister's delivery?

Hatcher gives a vivid picture of the delivery of an original old-time preacher:

> And gestures! He circled around the pulpit with his ankle in his hand; and laughed and sang and shouted and acted about a dozen characters within the space of three minutes. Meanwhile, in spite of these things [*because of these things, he should say*], he was pouring out a gospel sermon, red hot, full of love, full of invective, full of tenderness, full of bitterness, full of tears, full of every passion that ever flamed in the human breast.[10]

That was the original old-time preacher's technique of delivery — action, action, action.[11] Indeed, "the old-time Negro preacher of parts was above all an orator, and in good measure an actor.[12] The old-time Negro preacher's descendant in Macon County also recognizes the importance of action in his delivery.

To understand the delivery of the Negro preacher, the setting and the occasion of the sermon should be pictured. Old-time religious Negroes come to church on Sunday in order, partly to escape from an "impossible world" (second-class citizenship). The people are depressed; the physical surroundings are depressing. Raper gives a clear picture of the Negro church building in Macon County:

> Of all the oddly shaped and oddly placed steeples and spires in Christendom, the oddest to be seen are on the rural Negro churches

in the Black Belt. In nearly every instance, the unsupported side and end walls of the church bulge in and out and lean this way and that as though the curious little steeple or spire were of tremendous weight. Negro rural churches have a scattered look — seem to be too big for the amount of lumber used.

✓ ✓ ✓

[Yet *these churches stand as symbols of*] self-directed efforts of a group of people who have little opportunity to exercise personal responsibility.

When the church is finished it is a box-like, one-room building which may or may not have window sash, or side or overhead ceiling. . . . The equipment within these warped and twisted buildings is of a very crude and uncomfortable type. In half of them the benches are made of rough pine boards and stand as uncertain as the church itself; now and then one is equipped with painted and varnished pews which stand erect. It is very unusual to see more than a scrap of carpet or rug.

There is a pulpit of some description in each church, perhaps nothing more than a wide board nailed across the top of two upright planks which are fastened to the floor; two pulpits were observed with props. Occasionally, however, one finds a very substantial and even beautiful pulpit.[13]

The churches in which the sermons of this project were delivered fit the above description. They are generally poorly-constructed. To this type of building (usually located in the woods or in the typical "run-down" Negro section of a small town) the tired, depressed, religious Negro comes, partly to have the preacher arouse his emotion.[14] Before this Christian leaves the church, his emotions will be aroused and he will return to a blissful quietness; and it will be the preacher's delivery, to a great extent, that will be responsible for carrying him aloft and then returning him to this world.

An analysis of the preacher's techniques of delivery in arousing the listener follows the minister and the audience step-by-step as the mood moves from calm to the climax of shouting and then back to calm.

✓ ✓ ✓

James Weldon Johnson's classic description of the delivery of the Georgia sermon which inspired his great poem on old-time Negro preaching "The Creation," serves admirably as a framework for these essential characteristics of the delivery of the old-time Macon County preachers:

[149]

I. APPEARANCE IS IMPORTANT

["*At last he* (the old-time Negro preacher) *arose. He was a dark-brown man, handsome in gigantic proportions.*"]

The implication is that the appearance of the preacher added effectiveness to his delivery. This is true of the Macon County preachers. Their appearance, however, is not always impressive because of "gigantic proportions;" it is often seriousness of purpose, the air of the "Man of God."

2. THE CONVERSATIONAL TONE CREATES THE PROPER ATMOSPHERE

["*He appeared to be a bit self-conscious, perhaps impressed by the presence of the distinguished visitor on the Platform.*"]

At least two Macon County preachers show the influence (in the early part of the delivery[d]) of the presence of the recording group:

" 'Thou shalt love the Lord thy God [*Reading from the Bible.*] with thy whole heart, [*Pauses for a 9-count.*] with your whole soul, with your whole mind, and your whole strength. [*Pauses for a 14-count.*] (I)

"We going to talk this morning — we very glad to have our visitors out with us from the Fort Valley High School. And we going to talk this morning from — er — we told that they're taking sermons from different churches. We going to talk this morning . . . ." (II)

[The recorder's presence did not cause this minister concern:] "May knock this down [*the microphone*]; I don't know." (VI)

But, in all instances, the minister begins his sermon with a conversational type of delivery. This is the calmness which contrasts so startlingly with the turmoil to come later.

---

d "The delivery of the (*old-time Negro sermon*) is divided into several stages. It begins with a congregation that is relaxed and at ease and achieves rapport as the minister in the first stage of delivery speaks in a conversational tone. A friendly atmosphere is thus created.

"The preacher apologizes for his voice's being hoarse due to 10 nights of revival preaching ["We had great service over there for 12 nights" (II); "Not feeling good; been on road, two weeks of service. . . . Don't feel good" (III).]. The intermediary stages each varied a degree or so in intensity from the first to the last stage which was highly demonstrative. After making apologies for his disabilities, the preacher proceeded to identify his congregation with the great workings of Christ. The sermon solicited response because it was a rehearsal or reference to Bible stories with which the audience was familiar. These references to things familiar did not require full statement. They permitted the hearers to call up familiar images and to react to them emotionally in terms of the sentiments and feelings suggested. Like music these sermons revive memories in which all have participated. The preacher referred in a familiar way, to their God and His great power as things of which they had had personal experience" (Jones, *op. cit.*, pp. 14-15).

3. INTELLECTUAL, CALM DELIVERY PUTS THE AUDIENCE TO SLEEP

["(He) *started in to preach a formal sermon from a formal text.*"]

Three Macon County ministers (I, III, IV) make such a beginning.

["*The congregation sat apathetic and dozing.*"]

This is true of the audience when a Macon County preacher attempts to be intellectual. One minister cries out at such a time:

"You all can hear, can't yer?" (III)

4. OLD-TIME DELIVERY REQUIRED TO AROUSE THE AUDIENCE

["*He sensed that he was losing his audience and his opportunity. Suddenly he closed his Bible, stepped out from behind the pulpit and began to preach.*"]

Only one Macon County preacher fails to arouse his audience; he is the teacher-preacher (I). And his audience is hardly satisfied when he completes his sermon.

5. FIRST SIGNS OF EMOTION IN THE MINISTER ARE AMPLIFIED BY THE AUDIENCE

["*He started intoning the old folk-sermon that begins with the creation of the world and ends with Judgment Day. He was at once a changed man, free, at ease and masterful.*"]

That is true of the Macon County preachers.

["*The change in the congregation was instantaneous. An electric current ran through the crowd. It was in a moment alive and quivering.*"]

And that, also, is true of the audiences in Macon County.[15]

6. GESTURES AND MOVEMENT

["*And all the while the preacher held it* (the audience) *in the palm of his hand. He was wonderful in the way he employed his conscious and unconscious art. He strode the pulpit up and down in what was actually a very rhythmical dance.*"]

Macon County preachers perform almost every gesture and pulpit movement imaginable in public speaking. The following description of Sermon II delivery suggests the typical delivery of these ministers:

(1) The minister frequently pulled or rubbed his nose while he spoke; (2) He shook both hands with both fists clinched; (3) He shook the right hand with the forefinger pointing forward; (4)

[151]

He used a white and green bath towel every few minutes to wipe away perspiration from his face and to remove saliva which was frequently accumulating in the corners of his mouth; (5) The minister frequently clasped his hands together; after which he suddenly thrust the thumbs of each hand into his pockets; (6) He looked upward with arms extended outward and slightly upward; (7) Occasionally he lifted his right hand with his forefinger pointed forward and shook it rapidly; (8) He picked up a small book and slapped it against the top of the altar several times; (9) He looked upward with his hands held upward, his elbows bent; (10) He moved rapidly to the right side of the pulpit and back again to the center; (11) He turned the pages of the Bible on the altar; (12) He slapped his open hands upon the altar; (13) He supported himself by leaning upon the altar with both hands.[e]

7. THE VOICE IS MOST IMPORTANT

[*"And he brought into play the full gamut of his wonderful voice, a voice — what shall I say? — not of an organ or a trumpet, but rather of a trombone, the instrument possessing above all others the power to express the wide and varied range of emotions encompassed by the human voice — and with greater amplitude."*]

The preachers of Macon County have excellent voices and they know how to use them to obtain the desired effect.[16]

[*"He* (the average old-time preacher) *often possessed a voice that was a marvelous instrument, a voice which he could modulate from a sepulchral whisper to crashing thunder clap."*]

The preachers know the power of voice modulation and the effect of change in volume and intensity.

8. RHYTHM

[*"He intoned, he moaned, he pleaded — he blared, he crashed, he thundered. . . .*[f] *His discourse was generally kept at a high pitch of fervency."*]

The rhythm[17] of the delivery of sermons is always an attribute of the old-time preacher's fervency in delivery. The Macon County preachers use rhythmical delivery. However, the language itself is not always rhythmical, as is true of poetry. But the minister delivers *everything* with rhythm by crowding words together, stretching words out, and

---

[e] Description by a member of the Recording Group.

[f] DuBois describes the similar delivery of another old-time preacher: "The black and massive form of the preacher swayed and quivered as the words crowded to his lips and flew at us in singular eloquence" (*Souls of Black Folk, op. cit., pp.* 190-1).

at times the complete absence of words (pauses). In fact, the minister often maintains the tempo of his delivery by striking the lecturn, stamping his foot, and regular pauses, which are observed with sudden inspiration and audible expiration. "This is a decided syncopation of speech — the crowding in of many syllables or the lengthening out of a few to fill one metrical foot. The rhythmical stress of this syncopation is partly obtained by a marked silent fraction of a beat; frequently this silent fraction is filled in by a hand clap.[18] Often the minister interrupts this flowing rhythm with a "holler."[g]

9. "CHANGE OF PACE" FOR EFFECT
   ["*But occasionally he dropped into colloquialisms and, less often, into humor.*"]

The Macon County minister does this apparently for effect. At one moment the minister is rushing along like a fast train; then suddenly he begins speaking in a quiet, normal voice. The audience bubbles over with excitement. For example:

"And then you'll say: 'Whatever it takes, [*Loud accent made by striking the speaker's stand rhythmically.*] I'm going on; I'm going in Jesus!' [*Suddenly begins to talk calmly.*] Going on in Jesus." (IV)
"He told Elijah, [*In his stride now.*] 'Now you go show your-self to Ahab and I'll give yer the rain; I'll give you the key and he can't get none, [*Stops suddenly the mad, rhythmical pace and be-gins to talk calmly; it is like the quiet after the storm.*] until he git it from you." [*Pauses while the audience "takes over," bubbling over with emotion.*] (VI)

10. INARTICULATE SPEECH ACCOMPANIES THE CLIMAX;
    THE AUDIENCE "GOES MAD"
    ["*He knew the secret of oratory, that at bottom it is a pro-gression of rhythmic words more than anything else. Indeed I have witnessed congregations moved to ecstasy by the rhythmic in-toning of sheer incoherencies.*"]

At the climax of the delivery, as well as at many other points in the sermons, words become unintelligible, often incoherent:

"Ahhhhhhh [*Sings it.*] Lord! Tell me — men — Elijah saw — let — praise God — me tell you — saw on the mountain — ain't dat right?" (II)
"Hold it! [*The shouting should be kept up, he means.*] Hold it! Sometimes make cry; sometimes make you cry; sometimes make

---

g The minister literally screams; the "holler" is essentially crescendo and diminuendo. This scream might occur on an intelligible or an unintelligible word.

you moan. . . . If it makes you cry, I'll be with you. . . . Mother cry — 'I'll be with you' — mother cry. . . . Hold it! [*Moans a song while the audience shouts.*] Go with you to the graveyard. He makes up your dying bed. Mercy! Hold it!" (III)

[*"There is, of course, no way of recreating the atmosphere — the fervor of the congregation, the amens and hallelujahs, the undertone of singing which was often a soft accompaniment to parts of the sermon."*]

From the beginning of the delivery of the sermon, there is an antiphonal reaction between the minister and the audience. One helps to arouse the emotions of the other — more and more until the climax is reached. At this point — the point toward which almost everything in old-time Negro preaching is aimed — the minister and the audience often become indeed wholly inarticulate. They then "speak in tongues."[h] Raper gives his impression of the delivery effect in working toward the point of climax, the final step of emotional escape:

> The whole congregation responds with a rhythmical, "Yas, Lawd! Umm-m!" which gradually gets louder and deeper like the waves of the incoming tide — until some quivering woman springs to her feet, head thrown back, arms and fingers rigid and out-stretched, every muscle in a tremor, eyes wide open; she sways as she screams; she moves by jerks; after a while she shuffles down into a seat or falls to the floor in a swoon; a pall of rumbling silence — like the spent breakers of the outgoing tide — falls over the responsive congregation.[19]

Dr. DuBois says of this ultimate state of escape:

> . . . The gaunt-cheeked brown woman beside me suddenly leaped straight into the air and shrieked . . . , while round about came wail and groan and outcry, and a scene of human passion such as I had never conceived before.[20]

[*"I sat fascinated; and more, I was, perhaps against my will, deeply moved; the emotional effect upon me was irresistible."*[21]]

That was James Weldon Johnson's classic description of the delivery of the original old-time Negro preacher. The Macon County preachers still use the techniques of the old preachers.

---

[h] An expression used among Negroes to mean that the shouting people speak in a language which God gives them at such times; they alone can understand the language. A student of sociology explains "speaking in tongues": "[Old-time Negro religion] is not a surface matter. Its foundation is laid in the very depth of the Negro's being. It is concerned with the soul which is buried deeply with every individual. The medium of expressing things of so deep a concern cannot be adequately expressed in surface symbols" (Jones, *op. cit.*, p. 35).

To summarize the techniques of delivery: (1) the delivery of the preacher is impromptu; (2) the old-time preacher's delivery is a study in contrasts: at one moment he is talking quietly to his audience, and at the next moment he is doing everything but tearing the top from the building with the storm of his delivery; (3) the preacher's appearance and his gestures (awkward, spectacular, bombastic, and dramatic) do much to aid in the delivery; (4) the preacher's faith in himself, his sincerity, and his thorough understanding of the purpose of his sermon, aid in his delivery; (5) the preacher's use of rhythm is important in arousing the emotions of the audience; (6) the minister's excellent voice and the control which the preacher has over it to intone, "holler," etc., are indispensable to his success; (7) education has done little to change the type of delivery of the old-time Negro preacher; he must make the people shout if he wants to keep his job and only the old-time type of delivery can make the people shout; (8) the response of the audience spurs the minister on to the emotional climax, the ultimate escape in shouting. When that point is achieved in the delivery, everything else is "going downhill." Delivery, at this point of climax, leads to the old-time Negro preacher's goal of delivery — a type of delivery in which "You don't have to think." (VI)

The old-time Negro preacher's delivery declares that, in the case of the American Negro, this country has nurtured and conditioned a human being who must *feel* but must not *think*. To deny the people the right to think is strange indeed in a democracy.

IX.　When It Comes Our Time to Die[a]

AMONG NEGROES in the United States today, old-time preaching (the uneducated Negro's emotional type of preaching which stems from slavery time) is still a vital element. Two fundamental reasons why the Negro clings to the old-time religion are: (1) the American Negro possesses an emotional, superstitious temperament whose historical roots reach back through the days of slavery to the jungles of Africa; and this emotional nature has always needed a means of outward expression, (2) the Negro has been without a means of normal outward expression, due to his domination by powers beyond his control — in Africa, the jungle and tribal custom; in America before the Civil War, the institution of slavery; in America today (especially in the "Black Belt" and to a lesser degree in other parts of the United States), the plantation system and/or "divine white right." In Africa and in America many Negroes have made their adjustment to an "impossible world" by means of an emotional escape — the frenzy and shouting of old-time religion.

To explain the preaching of this old-time religion, the author (1) investigated the African and slavery time characteristics of this type of preaching, and (2) compared and contrasted these findings with the characteristics of the preaching which was recorded in Macon County, Georgia.

Besides the religious motive, the chief purpose of old-time Negro preaching appears to be to "stir up," to excite the emotions of the audience and the minister as a means for their escape from an "impossible world." The old-time purpose of persuading people to come to Jesus is still present in varying degrees, but the emphasis here seems to be a secondary one. The method of instructing the audience unemotionally is being ushered in by the more highly-educated Negro ministers. Another modern influence seems to be the underlying purpose of soliciting money.

The subject-matter (or ideas) of old-time Negro preaching, now as formerly, comes mainly from the Bible. These ideas of God, Heaven,

---

[a] The minister, closing Sermon IV: "May the Lord bless us, may He help us, and may He save us when it comes our time to die. Amen."

Sin, the Hebrew Children, etc., form the religious basis of the Negro's emotional escape from the world of reality. But education and enlightenment are injecting new ideas into the preaching — ideas unlike those of earlier old-time Negro preaching. The ultimate result of these influences might very well be the death of old-time Negro preaching.

The methods of persuasion of the Macon County preaching demonstrate that emotional appeal remains dominant; appeal through the character of the preacher (the "Man of God") runs a close second. Logical argument is not entirely absent. Especially in the sermons of the more highly-educated ministers, there appear evidences of both inductive and deductive reasoning (at the less emotional points of the sermon).

The style of Macon County preaching is basically simple: short words which are familiar to the audience (with a long word thrown in occasionally for effect). Sentences are often elliptical (without complete subject and predicate). Such sentences, however, are joined by conjunctions, to help maintain the speaker's rhythmical flow of words. Slang and Negro dialect (the language of the audience) form the level of expression. But the style is figurative, with the use of metaphor, based on the experiences of the audience or drawn from the Bible, taking the lead. The style is narrative — for the listener rather than for the reader. The amount of poetic, Biblical prose is decreasing, perhaps because education (newspaper, magazines, radio) is bringing in new expressions — a condition which is unlike the original complete dependency upon the Bible.

The arrangement (organization) of the recorded sermons follows the traditional (and old-time minister's) divisions of Introduction, Statement, Discussion, and Conclusion. But each of these units is unique. The Introduction sets the stage emotionally, so to speak, for the climax to come later. The Statement continues this atmosphere-setting activity; it is usually Biblical. The Discussion merely has the appearance of organization, for it is often a series of digressions aimed to arouse the emotions of the audience; the more highly-educated minister does use logical organization in the Discussion. The Conclusion is omitted entirely if the emotional climax is of sufficient intensity to make articulate speech impossible. Usually the Conclusion serves to emphasize the text and as an opportunity for persons to join the church. The Conclusion also allows the emotions of the preacher and the audience to return to normalcy. The arrangement is made while the minister is speaking (evidence of the preacher's use of his memory).

The delivery of the Macon County sermon is most characteristic of earlier old-time Negro preaching. Entirely impromptu, it is rhythmical — which helps to heighten the emotions of the minister and the audience. It gains effect by the change from conversational to rhythmical speaking. The delivery is also made more effective by the preacher's appearance, his sincerity, his bombastic gestures, and his many movements in the pulpit. Possibly most important, the preacher's delivery is aided by his masterful modulation and control of his excellent voice.

The recorded Macon County sermons indicate that old-time Negro preaching today is still a vital part of the Negro's existence. Preaching is still the soul expression of a frustrated people. But, as Hodding Carter points out,[b] because doors to education and new opportunities of normal expression are being opened wider and wider to the black man in the United States,[1] the degree of frustration is being lowered. The result of this process, if it continues, might be oratory's complete loss of one of the most peculiar types of public speaking that perhaps the world has ever known.

CONCLUSION

IN showing that the background of the American Negro, "A People in Bondage" (from the African jungle, to American slavery, and to present-day second-class citizenship), explains old-time Negro preaching partly as an escape mechanism for a frustrated people, this study also points up two conclusions: (1) the Negro race in the United States has made unparalleled progress in normal adjustment (against odds), but the Negro should not expect to exercise first-class American citizenship immediately — unless America herself decides (probably beginning with a Supreme Court decision) to practice true democracy *for all people*: to remove from the American scene the half-century-old concept (based on a ruling of the United States Supreme Court) of "separate-but-equal"; (2) the crying need of the Negro race in the United States is for improved leadership, regardless of the time-table of democracy: first-class citizenship for the Negro *now* as his American right or a *gradual*, step-by-step acceptance of the Negro as an American citizen based upon the preparedness of the Negro to exercise this right and the willingness of the "Lords of the South" to grant it.

---

[b] "It is true that there still remains a lack of equality among Negroes and whites in many places in the South; however, the South is definitely on the up-grade'" ["*Carter Says South Holds Destiny of Nation in Hands*," Jackson (Miss.) *Daily News*, March 5, 1949, p. 10, quoting Hodding Carter]. Is merely being "on the upgrade" in granting equality to the Negro good enough for the world's greatest democracy?

FIRST-CLASS CITIZENSHIP FOR THE NEGRO NOW — If the masses of United States Negroes are to have their frustration-producing condition eliminated permanently in the near future, America must somehow come to realize the menace to the nation of racial prejudice in an Atomic Age; she must realize in deed as well as in word that it is the American creed and law that no man deserves second-class citizenship because of race, color, or previous condition of servitude; she must realize that the best *preparation* for the Negro's wise use of first-class citizenship is to be found in the Negro's *practice* of first-class citizenship.

Since a United States Supreme Court decision in 1896, the "separate-but-equal" doctrine has been the basis for forcing second-class citizenship upon the Negro, especially in the "Black Belt." But the Supreme Court moved in the correct direction recently when it banned the segregation practiced at the Texas and Oklahoma state universities and on railway dining cars. However, the court evaded ruling on the fundamental question of whether segregation is discrimination, despite the convincing brief challenging the doctrine of "separate-but-equal." The brief declared (in the name of the United States Constitution, past court decisions, the Charter of the United Nations, and the science of anthropology and sociology) that segregation is wrong, that "equal" is "the same"; therefore, there can no such status as "separate-but-equal." Unless the country accepts this basic democratic conception, the American Negro cannot expect first-class citizenship immediately.

FIRST-CLASS CITIZENSHIP FOR THE NEGRO GRADUALLY—Long-range first-class citizenship will come to the Negro mainly through the unity of effort on the part of Negroes themselves; this unity of effort must be used to prepare the race to exercise wisely his rights as a citizen and to prepare the minds of Southern white people to permit such democracy. (If the Negro is frustrated because of persecution, the mind of the white man is warped because of the un-American practices of enslaving and degrading the Negro; Booker T. Washington stated it in this manner: "You cannot hold a man down in a ditch without remaining there yourself.") [c]

Freedom for the Negro through unity of effort on the part of Negroes themselves? Is this not the blind leading the blind? Certainly, united action on the part of "Black Belt" Negroes is in the distant future, for the Negro (due to his background of bondage) is far from be-

---

[c] "The laws of changeless Justice bind
Oppressor with oppressed;
And close as sin and suffering joined.
We march to fate abreast."

longing to a race that has solidarity. Old-time Negro ministers often declare, "Negroes just won't stick together." As Gunnar Myrdal shows, however,[d] the masses of a people *must* have education and some degree of economic security before they can unite to improve themselves permanently in a social, economic, and political way. The Negro as a group is still a semi-illiterate proletariat and, hence, cannot be expected to unite to improve the masses of his people until a sizable group of Negroes are both more highly educated and more economically secure. The Negro himself cannot make this a fact within the near future, nor is the white man[e] likely to clear his mind of prejudice voluntarily within the near future. American democracy never had a greater opportunity — for when the Negro is denied first-class citizenship, American democracy as a whole is debased.

IMPROVED NEGRO LEADERSHIP A NECESSITY — Undoubtedly, the old-time Negro preacher is *the* Negro leader today; it is to him that the great majority of Negroes in this country look for guidance. The degreed and trained Negro educators, ministers, writers, *et al,* should not delude themselves into thinking that they are the true Negro leaders. The masses of Negroes seldom get to know these "leaders" and even when the opportunity does bring the highly-trained leader into contact with the average Negro, the latter either does not understand the "highbrow" leader or distrusts his motives — and not always unjustly. But the old-time preacher is "one of the flock." He is trusted, listened to, and understood. Therefore, the crying need in improving the Negro masses (whether first-class citizenship comes immediately or in the distant future) is for improved Negro leadership.

As Dr. Richardson pointed out in a recent study,[f] improvement of the Negro ministry can do much to improve the condition of the Negro masses,[g] but the author is dubious of the leadership of any Negro who is economically dependent on the goodwill of prejudiced white persons (which eliminates many college presidents and teachers) or who is economically dependent upon the masses of Negroes (which seems to minimize the effectiveness of the leadership of the average Negro minister, who is dependent upon Negroes for his income). Government workers (postal clerks, etc.), housewives, and retired persons seem to offer the best examples of the most effective type of Negro leaders: they are not always economically dependent on the masses of Negroes or upon prej-

[d] *An American Dilemma,* Harper, New York, N. Y., 1944, p. 72.
[e] The one who is sick with prejudice.
[f] H. V. Richardson, *op. cit.,* pp. 190-192.
[g] The Phelps-Stokes Fund has rendered inestimable service in this direction.

udiced white people and they have some time to devote to the improvement of their people.

Little is said here concerning the great help which has come from friendly white people and from Foundations for the improvement of the Negro's condition. It is hoped that these persons and groups will continue help, but improvement of the race, as a whole and permanently, must come either (immediately) from America or (gradually) through the united efforts of Negroes themselves. The first step in this gradual process is well underway — the improvement of the Negro educationally and economically. When enough Negroes have thus been improved, and when enough prejudiced whites have been "converted" or buried, the Negro will then stand up and walk mainly through the unity and the coordination of his own efforts.

Without a feeling of despair or pessimism (but trying to read the time-table correctly, which is essential for the Negro race in making the journey himself to first-class citizenship), the author does not conceive of Negroes possessing within the immediate future the educational and economical improvement necessary to wrest first-class citizenship from a reluctant South — and the South will be reluctant for some time to come. Will the greatest democracy on earth meet the challenge? Will the "Land of the Free" return to *her* old-time religion, *freedom for all people*: "All men are created equal and from that equal creation they derive rights inherent and unalienable, among which are the preservation of life and liberty and the pursuit of happiness"[2]?

If America really wants to return to *her old-time* religion of freedom for all people, then let her say in deed—"Amen, Brother!"[h]

---

[h] "Benches can't say 'Amen.' You all can hear, can't yer?" (III)'

Notes

Chapter i

1 Negroes constituted 9.8% of the total population of the United States on April 1, 1940. *Sixteenth Census of the United States,* Department of Commerce, Washington, D.C., Series P-10, no. 1, 1942.

2 W. A. Daniel, *The Education of Negro Ministers,* Doran, New York, N. Y., 1925, p. 13. See also: Benjamin E. Mays and Joseph W. Nicholson, *The Negro's Church,* Institute of Social and Religious Research, New York, N. Y., 1933, pp. 7-10, 58.

3 "Old-time" and "old-fashioned" refer to the more emotional preaching of the uneducated Negro ministers (originally of the slavery days), whose preaching is "old-time" in comparison with the more intellectual and less emotional preaching of the educated Negro of today; the latter type of preaching is not unique.

4 J. W. Johnson, *God's Trombones,* Viking Press, New York, N. Y., 1932, p. 3. See also: Willis D. Weatherford and Charles S. Johnson, *Race Relation,* D. C. Heath, New York, N. Y., 1934, pp. 287, 496-7; Edward B. Reuter, *The American Race Problem,* Thomas Y. Crowell, New York, N. Y., 1927, pp. 326-27; Mays, *op. cit.,* p. 58.

5 Hortense Powdermaker, *After Freedom,* Viking Press, New York, N. Y., 1939, p. 223. See also: Edward B. Reuter, *op. cit.,* p. 324; Trevor Bowen, *Divine White Right,* Harper and Brothers, New York, N. Y., 1934, pp. 124 ff; 150-51; Thomas Pearce Bailey, *Race Orthodoxy in the South,* Neale Publishing, New York, N. Y., 1914, p. 93; R. C. Angell, *The Integration of American Society,* McGraw-Hill, New York, N. Y., 1941, p. 156; Alvin Good, *Sociology and Education,* Harper and Brothers, New York, N. Y., 1926, p. 500; Mays, *op. cit.,* p. 279.

6 C. G. Woodson, *History of the Negro Church,* Associated Publishers, Washington, D.C., 2nd edition, 1921, pp. 267-68. See also: W. E. B. DuBois, "Efforts for Social Betterment," *Atlanta University Publications,* University Press, Atlanta, Georgia, 1909, no. 3, p. 4; George E. Haynes, "The Church and Negro Progress," *Annals of the American Academy of Political and Social Science,* vol. cxxxx, Nov. 1928, p. 266; Maurice S. Evans, *Black and White in the Southern States,*

Longmans, Green, London, pp. 114, 116; Reuter, *op. cit.*, pp. 331-33; Ira D. A. Reid, *In a Minor Key*, American Council on Education, Washington, D.C., 1940, p. 83; Frank W. Blackmar and John L. Gillin, *Outlines of Sociology*, Macmillan, New York, N. Y., 1915, p. 239; Forrest B. Washington, "Recreational Facilities for the Negro," *Annals of the American Academy of Political and Social Science*, Nov. 1928, p. 279.

7 Mary Rodgers, "All is Peaceful in Their World," Louisville (Ky.) *Courier-Journal*, Sept. 15, 1940, p. 1. This article is quoted at length because it sets the stage, so to speak, for this study.

8 This minister, although not an educated Negro, did have some training; but, as will be seen, he is definitely in the vein of old-time Negro.

9 They are, for the greatest part, sermons of uneducated preachers.

10 Phillips Brooks, *Lectures on Preaching*, Dutton, New York, N. Y., 1894, p. 5. "Truth," of course, is difficult to define. Emerson said that truth is one's own innermost belief ("Self-Reliance"). No one questions the Negro's sincerity, as a rule, in his preaching.

11 "And now we shall listen to genuine oratory [*the reference is to a Negro sermon*], if by the term is meant the power which moves the heart in spite of all resistance." Wm. S. Gordon, *Recollections of the Old Quarter*, Moose Brothers, Lynchburg, Va., 1902, pp. 109-10.

12 James Weldon Johnson, *op. cit.*, p. 1. This work was the first full attempt to portray seriously the Negro preacher in his important characteristics. Johnson's conception of the old-time preacher will be presented in the course of this work.

13 There is scarcely an important sociological work on the Negro that does not at least mention the Negro church.

14 He was in the Merchant Marine during the last War.

15 See H. B. Allen's "The Minister of the Gospel in Negro American Fiction," M.A. thesis, Fisk University, Nashville, Tenn., 1937, and N. B. Woolridge's "The Negro Preacher in American Fiction Before 1900," Ph.D. thesis, English, University of Chicago, 1942.

16 Woodson, *op. cit.*, p. 305. The Negro minister's sermons thus also become important, because the preacher and the sermon are bound closely together.

17 W. E. B. DuBois, *The Souls of Black Folk*, McClurg, Chicago, Ill., 1903, p. 190.

18 In the future these two words are used interchangeably to refer to present-day Negro ministers who still preach to some extent in a manner similar to that of the uneducated and emotional colored preachers of the past, during the slavery days.

19 Johnson, *op. cit.*, pp. 2-3.

20 *Ibid.*, p. 11. The sermons recorded in this project show varying degrees of this change from the old to the new (the more rational and less emotional) type of preaching.

21 These records are unique and cannot be duplicated. The reader should hear these records, if at all possible.

22 Johnson, *op. cit.*, p. 10.

23 Arthur Raper, *Preface to Peasantry: A Tale of Two Black Belt Counties*, Univ. of North Carolina Press, Chapel Hill, N. C., 1936, p. 10.

The "Black Belt" is the name given to some two hundred counties which stretch, crescent-like, from Virginia to Texas. The name has no reference to the color of the many Negroes who live in this section of the country, but to the rich, black soil of these counties. During slavery days, the large slave plantations (on which were to be found most of the Negroes in the United States) were to be found in the "Black Belt." Raper, p. 10.

It became a formidable task to record representative Negro sermons which are delivered in almost every part of the country. Because the vast majority of Negroes live in the South, the problem became one of finding a typical Southern locality.

Dr. H. M. Bond, who was president of Fort Valley State College, Fort Valley, Georgia, where the investigator was employed as a teacher, suggested that Arthur Raper's book (*op. cit.*) be considered. There was also Powdermaker's study of a Mississippi county (*op. cit.*). Raper's study seemed to give a better basis for the election of Macon and Green Counties as being typical respectively of two types of Negro communities. (1) the more backward, and (2) the more progressive. Raper offers proof that these two counties "are typical" of the section most densely populated with Negroes "the Black Belt" (*op. cit.*, pp. 7-8, 10). Thus, in a study of old-fashioned preaching, Macon County (Raper's selection as the more backward of the two counties) was acceptable as the "Middletown" of Negro society.

24 The author knows this to be true from actual experience as a member of a Negro family in the "Black Belt." In the course of this work, he often draws upon this experience, but only when there is no better source of information available. His grandfather, a former slave, furnished much information concerning the days of slavery in the "Black Belt."

25 The fact (Powdermaker, *op. cit.*, pp. 245-46) that only on the large plantations of the "Black Belt" (which resemble so closely the days of slavery) has the old-time preaching remained almost intact leads to important conclusions. It would seem that this type of preach-

ing has a definite relationship with the status (economic, social, educational, political, etc.) of the Negro. To understand this preaching, then, one must consider these things also.

26 Raper, *op. cit.*, pp. 10; 7-8.

27 *Ibid.*, p. 10.

28 Cf. footnote 16 above.

29 This would include information on the ministers.

30 The opinion of advisers was that half a dozen sermons would be a representative number.

31 These churches usually "hold services" (with preaching) on one regular Sunday in each month; every first Sunday, for example. This situation exists because one church alone is unable to pay a preacher a full salary. Consequently, a minister usually pastors four churches and preaches one Sunday a month at each church.

32 Caution along this line was most important. An outsider has a difficult time learning anything about the real, inner thoughts and beliefs of Negroes in the "Black Belt." They smile and act "nice," and the outsider thinks he has the facts. But the real truth is often concealed from him. There are numerous sociological "investigations" which are supposed to reveal facts about the Negro; many of them only confuse the facts. As a Negro who was born on a cotton plantation in the heart of the "Black Belt" and who grew up picking cotton and plowing as a typical "Black Belt" Negro (before leaving for Tuskegee Institute), the author knows this to be true from experience. It would be all but impossible for a white man to record sermons in Macon County, Georgia, without destroying the normalcy of the situation. (To make a successful study of the county, Raper, a white man, had to live in the county for the greater part of a year.) It was fortunate for this study that the author was able to joke with the people before church, talk their language in church and Sunday School, sing and pray and, in general, become one of them.

33 The greatest difficulty in carrying out the recording project was beyond the power of this board: (1) recording discs (because of their rubber base) became almost unobtainable; the regular price doubled and tripled and then they were not obtainable at any price; (2) gasoline rationing had come to Georgia. The four gallons per week would hardly take the group to some places in Macon County and back to Fort Valley. One student in the group was a minister himself and had an "X" card; he saved the project.

34 Raper, *op. cit.*, p. 360.

35 Missionary Baptists and Primitive Baptists are essentially alike.

36 Very little consideration was given to the distinction between

town and country, because a pastor usually has churches in both. The largest church was located in the country.

37 Knowing the power of womanly charm, the author selected this member of the group very carefully.

38 The investigator's wife also took pictures and shared the work in every respect.

39 This was not always the case. At one church the minister very obviously did not want to make the recording. The recording group had been at the church for some time before he arrived, and had "won over" the people. The minister said he was afraid the deacons would not permit the recording. But such a favorable impression had already been made on the deacons that when the pastor suggested to them that records should not be made, the deacons over-ruled him and told the group to remain. Then the pastor tried to send the group to another church, where, as he put it, "Dere's a real mess of folks today." When the group remained for his sermon anyway, he deliberately avoided speaking into or near the microphone and he said "in conclusion" before he had even started the old-time preaching. It worked as he had hoped it would: all the discs were used before he really hit his stride. He is the only minister on whom the group doubled-back for a second recording (with a large number of discs and no inclination to be influenced by his "in conclusion"—which *was* tried again).

A second objection to the recording came from another Church when the minister (a blind man who had never really understood the nature of the recording project) said very truthfully, "I believe in doing everything where it ought to be done at. I believe when you have a car, don't put no gas in no, no radiator; it don't belong dere. Put de water in de radiator and the gas in the tank whar it belong and it'll do good. Put things whar dey don't belong, won't do no good, it'll do harm." The minister who spoke after him said, "I may knock this thing down" (referring to the microphone). But in all instances, the ministers were finally won over completely.

40 The author, having attended such services from childhood days, knows when the "spirit" is really having its way.

41 For the facts concerning this insurrection, see "Nat Turner's Insurrection," *Atlantic Monthly*, 8, Aug. 1861, pp. 173-187.

42 Thomas Jefferson, The Declaration of Independence, cited by Ernest S. Bates, *American Faith*, 1940, pp. 275 ff.

CHAPTER III

1 G. C. Lee, *The World's Orators*, International Pub., Philadelphia, Pa., vol. 4, pp. 1-3.

2 Aristotle states in his *Rhetoric*: "The premises from which our conclusions are drawn must be not only such as are necessary but such also as are generally true" and adds that "the proper materials of enthymemes must be not all opinions indiscriminately, but certain definite opinions. . . held either by our audience or by persons in whom they believe, and in the latter cause, the fact of such an opinion being entertained must be well-known to all or the great majority of our audience" (*The Rhetoric of Aristotle*, translated by Lane Cooper, Appleton, New York, N. Y., 1932 bk. 2, chapter 22, pp. 154, 155, 156). Invention is concerned with ultimate sources of material and ideas (Cicero, *Orations of M. T. Cicero*, edited by C. D. Yonge, G. Bell, 1919, *passim*). Therefore, chapter III of this book treats the ultimate sources of ideas of old-time Negro preaching.

3 It cannot be over-stressed that the "real" old-time Negro preaching—undiluted by education and freedom—existed in America only during the days of slavery. Preaching in Macon County, is merely its most immediate descendant.

4 Chapter II, pp. 39-43.

5 Huxley says we are influenced by our environment "to an extent that most of us do not realize and would perhaps be horrified if we did realize it" (Julian Huxley, *Science and Social Needs*, Harper, New York, N. Y., 1935, p. 199).

6 See Professor Thomas O'Gorman, *A History of the Roman Catholic Church in the United States*, Christian Literature Co., New York, N. Y., 1895, pp. 3-4.

7 *Ibid.*, p. 15.

8 O'Gorman, *op. cit.*, p. 17 ff. In 1565, Spain's first permanent settlement was made at St. Augustine, Florida (America's oldest city). Father Francisco Lopez was the leading priest and chaplain in Captain Pedro Menendez's expedition (*op. cit.*, p. 30).

9 Leonard W. Bacon, *A History of American Christianity*, Scribners, New York, N. Y., 1898, p. 152.

10 Settlement was made at Jamestown in 1607, under a charter from James I.

11 " 'About the last of August (1619),' says John Rolfe in John Smith's *Generall Historie*, 'came in a Dutch man of warre, that sold

us twenty Negars.' These Negroes were sold into servitude, and Virginia. . . ; and thus slavery gained a firm place in the oldest of the colonies" (Benjamin Brawley, *A Social History of the American Negro,* Macmillan, New York, N. Y., 1921, p. 9).

12 John S. Bassett, *A Short History of the United States,* Macmillan, New York, N. Y., 1918, pp. 45-52; George Bancroft, *History of the United States,* Little, Brown, Boston, Mass., 1853, 15th edition, vol. I, pp. 223-35; Joseph I. Gullick, *A Survey of American Pulpit Eloquence,* M.A. thesis, George Washington University, Washington, D. C., 1933, p. 14.

13 The author is not unaware of Frazier's insistence that "African traditions and practices did not take root and survive in the United States" (E. Franklin Frazier, *The Negro Family in the United States,* University of Chicago Press, 1939, pp. 7-8). Frazier attempts to destroy the contentions that Negro religious practices in the United States may be attributed to African sources, but his attempts are feeble. For example, he states: "Of the same nature is the claim of Herskovits that the practice of baptism among Negroes is related to the great importance of the river-cults in West Africa, particularly in view of the fact, that as has been observed, river-cult priests were sold into slavery in great numbers ("Social History of the Negro" in *A Handbook of Social Psychology,* Worcester, Mass., 1935, pp. 256-57). It needs simply to be stated that about a third of the rural Negroes in the United States are Methodists and only in exceptional cases practice· baptism" (Frazier, *op. cit.,* p. 9). Frazier's refutation is fallacious for two reasons. First, he simply states (without proof) that "about a third of the rural Negroes in the United States are Methodists." Second, even if one accepts his unsupported statement that a third of the rural Negroes in the United States do not baptize (the author knows from experience that some Methodists baptize), Herskovits' contention that the American Negro's practice of baptism is related to the river-cults in West Africa may still stand. Over a period of 320 years, without contact with African religious practices, the American Negro naturally has lost much of the African heritage; it is possible that he could have lost entirely the practice of baptism. Frazier ignores these lines of reasoning, and labels as "uncritical" and "absurd" the assertions of Herskovits, Woodson (Carter G. Woodon, *The African Background Outlined,* Washington, D. C., 1936, pp. 168-75), and others (Frazier, *op. cit.,* p. 9). However, it does seem reasonable that these Africans who were brought to America retained something of their African backgrounds. That time and American influences modified and even eliminated this background cannot be denied. But it is in-

conceivable that a people could suddenly lose all their religious practices. As Robert E. Park says, "It is in connection with his (the Negro's) religion that we may expect to find, if anywhere, the indications of a distinctive Afro-American culture" "The Conflict and Fusion of Cultures With Special Reference to the Negro," *Journal of Negro History*, vol. 4, no. 2, April 1919, p. 118).

14 Park, "Conflict and Fusion. . . ," *op. cit.*, p. 130.

15 Alvin Good, *op. cit.*, p. 494.

16 W. E. B. DuBois, "The Negro Church," *Atlanta University Publications*, Atlanta University Press, Atlanta, Ga., 1903, no. 8, p. 5.

17 Melvin J. Herskovits, "The Negro in the New World," *American Anthropologist*, vol. 32, no. 1, 1930, pp. 149-150.

18 W. D. Weatherford, *The Negro from Africa to America*, Doran, New York, N. Y., 1924, p. 43. See also: Sir Richard F. Burton, *A Mission to Gelele, King of Dahome*, vol. 2, p. 88; Melvin J. Herskovits and Frances S. Herskovits, "An Outline of Dahomean Religious Belief," *American Anthropological Association*, no. 41, 1933, pp. 7 ff.

19 Robert H. Nassau, *Fetichism in West Africa*, Duckworth, London, 1904, p. 36.

20 Wilson (quoted in Weatherford, *The Negro from. . . , op, cit.*, p. 44), *Western Africa*, p. 209. See also Arthur G. Leonard, *The Lower Niger and Its Tribes*, Macmillan, New York, N. Y., 1906, Introduction, p. 11.

21 Weatherford, *The Negro from Africa to America, op. cit.*, p. 45. Cf. Notes for chapter III, no. 110.

22 Mary H. Kingsley, *Travels in West Africa*, Macmillan, New York, N. Y., 1897, p. 300.

23 Leonard, *op. cit.*, p. 166.

24 Weatherford, *The Negro from. . . , op. cit.*, p. 49.

25 *Ibid.* Many Southern Negroes still carry an asafetida bag, a dime, a rabbit's foot, or some other charm hung around their necks.

26 Weatherford, *The Negro from. . . , op. cit.*, p. 51.

27 *Ibid.*, p. 53.

28 Weatherford, *The Negro from. . . , op. cit.*, p. 55.

29 See Leo Frobenius, "Early African Culture as an Indication of Present Negro Potentialities," *Annals of the American Academy of Political and Social Science*, vol. cxxxx, no. 229, Nov. 1928, pp. 153 ff.

30 Weatherford, *The Negro from. . . , op. cit.*, p. 65.

31 Franz Boas, *The Mind of Primitive Man*, Macmillan, New York, N. Y., 1938, pp. 98-99.

32 Frederick M. Davenport, *Primitive Traits in Religious Revivals*, Macmillan, New York, N. Y., 1905, pp. 14 ff.

33 William James, *Psychology,* Holt, New York, N. Y., 1900, p. 408.

34 In other words, it would seem that, even in Africa, the Negro found himself humbled, cramped and enslaved by forces stronger than himself—an ideal specimen for the Negro's future life in America. And his religion gave him release in Africa, as it was to do in America.

35 John Murray, *Travels of Mungo Park,* London, vol. I, p. 487. Emphasis supplied by author.

36 "Death" plays an important part in the Negro's old-time religion—his ability to escape from the reality of this world by thinking of a better life after death.

37 Hence, religion was a necessity.

38 This is an important characteristic: as a slave and as a tenant farmer in Macon County the Negro remained without real freedom of speech; the place of the chieftain (and the jungle, with its dangers) was taken, in slavery days, by the master and, in Macon County, by the plantation owner (and white people in general).

39 See Winifred DeWitt Bennett, *A Survey of American Negro Oratory,* M.A. thesis, George Washington University, Washington, D. C., February 1936, ch. II, pp. 3-4. Audience participation is another characteristic which has not been lost, as the records affirm.

40 Bennett, *op. cit.,* p. 4. Each of these characteristics still exists.

41 DuBois, *The Negro Church, op. cit.,* p. 3.

42 "Adahoonzon's Speech," New York *Weekly Magazine,* vol. 2, no. 95, April 26, 1796. This very short and incoherent speech is cited by the magazine, but doubts may be raised over its authenticity.

43 The effect of this restriction in America was a swing to another extreme—numerous Negro ministers.

44 Bennett, *op. cit.,* p. 9.

45 It is not entirely a matter of belief; the records prove this.

46 "The church is the door through which we first walked into western civilization; religion is the form in which America first allowed our personalities to be expressed" (Richard Wright, 12 *Million Black Voices, A Folk History of the Negro in the United States,* Viking Press, New York, N. Y., 1941, p. 131).

47 In the course of approximately 200 years, it is estimated that between 10 to 15 million Negroes were taken from Africa and brought to America" (Bennett, *op. cit.,* p. 10).

48 "That the Negro has succeeded in fitting himself into the life of the new world is one of the highest achievements ever brought about by any race" (*Ibid.*).

49 The Negro would have perished literally; if he had not found

a means by which he could bear his trials with some degree of contentment, he could not have been a good worker and poor workers perished during slavery days; as did unruly slaves.

50 This is important, and a basic cause of the shouting and frenzy of old-fashioned Negro preaching.

51 Bennett, *op. cit.*, p. 11.

52 The Negro adopted this code entirely. For additional information on the colonial history of Virginia, see E. D. Neil's: *The English Colonization of America During the Seventeenth Century; History of the Virginia Company; Virginia Vetusta; Virginia Carolorum;* and *Life of Patrick Copland.*

53 Bennett, *op. cit.*, p. 11. This was "ready-made" for the Negro, because, as a slave, he dared not let politics enter into his preaching; the same situation exists in Macon County—sermons seldom mention the war being fought at the time of the recording; certainly they avoid mention of state and local politics.

54 The years of George Whitefield.

55 Bacon, *op. cit.*, p. 155.

56 This pleased the Negro slave.

57 Bacon, *op. cit.*, 163 ff.

58 *Ibid.*, p. 126.

59 For information on the settlement of the Georgia Colony by General James Oglethorpe in 1733 and the history of religion in Georgia during colonial days, see Bacon, *op. cit.*, pp. 122-26, and the *American Church History Series*, vols. 4, 5, 7, and 8.

60 Bacon, *op. cit.*, pp. 163-65.

61 *Annals of the American Pulpit* (quoting from *Benjamin Franklin's Autobiography*), vol. 5, p. 107.

62 *Ibid.*, vol. 15, pp. 106-7.

63 Gullick, *op. cit.*, p. 79.

64 Similar to the Macon County ministers.

65 "The emotional preaching of Whitefield brought to the Negro a religion he could understand and which could stir him to self-expression. He responded to it with enthusiasm, allowed his imagination to run riot with it, loved it with passion. It afforded him a mental escape from the wretchedness of his social position, whether he was a slave or free, and it stimulated him to assert himself as a human being. More than any other force it aided him in adapting himself to the ways of Western civilization" (Vernon Loggins, *The Negro Author*, New York, N. Y., 1931, p. 4).

66 In the Negro congregation in Macon County there are weak-

minded (sometimes almost insane) people who should be in institutions. These people remain in society; they come to church and shout.

67 Gullick, *op. cit.*, p. 85.

68 Many Negroes got their first taste of American religion at camp meetings, which "were social as well as religious and sometimes partook of a festive nature. . . . While an Episcopal clergyman with his ritual and prayer book had difficulty in interesting the Negroes, they flocked in large numbers to the spontaneous exercises of the Methodists and Baptists, who, being decidedly evangelical in their preaching, had a sort of hypnotizing effect upon the Negroes, causing them to be seized with certain emotional jerks and outward expressions of an inward movement of the spirit which made them lose control of themselves. The program of the day was a delivery of sermons at intervals, interspersed here and there by appeals to sinners to come forward to be prayed for. . . . Seeing that they were made a special object of the philanthropy of these new workers, the Negroes became seized with hysteria because of this new boon; and the interest in the work. . . spread. . . . Persons fell helpless before the altar of the church and had to be carried out. . . . And when they emerged from their semi-conscious state, they came forward singing the songs of the redeemed who had been washed white in the blood of the Lamb" (Woodson, *History of the Negro Church, op. cit.*, pp. 142-44).

69 *Atlanta University Publication*, no. 8, *op. cit.*, 1 ff.: slavery in America almost destroyed the Negro's African heritage; then the Negro Church arose slowly; at first it was voodooism, heathen.

70 Woodson, History of the Negro Church, *op. cit.*, p. 6.

71 *Ibid.*, p. 7.

72 *Ibid.*, John Wesley's diary tells of the first Negro Methodist, November 29, 1758: "I rode to Wadsworth, and baptized two Negroes belonging to Mr. Gilbert" (Daniel, *op. cit.*, p. 21).

73 Woodson, *The Negro in Our History, op. cit.*, p. 118.

74 *Ibid.*

75 "It was not, however, until the coming of the new free and evangelistic types of Christianity, the Baptists and the Methodists, that the masses of the black people, that is, the plantation Negroes, found a form of Christianity that they could make their own" (Robert E. Park, "The Conflict and Fusion of Cultures with Special Reference to the Negro," *op. cit.*, 119).

76 His influence is discussed earlier in this chapter.

77 Bennett, *op. cit.*, II, p. 4.

78 Other religious denominations failed to attract the Negro because their preaching placed too little emphasis on the emotion. "The

Latin ceremonies of the Catholic Church and the ritualistic conformity required by the Anglicans too often baffled the Negro's understanding. . . . The simplicity of the Quakers . . . equally taxed the undeveloped intellect of certain Negroes who often wondered how matters so mysterious could be reduced to such an ordinary formula. . . . [*But the Baptists, Presbyterians and the Methodists attracted the Negro because they*] imbibed more freely than other denominations the social compact philosophy of John Locke and emphasized doctrines of Coke, Milton, and Blackstone as a means to justify the struggle for an enlargement of the domain of political liberty, primarily for the purpose of securing religious freedom denied them by the adherents of the Anglican Church" (Woodson, *op. cit.*, pp. 24-26).

But even the Presbyterians were "too intellectual. [*And*] because Baptist churches were independent of the national organization and because as few as four Baptists under the direction of a minister could organize a congregation [*which accounts for the large number of Negro Baptist churches*] it was easy for this sect to multiply. . . . Both Methodists and Baptists offered a form of worship to which the Negro converts readily responded and both denominations were fired with evangelican zeal. The Camp Meeting Methodists, the Primitive Baptists and other groups, whose religion took a similar form of expression were the ones who set the patterns accepted and later adapted by the Negroes" (Powdermaker, *op. cit.*, p. 230).

79 See Part II of this chapter for a discussion of this fundamental of all old-fashioned Negro preaching.

80 Powdermaker, *op. cit.*, pp. 231-2. All sects, Powdermaker adds, of the Methodists and the Baptists "had in common their belief *that man was sinful; that the Bible was to be interpreted literally; that the body and the present life are nothing, the soul and the future all; that Jesus alone can save; and that the Lord is a stern but just Father who will punish the sinner and reward the righteous*" (p. 230).

81 Woodson, *History of the Negro Church*, *op. cit.*, p. 41. This freedom to preach was permitted until after the Revolutionary War, when opposition to the Negro's cry of a new day to come became more pronounced.

82 *Ibid.* (quoting Jonathan Boucher), p. 24.

83 Paul the Apostle, "The Epistle to the Romans," *Holy Bible*, authorized version, chapter 10, verses 13-14.

84 Johnson, *op, cit.*, p. 3.

85 Woodson, *History of the Negro Church*, *op. cit.*, p. 56.

86 *Ibid.*, pp. 56-7.

87 This is true even today. Negro ministers "put on a show for white listeners every Sunday over radio stations.

88 Bennett, *op. cit.*, vi, p. 7. Jasper was typical of the original old-time Negro preachers of the slavery days.

89 Bennett, *op. cit.*, ii, p. 20.

90 "The church buildings were always constructed so that white people and Negroes could worship in the same house" (Wm. E. Hatcher, *John Jasper*, New York, N. Y., 1900, p. 44).

91 Bennett, *op. cit.*, ii p. 20.

92 Hatcher, *op. cit.*, pp. 24-29.

93 Hatcher, *op. cit.*, p. 47.

94 Bennett, *op. cit.*, ii p. 24.

95 Hatcher, *op. cit.*, p. 11.

96 *Ibid.*, pp. 7-8.

97 In this work, the Macon County sermons are not evaluated critically according to classical standards, but interpretations according to the basic principles of these standards are made.

98 Hatcher, *op. cit.*, p. 164.

99 Bennett, *op. cit.*, vi, p. 8.

100 *Ibid.*, ii, p. 25.

101 In 1794, Absolem Jones and Richard Allen established the Negro African Methodist Episcopal Church in Philadelphia; it became National in 1821 (Bennett, *op. cit.*, ii, p. 18). The first Negro Baptist Church in America was established in Silver Bluff, South Carolina, in 1773 (Daniel, *op. cit.*, p. 21). The second Negro Baptist church was established by George Liele in Savannah (Woodson, *History of the Negro Church*, *op. cit.*, p. 43). John Glouschester established the first African Presbyterian Church in Philadelphia, in 1807 (Woodson, *History of the Negro Church*, *op. cit.*, p. 65).

102 There were many Negro Baptists, for example, who were members of white churches. The First Baptist Church of Charleston, South Carolina, once reported 1,643 members, including 1,383 Negroes (Daniel, *op. cit.*, p. 22).

103 William Lemon, Lemuel Haynes, George Liele, Andrew Bryan, Henry Evans, Black Harry, John Stewart, Lott Carey, John Chavis, Uncle Jack, Nat Turner, *et. al.* Many of these preached to both black and white congregations.

104 Griffin, *op. cit.*

105 Broadly speaking, the original old-fashioned Negro preaching lasted from 1619 to 1832. But since 1619 marks the first appearance of Negro slaves in America, it is reasonable to believe their new religious life did not actually begin that early. Not until the time of Whitefield

(about 1732) did this period begin to influence the Negro's religion. On the other hand, 1832 marks the reaction against Nat Turner's slave insurrection. From then on, old-fashioned Negro preaching has been on the decline. First, there were slave laws against Negro religious meetings and against Negro preaching. Then came freedom for the Negro slave, which tended to release, to some extent, the Negro from bondage (a necessary condition for old-time Negro preaching). During the Negro's freedom, education has tended to continue the decline of old-fashioned Negro religion. The Negro's emphasis upon old-time preaching varies inversely with the amount of the Negro's education and freedom. (This does not mean that the educated Negro is always a disbeliever.)

106 "It is this historic fact, that the Negro Church of today bases itself upon the sole surviving institution of the African father-land, that accounts for the extraordinary growth and vitality" (DuBois, *The Negro Church, op. cit., p.* 188).

107 Griffin, *op. cit.,*

108 Negroes are a people who, except for the period of relief during church services, are mentally, physically, and socially subdued. The word *slavery* is no longer used; but the "Black Belt" Negro is still enslaved.

109 This concept of escape is not without scientific basis. One hesitates to follow Sigmund Freud all the way when he says: "Religion is a clinging to childhood desires and illusions which the weakness of the individual and his fear of life or lack of preparation to deal with it forces him to nourish since, were he to face the facts as they are, he would suffer from utter helplessness" (*Future of An Illusion,* p. 85).

Yet, for suppressed, primitive, emotional and backward people (the Negro of slavery days and many Negroes of Macon County today), the psychoanalytic explanation seems appropriate; for ignorance *is* essential to religious escape. According to Ernest R. Groves (*Introduction to Mental Hygiene,* Holt, New York, N. Y., 1930, p. 308): "Primitive man found his environment saturated with fear, born of his ignorance, and *in his efforts to escape* from the dangers that faced him on every side he was irresistibly drawn toward the supernatural, pulled both by his yearnings and his need of security. This interpretation is at least closest to the attitude that mental hygiene has to take as it deals with religious experience in the modern world."

A. G. Leonard (*op. cit.,* p. 88) speaks of primitive man's inability to check his emotions: "Primitive man made no effort to develop a religion." "On the contrary, his suspicions and fears, his confidence and veneration, were but the spontaneous outcome of his natural instincts—

*an outcome of the emotions that he could no more check than he could
cease to exist or to propagate.*"

Fear may be a reason for man escaping instinctively from reality
by means of religion: "Fear is the determining stimulus to the repres-
sive myth-making phantasy. Of course the fear that stimulates modern
religious faith is not a primitive fear of certain places or persons. It is
rather a complex dread of life and its tasks as a whole. When dangers
threaten mental peace or physical health, the instinct of fear counsels
men to *retreat from an intolerable situation.* Viewed thus *religion appears to be a psychical flight from a dark and threatening reality.* The
sensitive person *who feels inwardly incapable of resisting the blows of
fortune seeks escape from the real present in a religious world of phantasy or faith. Religion is indeed a safety valve for the strained mind*
(C. Dixon, "Religion in the Light of Psychoanalysis," *Psychoanalytic
Review*, Jan. 1921, p. 96).

When Groves says that "the monotony of life in the country-side
and village encouraged the [*religious*] revival [*meetings*] which afforded
relief from the barren life of toil endured by many [*op. cit.*, p. 317],"
he touches directly the condition of Macon County Negroes, who, as a
rule, are without newspapers, radios, magazines, or movies to give them
relief from their bitter existence—they have only their religion. "The
emotional type of church worship has very little influence on the practical affairs of life; it is, indeed, rather to be understood as a method
of escape from the repressions of daily existence" (Reuter, *op. cit.*,
pp. 330-31).

Kilton Stewart, psychologist and anthropologist, told an audience in
New York recently that "civilized Western man is not so well off
emotionally as are the Negritos of the Bataan Mountains in the Philip-
pines." The New York *Times* (Oct. 30, 1949, p. E-9) continues: "The
Negritos have no written language and seldom even talk to one another.
They rely more on gestures, rhythms and expressive movements than
we do for emotional release. It may be, thinks Dr. Stewart, that the
highly complex mind of Western man has lost its ability to readjust
itself in this manner. The Negritos believe that spirits are everywhere
and in all things, so that dances are held both before and after food-
hunting expeditions to dispel fear while hunting and guilty feelings for
having taken food which is haunted. According to Dr. Stewart, the
dance, which follows food-gathering, releases body tensions and feelings
that we would describe as a fear of reprisal or a sense of guilt—both
primary causes of civilized man's neurotic instability.

"Whether he is civilized or not, man prepares for any one of many
activities with particular sets of muscles, like a runner who is on his

mark. The glands play a chemical part in this preparation. The Negrito dance which precedes food-gathering sets the whole adjusting apparatus in motion.

"Negritos believe that the spirits that supposedly haunt animals and plants which have been destroyed participate in the dance. The images of the animals or plants that have been killed are still in the minds of the Negritos and cause psychic difficulties.

"For this reason Dr. Stewart sees nothing absurd in the Negrito attitude. In fact, the Negrito ability to project both images and actual hallucinations into the dance or to have emotional feeling makes the ceremony real rather than symbolic. Thus the Negritos sensibly re-adjust their drives and tensions and in the process land on their psychic feet, even though the spirits to be propitiated are imaginary.

"This method of adjustment is also practiced at funerals. At a funeral the participants engage in a dance which approaches, or even surpasses, the type of psychotherapy upon which the West depends. Children are taught that parents will not completely break with them after death. An expectancy is built up that the dead parent will come back and communicate through dreams. All of the Negritos with whom Dr. Stewart talked on the subject had been thus visited and instructed, encouraged and reproved as in life. Dream visitations continue for a year or two, whereupon the parent instructs the child to arrange a ceremony with dancing and feasting which will release his spirit from the necessity of further communication. w. k."

Irving Kristol, in a recent issue of *Commentary*, states: "the willingness of many clergymen and psychoanalysts to say soothingly that religion and Freud can get along fine with each other makes no sense. . . ; the peacemakers between the two camps are talking through their hats." *Time* (Nov. 14, 1949, pp. 64-65) continues: "One of the basic tenets of Freud's psychoanalysis, Kristol says, was the conviction that religion is nothing but a combination of neurosis and illusion. Today, Author Kristol complains, many clergymen and psychoanalysts are trying to take over Freud's conclusions while ignoring the premises on which they were based.

It was in the U. S., he writes that the idea first took root that psychoanalysis and religion could somehow lie down together and live happily ever after. "In America all races and creeds live and work peacefully side by side—why should not ideas do likewise. . . . It is. . . in such a benign climate of opinion that the current love affair between psychoanalysis and religion has been, time and again, consummated. There have been bickerings. . . and the Catholic Church has shown itself to be rather a frigid partner, but all in all, things have gone well, and the occasional Catholic reserve has been more than made up for by Protestant acquiescence and Jewish ardor.

"Psychoanalysts and the friendly clergymen, says Author Kristol, tend to talk about human happiness instead of truth: they blithely agree that religion and psychoanalysis have at heart the same intention: to help men 'adjust' . . . to make them happy or virtuous or productive. . . .

"Moses did not promise the Jews 'happiness,' nor did he say they should walk in the path of the Law because he thought it a virtuous law. The Law was true because it was divine—it was God's Law, a revelation of man's place in the fundamental constitution of existence. . . . Men's true happiness and virtue are in adhering to this truth —because it is true. . . .

"Orthodox psychoanalysis and religion, says Kristol will never agree on truth. The issue between them is simple and clear-cut. Religion asserts "that the understanding of psychoanalysis is only a dismal, sophisticated misunderstanding, that human reason is inferior to divine reason, that the very existence of psychoanalysis is a symptom of gross spiritual distress. . . Psychoanalysis, religion might say, comes not to remove insanity, but to inaugurate it."

110 Summer 1942.

111 Cf. footnote 109.

112 "Both Old and New Testament offered much with which they [*Negro slaves*] could immediately identify themselves. They could and did fit into the concept of God's chosen people. They, like the ancient Hebrews, were in bondage, longing for the promised land. . . . But Jesus died for them. . . . The Lord would lead them out of the wilderness" (Powdermaker, *op. cit.*, 231-32).

113 The Macon County Negro (who is supposed to be free) still uses this means of escape.

114 Loggins, *op. cit.*, p. 4.

115 Significant expressions have been underlined by the author.

116 "The individual who maintained his self-respect by referring all conduct to an ethical-religious basis is typical of a large class [*of Negroes*]. . . . Slavery and peonage are by this mechanism compared to the enslavement of the Israelites by the Egyptians, and is merely God's plan for the ultimate salvation of his people" (H. M. Bond, "Self-Respect as a Factor in Racial Advancement," *Annals of the American Academy of Political and Social Science*, Nov. 1928, p. 23).

117 Bowen, *op. cit.*, pp. 110-111.

118 That is, for a while.

119 Vernon Loggins, *op. cit.*, p. 51. In any of the recorded sermons

the minister stresses the importance of right living "here below" so that one may receive a better life after death.

120 Bennett, *op. cit.*, II, p. 11.

121 Macon County Negroes "are descended from various African peoples, including the Sudan and Bantu stocks, with a considerable admixture of other groups, particularly the Arabs, the American Indians, and the American whites. . . . " (Raper, *op. cit.*, p. 21). This mixture might account, in part, for the swing away from old-time Negro preaching. However, racial identity seems to be no absolute requisite for following old-time religious principles. Mulattoes indulge in some of the extremest manifestations of this religion (shouting, etc.) Father Divine's group includes whites and blacks. The need for a means of escape seems to be a basic reason for following old-time religious practices.

122 Macon County has a 332-square-mile area; population density, 50.1 [5,451 whites and 11,112 Negroes (Raper, p. 184)]; location, midway between Macon and Albany; the Flint River bisects it; Oglethorpe is the County Seat (Raper, pp. 11, 18). Of the County's 33 Negro churches, 32 have preaching once a month; 1, twice a month; one pastor serves 1 church; one pastor serves 5 churches; the others serve from 2 to 4 churches per month (Raper, p. 363).

123 Old-time Negro preaching, too, has undergone a change—it is disappearing.

124 Raper, *op. cit.*, p. 10.

125 *Ibid.*, p. 99.

126 Reference is to the cotton plantation tenant system. The landlord owns the land and "furnishes" [lets the Negro "take up" (get on credit) food, clothing, etc., the cost of which is deducted from the receipts from the sale of the cotton] the Negro, who, in turn, cultivates the crops and repays the landlord for his food, etc., plus 10% interest." This interest rate is sometimes higher, seldom lower. For example before the tenant sells his cotton, he is indebted to the landlord for $100; he repays the debt plus interest of in reality about 35%, because as a rule the Negro's loan has been for only three or four months. Furthermore, the credit prices which he pays when "takin' up" goods are often much higher than regular cash prices. Add to this (1) the Negro cannot (does not dare) keep a record of the things he purchases on credit, and (2) the landlord is seldom honest. Often at "settlement time," the Negro finds that he owes the landlord $200 to $300 above the income from his cotton. Therefore, he cannot "move to another place," but works on, year after year, bound to the soil, always in debt. Fear

of being lynched, etc., keeps him quiet. He finds release in his religion—or in his Saturday night drunks and cutting sprees.

127 T. Arnold Hill, *The Negro and Economic Reconstruction,* Assoc. in Negro Education, Washington, D. C., p. 38. See Weatherford, *Race Relations, op. cit.,* p. 325: "Among Negro farmers one-third of the owners and two-thirds of the tenants received credits from time merchants at an average interest of 25%.

128 The average income for Negroes in Macon County is less than 20c a day per person (Raper, *op. cit.,* p. 37) ; his diet is unbalanced; his dwelling place is leaky, glass-less, and screen-less; he literally lives in overalls; 29% are illiterate (Raper, p. 344) ; the average educational level is the third grade (*Ibid.*) ; of 323 homes, 68 had no printed matter at all, two-thirds had Bibles and one-fourth had school books (*Ibid.,* pp. 66-7) ; he does not (usually cannot) vote. Is this situation a result of the South's general attitude toward the Negro? Thomas Pearce Bailey, formerly Dean of the Department of Education and Professor of Psychology, University of Mississippi, summarizes this general attitude: "Blood will tell. The white race must dominate. The Teutonic peoples stand for race purity. The Negro is inferior and will remain so. This is a white man's country. No social equality. No political equality. In matters of civil rights and legal adjustments give the white man, as opposed to the colored man, the benefit of the doubts; and under no circumstances interfere with the prestige of the white race. In educational policy let the Negro have the crumbs that fall from the white man's table. Let there be such industrial education of the Negro as will best fit him to serve the white man. Only Southerners understand the Negro question. Let the South settle the Negro question. The status of peasantry is all the Negro may hope for, if the races are to live together in peace. Let the lowest white man count for more than the highest Negro. The above statements indicate the leadings of Providence" (*Race Orthodoxy in the South,* Neale, New York, N. Y., 1914, p. 93).

Raper says the white man in Macon County, as in slavery days, uses the Bible to justify the Negro's lowly condition. "The vast majority of the white people, whether landed aristocrats or tenants, believe that the Negro was made to serve the white man. A Biblical sanction for this they find in the latter part of the ninth chapter of Genesis [*"And he (Noah) drank of the wine, and was drunken; and he was uncovered within his tent. And Ham, the father of Canaan, saw the nakedness of his father, and told his two brethren without. And Shem and Japheth took a garment . . . and covered the nakedness of their father . . . and they saw not their father's nakedness. And Noah awoke from his wine, and knew what his younger son had done unto him. And he said, Cursed be Canaan; a servant of servants shall he be unto his brethren" (verses* 21-25)]. This story which makes no mention of anybody's being turned black, is well-nigh universally used in the Black Belt as Biblical proof that the Negro was created to serve the white man" (Raper, *op. cit.*, p. 164).

129 But conditions are changing. The New Deal, the Fair Deal, the Red Cross, and the Wars (wars seem to improve the Negro's lot in America!) are partly responsible. Old-time Negro preaching can in time disappear entirely.

130 The singing of this song is on the records of one of the sermons.

131 Raper, *op. cit.*, p. 372.

132 Powdermaker, *op. cit.*, pp. 246-7.

133 Reinhardt echoes this same idea when he says: "The possibilities innate in him [*the actor*], but not realized in life, open their dark wings and carry him far beyond his understanding, out into the midst of quite strange happenings" (Hans Rothe, Max Reinhardt: 25 *Jahre Deutsches Theater*, Piper, Munchen, 1930, p. 12).

134 Wright, *op. cit.*, pp. 68, 73

135 Powdermaker's description of Negro preaching in a Mississippi community in the "Black Belt" is true of the sermons in Macon County: "In certain respects most of the sermons preached in the Negro churches of this community resemble those preached to Negroes by white ministers before the Civil War. The formal dogma is essentially unchanged. The Bible is still accepted literally, as it was a hundred years ago. Most Negro ministers today, as did their former white preceptors, stress the sins and faults of the colored people and the glories of the future world, counseling patience, endurance, repentance, so that they may win the Kingdom of Heaven" (Powdermaker, *op. cit.*, pp. 245-6).

136 DuBois, *Souls of Black Folk, op. cit.*, pp. 67-68.

CHAPTER IV

1 This study does not intend to restrict old-time Negro preaching to classical standards of rhetoric. However, for this phase of the treatment of the sermons, no better units of organization than *invention, style, disposition*, and *delivery* present themselves. Therefore, chapters IV-VI will be concerned with the interpretation of that element of the Macon County sermons which has to do with, as Cicero conceived it, the *invention* of what is said (*De Oratore*, Bohn edition, p. 242): audience analy-

sis (already touched upon), purposes of the sermons, topics or subject matter, methods of persuasion, and preparation of the sermon (to be treated in a later chapter).

Because the preacher, his sermon, his delivery and his audience are so closely united, there must be, of necessity, overlapping of treatment in the chapters, despite the units of division. In fact, the interpretation throughout is concerned with all four elements of the preaching (just as the records are); the chapter units denote changes of emphasis.

2 Brooks, *op. cit.*, p. 110. Another writer says: "The primary intention of preaching is the reformation of mankind . . . , a reformation of life and manners. . . . To restore the sinner to the likeness and favor of God" (W. Gresley, *Ecclesiastes Anglicanus,* Appleton, New York, N. Y., 1843, pp. 9-10).

3 Cf. footnote 4 below, par. 4.

4 This emotional escape of pent-up feelings. The purpose of winning souls to Christ has not been lost entirely, but it seems to be a remote purpose.

The strangeness of the Negro's "getting happy" and shouting lies at the heart of an explanation of the Negro's old-time religion. This type of religious expression seems to be an indication of primitiveness. The following description of the primitive dances of Australian Aborigines is suggestive of the American Negro's old-time religious practices: "When they are once come together, a sort of electricity is formed . . . which quickly transports them to an extraordinary degree of exaltation. Every sentiment expressed finds a place without resistance in all the minds . . .; each re-echoes the others, and is re-echoed by the others. The initial impulse thus proceeds, growing as it goes, as an avalanche grows in its advance. And as such active passions so free from all control could not fail to burst out, on every side one sees nothing but violent gestures, cries, veritable howls, and deafening noises of every sort. . . . And since a collective sentiment cannot express itself collectively except on the condition of observing a certain order permitting co-operation and movements in unison, these gestures and cries naturally tend to become rhythmic and regular; hence come songs and dances. . . . When arrived at this state of exaltation, a man does not recognize himself any longer. . . . It seems to him that he has become a new being. . ." (Emile Durkheim, *The Elementary Forms of the Religious Life,* London, 1915, pp. 215-216; 218-219).

The purpose of "getting happy" does not seem to be solely a religious one; the records show that the excitement is really festive in nature. They [*Negro folk services and sermons*] seem often to have at once, religious and secular character. They are secular in so far as people attend them in order to participate in the spectacle, the drama and the excitement of the event. They are religious in so far as they seem to give a renewed sense of communion and solidarity of the members of the congregation with all the remembered dead . . .; they encourage hope and belief in some happy reunion with 'those who have gone before.' They are moral. . . .

"There seems to be no escaping the fact that, for a considerable part of the congregation, the preaching and the service are rather more a form of entertainment than a religious experience. It is an experience which, like a work of art, is valued for its own sake and not for any more remote and ulterior moral or religious purpose connected with it.

"In this sense, these folk religious services are comparable with those orgiastic exercises of primitive people in which not only religious, but eventually all the more specific forms of religious expressions, the ritual, the hymns, prayers and sermons, have evolved.

". . . The question which has interested students of art and religion is this: Just when did the song and the ritual, which among primitive people is mainly dance, cease to be religion and become a form of art? It seems to be true that not only religion but most of the expressive arts, the dance, the drama and music have evolved from this same generative nucleus or core," Robert E. Park, *Unpublished Lectures* (quoted by Jones, *op. cit.*, pp. 82-3; 84).

Found in Negro folk service is what is apparently an elementary and immature form of religious expression. That is, a form of expression which is the first and most natural manner of expression utilized by a person or a group of persons. Such are the inarticulate expressions of the baby who makes random noises to express his feelings, before he acquires the customary forms which are called language, or of the group which spontaneously expresses itself as natural tendencies led it to do, rather than according to a formalized mode of conduct. Therefore, the elementary or immature stage of expression apparently is one of spontaneity rather than of conventionality, and is guided by impulse and the way one's feelings direct one to act, and not by a standardized pattern. The expressive stage found in Negro folk service seems to be elementary in this sense of the word.

". . . Apparently there is taking place again in the case of Negro folk the process by which religious expression passes from an elementary form to a mature form and at the same time gives rise to various expressive arts. Hence, here, as among the Greek people, we have the development of art out of religious practices. Perhaps religion, then can be said to furnish the foundation upon which much of our art is built" (Jones, *op. cit.*, pp. 77; 86).

[184]

5 Emotional sermon.

6 DuBois, *Souls of Black Folk, op. cit.*, pp. 191-192.

7 "Open the doors" is a figurative way of saying the church is now ready to accept new members.

8 "Obligations" refers to the paying of dues. These ministers always seem to have the economic purpose in the background. "The more members I have, the more money I *should* get; the more members that pay their dues, the more money I *do* get," seems to be the thought.

9 This is discussed further, in the chapter on organization.

10 Raper, *op. cit.*, p. 368.

11 The author has seen as many as five "collections" (asking the audience for money) at one preaching occasion. And each "collection" is a long, drawn-out affair. The minister stands in the pulpit looking down at the collection table, occasionally leading a song (and always encouraging the people to give), while the deacons plead for more money. They always ask for a certain amount at the beginning of the "collection" — say, $5. When the money is counted, after a period of pleading, the deacons often say that they need additional money (say 85c) to make the amount "even" $5 or $6 "even." There is more singing and more money is collected. This final amount usually exceeds the amount asked for and additional money is needed to make the new amount "even." (As a boy, the author often wondered why it was so necessary to make the amount "even" — precisely $3 or $4, no fraction of a dollar.) This goes on and on, with the audience digging out more and more nickels and dimes, until the minister and the deacons are satisfied that no additional money can be secured. Then the minister takes the money, as a rule, then and there. "Officers are all right," one minister confided to the author. "Don't know what I'd do without 'em; may the Lord bless 'em, but I feel better with the money in *my* pocket. Plain business, you know."

12 "Five dollars or $8 ain't gwine to speak to no good preacher" (III). Money ("taking up collection") colors the services to a very great degree.

13 This study moves directly to the subject matter of the sermons without considering the types of sermons, because — although delivered at various occasions: regular Sunday services, funerals, revivals, Union Sunday sermons, conventions — the majority of old-time Negro sermons are essentially alike. Topics has to do with the ideas of the sermons. These ideas might consist in "simple texts and broad truths; . . . [*the subjects of sermons should be*] mostly eternal truths," Kenneth G. Hance (quoting Phillips Brooks), "The Elements of the Rhetorical Theory of Phillips Brooks," *Speech Monographs*, Dec. 1938, vol. 5, no. 1, p. 19.

14 Hance (quoting Frank W. Gunsaulus), *Ibid.*, p. 16.

15 Brooks, *op. cit.*, p. 172.

16 A PRAYER, SERMON I.

17 The names of some sermons are colorful ideas based on the Bible: "Dry Bones in the Valley," and "As the Eagle Stirreth Her Nest."

18 The minister did not give the Biblical location of this text, but it seems to be based on two Bible passages: (1) "Thou shalt love the Lord thy God with all thy heart, and with all thy mind" (MATTHEW, 22: 37).

19 "Then spake Joshua to the Lord in the day when the Lord delivered up the Amorites before the children of Israel, and he said in the sight of Israel, *Sun, stand thou, still upon Gibeon; and thou, Moon, in the valley of Ajalon.*" JOSHUA, 10: 12.

20 This preacher's talk is included as Sermon V because it is characteristic of this type of preaching.

21 The themes of the nine Negro sermons which were recorded for the Files of the Department of Social Sciences at Fisk University are as follows:

1. "And though I bestow all my goods to feed the poor and though I give my body to be burned and have not love it profiteth me nothing."
2. "Now we are interested in victory. My life in Christ, your life in Christ doesn't mean anything if you haven't got the victory."
3. "Stay 'round the feeding place."
4. "There's a great day coming."
5. "Lord, what wouldst thou have me ter do."
6. "That makes us know we got to get on our traveling shoes so we can march right up to our heavenly glory."
7. "Feed my sheep."
8. "I am talking tonight on Obedience and the way to go."
9. "It just takes being born again." (Funeral sermon.) (Jones, *op. cit.*, p. 42.)

22 Can people, who practice old-time Negro religion, think? These quotations indicate that the ministers *are* able to think. The following statement, directed at the author and the recording group, is further indicative: "Dere's people done come for one thing and some come for annuder. Some uv 'em done come here lookin' for mistakes. Well, now, I know dat feller ain't gwine be disappointed, 'cause I'se full uv dem" [*Laughter.*] (VI). At the highest emotional point, the Negro shouter *does not* think, but it is not because he *cannot think.* The distinction is important: the *ability* to think is a distinguishing characteristic of *Homo*

sapiens. To say that the shouting Negro cannot think is to say that he is not a human being.

23 Desire for success is a compelling motive; to be discussed later.

24 The Negro thinks of each member of the Trinity as being all-powerful and thinks of the Trinity as being one.

25 The discussion of pathetic appeal will show that fear of death and the hope of a new life play a part in this preference.

26 Young people often questioned this. When told that God knows everything and, at the same time, ordered to pray to God, they cannot understand why it is necessary to *inform* one who already knows everything and who is good and kind. Since he knows what one has in mind before one asks it, wouldn't the kind Man give it without the asking?

27 *Cf. footnote* 4, chapter IV.

28 *Ibid.*

29 Could the Negro be living in an age which has passed? Raoul De Roussy De Sales could have had the Macon County Negro in mind instead of people of another period in history when he says: ". . . For our forefathers the idea of happiness was not connected with this earth. . . . The whole moral outlook of the Western man was indeed based on the fundamental precept that the purpose of life was to deserve a place in Heaven, and that earthly ambition or satisfaction were more of a handicap than an asset to those who, one day, would have to appear before their Creator. . . . Men were expecting the end of the world, sometimes in terror, sometimes in hope. They were not expecting that life on earth could ever be anything but miserable. To live was admittedly a punishment" ("The Idea of Happiness," *Saturday Review of Literature*, v. 25, no. 7, Feb. 14, 1942, p. 3.).

CHAPTER V

1 The classical tradition places "modes of persuasion" below invention and recognizes three modes: (1) through character (Ethos); (2) through the emotion (Pathos); and (3) through logical argument. This chapter considers Ethos.

2 Hance (paraphrasing Brooks, *op. cit.*, p. 109), *op. cit.*, p. 20.

3 "Apart from the argument [*in a speech*] there are three things that gain our belief, namely, intelligence, character, and good will" (Aristotle, *op. cit.*, bk. 2, p. 92).

4 Even a Negro theological student said, "I believe men are called

to the ministry not by any actual sound they hear, but I believe they see a vision from God. . . ." (Daniel, *op. cit.*, pp. 71-2).

5 Such are the elements of ethical proof. See Aristotle, *op. cit.*, bk. II, ch. 1. Joseph Glanville thinks the preacher should be a pious man himself, endeavoring to set the example for the people (*An Essay Concerning Preaching* . . , London, 1678, p. 28).

6 This was during World War I.

7 *God Struck Me Dead: Conversion Experiences and Autobiographies of Ex-Slaves* (quoted by Jones, *op. cit.*, pp. 41-2), Source Department, series no. 1, Department of Social Sciences, Fisk University, Nashville, Tenn., unpublished, p. 55.

8 Booker T. Washington implies that the Negro preacher is not always sincere in his claim that he has been called to preach. He tells the story of the Negro who, working along in the cotton field one day, suddenly stopped and cried in a pulpit voice: "De sun am so hot and dis Nigger am so tired, bless my soul, I believe I done been called to preach! Glory!" (*Up From Slavery*, Doubleday, New York, N. Y., 1924, p. 82).

A common joke among Negroes is that such-and-such a preacher thought God said, "Go *preach*," when what He really said was, "Go *plow!*"

9 Jerry believed his "call" had been merely imagination and coincidence; perhaps he still remembered his unemotional conversion.

10 Daniel, *op. cit.*, p. 65. For more information on the "conversion" and "the call," see pp. 68-78, same book.

11 "The church-goers of lesser intellectual and social average believe that the minister is the mouthpiece of the Almighty and hang to every word that falls from his lips" (Daniel, *op. cit.*, pp. 71-2).

12 "The combination of a certain adroitness, with deep-seated earnestness of tact, with consummate ability, gave him [*the old-time Negro preacher*] his preeminence, and helps him maintain it" [*Ibid.* (quoting DuBois), p. 29].

13 Johnson, *op. cit.*, pp. 4-5.

14 Raper, *op. cit.*, p. 365.

15 Daniel, *op. cit.*, p. 41.

16 Raper, *op. cit.*, p. 367.

17 *Ibid.*, p. 368. This amount is greater than the income of the average rural family or the average rural school teacher.

18 Johnson, *op. cit.*, pp. 4-5.

19 The regular pastor of the church had been ill for some time and this minister was substituting.

20 J. Saunders Redding's description of a "Black Belt" Negro

preacher who was attending a "wake" (sitting up all night with the dead) is suggestive of this minister: "We had nearly finished eating when the dining-room door opened again and a heavy-muscled black man not much over five feet tall, stood there. Above his piped vest his shirt was wet with perspiration. His face was black as a thundercloud. It quivered in a fixed, beatific smile. Behind him the room seemed more crowded than it had been when Jamie flung open the door. A thick murmur of hushed voices beat gently behind the preacher. He was looking at us, but he seemed also to be listening in pious satisfaction to the murmur behind him.

" 'I brings you the word of the Lord, brethren,' he said, raising his short, heavy arms in a gesture at once grotesquely pompous and reserved. 'Weep not at the outgoin', but take joy an' be comforted that Gawd's great will is done. Amen! Who's goin' a say amen?'

"From the women behind him there was a chorus of amens; from the men, not a word, only a shifting of feet and a dropping of eyes. Arms still upraised, he began his prayer" (*No Day of Triumph*, Harper, New York, N. Y., 1942, p. 273). The audience reaction is indicative of the change in attitude on the part of the men toward the preacher. The women appear to be more impressed.

21 Seven times, according to a single typewritten page of his sermon.

22 That is, he is to be a "good" old-time preacher, but his success will be based upon ignorance and emotional escape.

23 An indication of the successful Negro preacher.

24 A Negro called "Son" Langs first brought this term forcefully to the author's attention: "I don't care what a Nigger preacher has — education, looks, sense, or whatnot —. If he wants to please the people, he's got to 'holler'." The recordings clearly emphasize that complete stop in the flow of words in order for the preacher to "holler."

25 Negroes frequently criticize one another for doing things late. A common expression is: "Do you mean nine o'clock or nine o'clock, c. p. t.?" Nine o'clock, c. p. t. (COLORED PEOPLE'S TIME) means about nine-thirty (or at least before noon).

26 He says John Smith was captain of the *Titanic*. (This ship sank in 1912.)

27 This is not the old-time Negro preacher, who did not always feel it necessary to point out the exact chapter and verse in the Bible. The other Macon County preachers are like the original old-time minister.

28 This is a short talk, really an introduction and a conclusion to

the other two sermons given at Deer Creek Church; but it has character-istics of Macon County preaching.

29 The author made this mistake. Attempting to "sell" the record-ing idea to the minister, the author pointed out the probable result of the project and expressed the hope that the sermons might some day be made into a book on preaching in Macon County and that the minister would "see" a copy of the book. There was a long pause; then the minister said simply, "I am blind."

30 He is known by his nickname; but no one could recall its origin.

31 Hatcher described Jasper in these words: "Jasper was an odd picture to look upon. His figure was uncouth; he was rather loosely put together, his limbs were fearfully long and his body strikingly short, a sort of nexus to hold his head and limbs in place. He was black but his face saved him. It was open, luminous, thoughtful, and in moments of animation it glowed with a radiance and exaltation that was most at-tractive" (Hatcher, *op. cit.*, p. 21).

32 "My belove' " is used 21 times on one typewritten page (selected at random) of his sermon.

33 "This combination of a certain adroitness, with deep-seated earnestness of tact, with consummate ability, gave him [*the old-time Negro preacher*] his preeminence, and helps him maintain it" [Daniel (quoting DuBois), *op. cit.*, p. 29].

34 And, as a result, they talk as if God, Christ, and the prophets are old friends of theirs.

CHAPTER VI

1 Aristotle said that "proof may be conveyed through the audi-ence, when it is worked up by the speech to an emotional taste. For there is a wide difference in our manner of pronouncing decisions, according as we feel pleasure, pain, affection or hatred" (Aristotle, *op. cit.*, bk. 2, Ch. 1). In other words, pathetic appeal is important.

2 Thomas Foxcroft, like other Colonial preachers (from whom the old-time Negro minister learned to preach), said the preacher should "press every duty . . . with all the artifices of persuasion. . . ." (*Some Seasonable Thoughts on Evangelical Preaching; Its Nature, Usefulness and Obligation*, Rogers & Fowle, Boston, Mass., 1740, p. 28).

Ebenezer Pemberton (*A Sermon Preached at the Ordination of the Reverend Mr. Walter Wilmot*, Apr. 12, 1738, Boston, Mass., 1738) and

Cotton Mather (*Manductio Ad Ministerium* . . . , Hancock, Boston, Mass., 1726) mention hope and fear most often as motives.

3 Glanville says pathetic proof was necessary because "the common people are incapable of much theory. . . . Their affections are raised by figures and earnestness and passionate representations. . . ." (Glanville, *op. cit.*, p. 38).

Bernard thought "the affections heere to be stirred up are foure: love to the thing: desire to the means: hope in the means: and joy respecting the benefits of the means" (Richard Bernard, *The Faithful Shepherd*. . . . Pavier, London, 1621, pp. 320 ff.).

4 Johnson, *op. cit.*, p. 5.

5 Brooks, *op. cit.*, pp. 130-31.

6 "We feel undeniably how hearty laughter frees us, a deep sob relieves us, a fit of anger can redeem us" (Max Reinhardt, *op. cit.*, p. 5).

7 This requires imagination, which the Negro has. Then, by concentration and suggestion, as in the induction of the hypnotic state, the subject goes off into a kind of hypnotic trance and makes of the Negro preacher something of a hypnotist.

8 Perhaps the Negro's emphasis on the great mystery of God is an aspect of his original (African) superstitious temperament.

9 The moving-picture producers capitalize upon this. Nothing is supposed to amuse a theater audience more than to see a Negro, in a haunted house, roll his eyes and talk about running.

10 Much of the effect here is due to the rhythm.

11 Some of the songs had piano accompaniment. This is the only church, of those visited, which had a piano.

12 Negroes in the "Black Belt" still observe the old custom of sitting up all night with the dead. Friends and relatives visit the house of the deceased on the night of the "wake;" the body is in plain view, and the night is spent in talking of death, of the dead person (especially, how the "end" — death — came), and in drinking coffee or something stronger.

13 Redding, *op. cit.*, pp. 273-74.

14 Dr. W. E. B. DuBois said "three things characterize the religion" of the backward Negro: the preacher, the music, and the frenzy. "The music is that plaintive rhythmic melody, which is touching in minor cadences, which, despite caricature and defilement, still remains the most original and beautiful expression of human life and longing yet born on American soil. Sprung from the African forests, where its counterpart can still be heard, it was adapted, changed, and intensified by the tragic soul-life of the slave, until, under the stress of law and whip, it

became the one true expression of a people's sorrow, despair, and hope" (*Souls of Black Folk*, pp. 190-91).

15 The *thought* is not all-important at all times.

16 He refers to a deacon in the audience.

17 It was not always a sorrowful feeling the minister suggests. Often his words are charged with memories of happy times, perhaps even another "good" religious service.

18 But much of the success of the Negro preacher's pathetic appeal depends on his delivery.

19 Logical proof is founded in formal logic and speaks to the listener's reason. Deduction and induction are the two general types of reasoning. On the basis of specific types of argument, these two main classes are further subdivided. Deductive proof consists of various classes of enthymemes, having as the basis for distinction the manner in which the propositions are stated. Inductive proof, on the other hand, consists of the following four types: (1) argument from specific instances; (2) argument from causal relation; (3) argument from authority; and (4) argument from analogy (Aristotle, *op. cit.*, bk. 2, chs. 20-24; Aristotle, *The Organon or Logical Treatises of Aristotle*, O. F. Owen, ed., Bohn edition, London, 1853, vol. 1, pp. 41, 42, 89-142, 232, 244, 347-352). The author does not attempt to make an exhaustive treatment of logical argument.

CHAPTER VII

1 "To clothe and deck his thoughts with language" is the speaker's duty, says Cicero (*De Oratore*, Bohn edition, p. 178). ". . . A good style is, first of all, clear. . . . The style, again, should be neither mean nor above the dignity of the subject, but appropriate. . . . (Aristotle, *Rhetoric, op. cit.*, 185-86). Quintilian said of style: ". . . Let the greatest possible care, then, be bestowed on expression" (*Institutes of Oratory*, J. S. Watson, ed., London, George Bell and Sons, 1891, vol. 2, pp. 74-77).

Since the sermons of this project were composed by men who had very little formal education and because the sermons (with the exception of I and II) were not written and published before delivery, it is not expected that the style of the sermons be polished and literary.

2 Aristotle, *op. cit.*, bk. 3, p. 182.

3 *Ibid.*

4 "A dialect is an irregular type of speech, estimated and in greater

or less degree condemned, by comparison with what is assumed to be a normal and approved set of speech habits. . . . There is no essential language, but only varieties of languages. . . . Dialects of all kinds are merely the convenient summaries of observers who bring together certain homogeneities in the speech habits of a group and thus secure for themselves an impression of unity. Other observers might secure different impressions by assembling different habits of the same groups" (G. P. Krapp, *The English Language in America*, Century, New York, N. Y. 1935, vol. 1, pp. 225-26). For a discussion of Southern dialect, see "Southern American Dialect" by C. M. Wise (*American Speech*, 8, 1933, p. 42). Wise has studied dialect in Louisiana, Mississippi, Texas, Arkansas, Tennessee, Kentucky, Alabama, Florida, Georgia, the Carolinas and Virginia. His definition: "Dialect is used here to mean any form of English, spoken by a literate or an illiterate group, which is phonologically different from the English spoken by some other group" (Wise, *op. cit.*, p. 37).

For a study of Negro dialect in the South, see William E. Farrison's thesis, "The Phonology of the Illiterate Negro Dialect of Guilford County, North Carolina" (*Ohio State Abstracts of Dissertations Presented by Candidates for Degree of Doctor of Philosophy*, Summer Quarter, 1936, Ohio State University Press, Columbus, O., no. 21, 1937), whose purpose was "to describe phonologically a fair sample of the illiterate Negro speech of Guilford County, North Carolina — a sample of what may be considered more or less ordinary illiterate Negro speech" (p. 71). Farrison's procedure was: (1) interviews with inhabitants of the county; (2) samples of the speech of the illiterate Negroes taken by a recording machine; and (3) a questionnaire. "Samples of the speech of ten different persons were phonographically recorded . . . on eighteen 12-inch and seven 8-inch double-faced aluminum discs. . . . Biographical sketches of the persons whose speech was recorded and samples of the transcriptions made from the phonograph records are given in an appendix to the dissertation" (p. 72).

For a "word-list" of Negro dialect in the South, see article in *Dialect Notes, American Dialect Society*, vol. 2 (quoting John Uri Lloyd), New Haven, Conn., parts 1-4, 1900-1904, p. 180. It describes the dialect of the old-time Negro: " 'Words were beheaded, curtailed, conglomerated, broken; and the Negro also had an *idiom* of his own: sentences were now and then run together, as if made of a few words. . . . Barbarisms that came from illiteracy were mixed with expressions peculiar to himself. . . . The letter *r* was often ruled out. . . . *E* might become *i*, as in ch*i*st for ch*e*st; or replace another letter instead of being itself displaced, as *r*, be altogether brushed away, as in p*u*sson for person, in which it became *u*. The final *g* was usually dropped, and the final letter *d* seldom touched, the determination *ed* being seldom if ever employed. . . . The letter *o* often became *u*, *th* became *f*. . . . The letter *v* became *b*. . . . With the Negro the aim seemed to be either to shorten and simplify words and to drop letters which require an effort, or to show his 'smartness' by using words took big for his comprehension.' ''

5 Hatcher, *op. cit.*, p. 9.

6 "It is hardly appropriate if fine language is used by a slave" (Aristotle, *Rhetoric, op. cit.*, pp. 185-186).

7 Johnson, *op. cit.*, p. 9.

8 Aristotle, *Rhetoric, op.cit.*, bk. 3, pp. 185-86.

9 Johnson, *op. cit.*, p. 5.

10 "A good style is, first of all, clear" (Aristotle, *Rhetoric, op. cit.*, p. 185).

11 The language of the sermon "should be full of vivid images" (Gresley, *op. cit.*, p. 115). Aristotle (*Rhetoric*) states the force of language consists in the thing being "placed before the eyes." Evidently he had images in mind.

12 The Negro preacher in expounding the Bible draws striking figures and portrays life, death, and the beyond in a dramatic fashion, replete with emotion (Woodson, *op. cit.*, p. 269).

13 Foxcroft thinks the minister should deliver his thoughts "with a natural turn of speech, and in the most entertaining images" (Foxcroft, *op. cit.*, p. 26).

14 Metaphor — comparison of an automobile and Baal.

15 Metaphor — a comparison of religious conversion and birth. So many metaphors may be surprising yet Aristotle says "in prose all the more attention must be devoted to metaphor because here the resources of the writer are less abundant than in verse. It is metaphor above all else that gives clearness, charm, and distinction to the style. . . . The speaker must find epithets and metaphors . . .; the simile also is a metaphor; the difference is but slight" (*Rhetoric, op. cit.*, bk. 3, Ch. 2-4, pp. 187, 192).

16 Metaphor — comparison of an aroused cat (or some such animal) and the people in the audience when they are aroused emotionally ("happy").

17 Metaphor and alliteration. The listener's condition is compared to that of an animal or of an insect which crawls, in its lowly condition, into its hole. Repetition of "t."

18 Metaphor and personification. Jealousy is compared with a dog.

19 Metonymy. Instead of saying that the one you scorn is going

to be kind to you, he uses the effect of this kindness (fanning the flies away from the face of a sick person) to represent kindness, which is the cause. Note the parallelism and periodic construction.

20 Maintaining the rhythmical stride in preaching is compared to staying on a moving horse.

21 A woman screams this comment. "Tear it up" might have a sexual implication. She compares the abandon of the climax of the preaching (and the effect on the audience) to the climax of sexual intercourse; the words "hon' " [*honey*] and "pull 'em down" suggests this interpretation.

22 The vividness of an image is due to its four attributes: "recency, original intensity, frequency of occurrence, and recency of recollection" (A. E. Phillips, *Effective Speaking*, Newton Co., Chicago, Ill., 1926, p. 33).

23 Raper, *op. cit.*, p. 368.

24 Woodson, *op. cit.*, p. 270.

CHAPTER VIII

1 Disposition is concerned with arrangement, the general plan of the speech, as well as the particular parts of the speech. Cicero is aware of the importance of disposition when he says the speaker should "dispose and arrange his matter, not only in a certain order, but with a sort of power and judgment" (*De Oratore, op. cit.*, p. 178). In fact, the importance of the arrangement of material has been stressed again and again in rhetorical treatises and in textbooks from Aristotle's time to the present. Aristotle thought organization aids in obtaining clarity, for "the average man cannot easily follow a long and complicated chain of reasoning." He believed "a speech has two parts. Necessarily, you state your case, and you prove it"; but he felt that "at most, the parts cannot exceed four—Proem [*introduction*], Statement, Argument, and Epilogue [*conclusion*]" (Rhetoric, *op. cit.*, bk. 3, ch. 13, p. 220). Quintilian also felt arrangement was important: "However, good the material, it will form but a confused mass and heap unless similar arrangement bind it together, disposed in regular order, and with its several parts connected one with another" (Quintilian, *op. cit.*, II, 1).

2 Cicero, *De Oratore, op. cit.*, p. 242.

3 The minister is not entirely without preparation; his entire life is usually one of general preparation.

4 Disposition and delivery go hand-in-hand. Such speaking also suggests that the old-time Negro preacher possesses a fine memory. Memory is a constituent of rhetoric and "to Aristotle, Cicero, and Quintilian, memory meant more than the retention of words. . . . 'It includes the speaker's whole command of his material. . . .'" [Hance (paraphrasing and quoting Harry Caplan's paper, "Mnemonics for the Ancient Public Speakers"), *op. cit.*, pp. 36-37].

5 "The Proem is the beginning of the speech; it answers to the prologue in poetry, or to the prelude in music for the flute. All three are beginnings, and, as it were, pave the way for what follows, . . . to make clear the end and object of your work. And hence, if your matter is plain and short, a proem really should not be employed" (Aristotle, *Rhetoric, op. cit.*, bk. 3, 13-14, pp. 221-23).

6 "Sun, stand thou still upon Gibeon; and thou, moon, in the valley of Ajalon" (*Bible, op. cit.*, JOSHUA 10:12).

7 Cf. footnote d.

8 In the Epilogue " you must put the audience into the right state of emotion" (Aristotle, *Rhetoric, op. cit.*, bk. 3, ch. 19, p. 240).

9 Aristotle says: "success in delivery is of the utmost importance to the effect of the speech" (*Rhetoric op. cit.*, bk. 3, ch. 1, p. 182). Cicero acclaims the importance of delivery when he says the speaker must "deliver it [*the speech*] with due action. . . " (*De Oratore, op. cit.*, p. 242).

10 Hatcher, *op. cit.*, p. 9.

11 "What is true of the Negro preacher and his swaying congregation, of the jazz-band leader and his cavorting man. . . . What they do. . . is seldom not alive and active" (Edith J. R. Isaacs, *Theater Arts*, Aug. 1942, p. 525).

12 Johnson, *op. cit.*, pp. 5-6.

13 Raper, *op. cit.*, p. 362.

14 Cf. Richard Wright's description, pp. 116-117.

15 "Tension rose as he [*the old-time preacher*] continued in a voice that was gradually assuming the character of a chant" (Jones, *op. cit.*, pp. 13-14).

16 "The art of delivery has to do with the voice: with the right management of it to express each several emotion—as when to use a loud voice, when a soft, and when the intermediate; with the mode of using pitch—high, low, and intermediate; and with the rhythms to be used in each particular case" (Aristotle, *Rhetoric, op. cit.*, bk. 3, ch. 1, p. 183).

17 "These are, in fact, the three things that receive attention:

volume, modulation of pitch, and rhythm" (Aristotle, *Rhetoric*, bk. 3, ch. 1, p. 183).

18 Johnson, *op. cit.*, p. 11.

19 Raper, *op. cit.*, pp. 369-70.

Raper (quoting a Georgia white man, *op. cit.*, p. 370) relates a story of shouting which, if it is true, implies that all of the "shouters" are not happy religiously: "Always will remember one night, when two stout women were sitting right in front of me, and as the arousements got on one of them turned to the other and said: 'Here, sistuh Herry, hole my hat; I'se gwine to shout!' 'Hole your own hat, I'se gwiner shout myself!' was the quick reply. I snickered; they looked around, got sullen and stayed in their seats."

20 *Souls of Black Folk, op. cit.*, pp. 190-91.

21 Johnson, *op. cit.*, pp. 5-10.

CHAPTER IX

1 The editor of the Jackson (Miss.) *Daily News* shocked a number of people when he ran the following article as a front page editorial:

OUR DISGRACEFUL NEGRO SCHOOLS
(quoted in *New South*, Feb. 1949, vol. 4, no. 2, pp. 5-6)

Whether we like it or not, the Supreme Court of the United States has declared that Mississippi, in common with other Southern States, must provide equal educational opportunities for Negroes.

No use fussing, cussing, or fuming about it.

That decision is the law of the land and we have no alternative save to obey.

It is far better to obey promptly, cheerfully, and in our own way, than to be forced to do so.

Moreover, that decision embodies justice and common sense.

In the matter of education we have for many years been treating Negroes most outrageously. The type of education we have been providing for them is nothing short of a disgrace. It might well be called a public scandal.

Some Ugly Facts

Let's face a few of the ugly facts — not all of the ugly facts, for it would take too long to tell the whole story. Statements that

[197]

follow are based on official reports in our state department of education.

The estimated value today of all school property in Mississippi being used for white children is $57,000,000.

The estimated value of all school property being used for colored children is only $11,000,000.

According to the latest survey there are in our State 3,700 Negro school-houses, but not all of them are school property. About 2,300 of these buildings are owned by counties and communities, and many of them are the old Julius Rosenwald school buildings constructed at the time when that great philanthropist was spending money freely in Mississippi — a goodly part of it being stolen and diverted to other uses.

Over 1,400 of the buildings now being used to house Negro schools belong to churches and Negro fraternal bodies. Some of them are tenant cabins used where no other structures are available. As a matter of fact, Negro churches and fraternal organizations in our State are furnishing nearly one-half of what little Negro children get in the way of educational facilities. It is a shame and a disgrace that such should be the case.

Our white rural schools, as a rule, are fairly well maintained, but Negro schools are poorly equipped, shabby, dilapidated, and unsightly. Go into any rural school building for Negroes and see for yourself how things are. Almost without exception they are one-room structures, rickety stoves are propped up on brickbats, black-boards are absent or worn to the point of uselessness, sanitation is sadly lacking, and the common drinking cup is still in use.

In many hundreds of instances it will be found that one Negro teacher is struggling along trying to teach children in all the grammar school grades.

Here in the county of Hinds, wealthiest in the commonwealth, our school facilities for Negroes are so poor and shabby that churches and lodges are furnishing 18 of the buildings in which Negro schools are housed.

Official Honesty Lacking

Moreover, in recent years we have not had official honesty in the matter of providing for Negro schools. During the administration of Governor Thomas L. Bailey a legislative survey committee, headed by Senator John Kyle, studied our public school system and submitted a report to the lawmaking body — a report that should have made our people blush for shame. It fully revealed the appalling conditions in our Negro schools and gave the legislature such a shock that it was decided to vote an appropriation of $3,000,000 for the purpose of aiding communities in the construction of new school buildings.

It was a sort of gentleman's agreement, fully understood among lawmakers who voted for the appropriation, that this money would be used for the improvement of Negro schools. But it didn't happen that way. The fund was administered by the State Building Commission. Due to political pressure, and other causes, most of that $3,000,000 was spent on white schools. It was explained by the commission that in most rural areas the Negro schools had no way of raising funds to supplement state allowances and they received practically no help from boards of supervisors.

In other words, that $3,000,000 appropriation — a sum wholly inadequate for the purpose — was a good gesture, a "noble experiment," and all that sort of thing, but the Negro schools for which it was intended didn't get the benefit.

Outmoded Theory

And it has been that way for so long that the mind of man runneth not to the contrary. It has been that way quite too long and it must quit being that way. Our educational theory of "all for the white folks and nothing for the Negro" must be abandoned.

The *Daily News* here and now serves notice that when the next legislative session is convened the newspaper, aided and supported by a large majority of the newspapers in Mississippi, is going to wage a fight to see to it that a good portion of that treasury surplus, about which there has been so much boasting, and on which so many avaricious eyes have been cast, is used to provide a decent educational system for Negroes.

It is well night unbelievable, but it happens to be a fact that in an area nearly two miles square in great and growing Jackson, Mississippi's biggest, best and most progressive city, there is not a single Negro school building.

It happen to be a fact throughout the State that in some Negro school buildings there is not even standing room for pupils. In many cases hard-working teachers are trying to do the best possible with a deplorable condition by teaching Negro children in two or three shifts each day. Under such conditions the children get little or nothing in the way of education.

Law of the Land

The United States Supreme Court has decreed equal educational opportunity for the races. That's the law of the land. It must be obeyed.

It is up to our lawmaking body to handle this question intelligently, to meet all phases fairly and squarely. Whatever may exist in the way of race prejudice must be thrust aside and a program prepared that will deal justly with the Negro race.

And the following newspaper article (*Commercial Appeal*, Memphis, Tenn., March 31, 1949, p. 1) is no longer unusual:

UNIVERSITY IS OPENED TO NEGRO GRADUATES
KENTUCKY'S SEGREGATION IS UPSET BY U. S. JUDGE

Lexington, Ky., March 30 (*AP*) — Federal Judge H. Church Ford Wednesday opened up the doors of the University of Kentucky Graduate School to Negro students.

He ruled that Negroes were entitled to entrance on the same basis as white students until the state provides a graduate school for Negroes "substantially equal" to that at the university.

The decision was handed down in a suit filed by Lyman Johnson, Louisville Negro school teacher who was refused admission to the university's graduate school to study for a degree of Doctor of Philosophy.

Unless the decision is reversed in an appeal to a higher tribunal, the university will become the first south of the Mason-Dixon line and east of the Mississippi River to admit Negroes.

As the result of a recent Supreme Court ruling, based on constitutional provisions that Negroes shall be provided educational opportunities equal to those of the whites, two Negroes have been admitted to the University of Arkansas and one is enrolled at Oklahoma University, states which normally follow the segregation policies of the South.

Counsel for the university and the state announced the decision would be appealed if authority is forthcoming from the school and the state attorney general.

2 Thomas Jefferson, The Declaration of Independence, cited by Ernest S. Bates, *American Faith*, 1940, pp. 275 ff.

Bibliography

BOOKS

Adams, John Q., *Lectures on Rhetoric and Oratory*, I, Hillard & Metcalf, Cambridge, Mass., 1810.

American Church History Series, vols. 4, 5, 8.

Angell, Robert Cooley, *The Integration of American Society*. McGraw-Hill, New York, N. Y., 1941.

Aristotle, *The Organon or Logical Treatises of Aristotle*, O. F. Owen, ed., H. G. Bohn, London, 1853, vol. I.

Aristotle, *The Rhetoric of Aristotle*, translated by Lane Cooper, Appleton, New York, N. Y., 1932.

Bacon, Leonard Woolsey, *A History of American Christianity*, Scribners, New York, N. Y., 1898.

Bailey, Thomas Pearce, *Race Orthodoxy in the South*, Neale, New York, N. Y., 1914.

Bancroft, George, *History of the United States*, Little, Brown, Boston, Mass., 1853, 15th ed., vol. I.

Bassett, John S., *A Short History of the United States*, Macmillan, New York, N. Y., 1918.

Bates, Ernest, *American Faith*, New York, N. Y., 1940.

Bernard, Richard, *The Faithful Shepherd. . .* , Thomas Pavier, London, 1621.

The Holy Bible, authorized version.

Blackmar, Frank W. and Gillin, John L., *Outlines of Sociology*, Macmillan, New York, N. Y., 1915.

Boas, Franz, The Mind of Primitive Man, Macmillan, New York, N. Y., 1938.

Bowen, Trevor, *Divine White Right, Harper*, New York, N. Y., 1934.

Brawley, Benjamin, *A Short History of the American Negro*, Macmillan, New York, N. Y., 1939.

——————, *A Social History of the American Negro*, Macmillan, New York, N. Y., 1921.

Brooks, Phillips, *Lectures on Preaching, Dutton*, New York, N. Y., 1894.

Burton, Sir Richard Francis, *A Mission to Gelele, King of Dahome*, vol. 2, 1864.

Cicero, De Oratore, J. S. Watson, ed., Harper, New York, N. Y., 1878.

——————, *Orations of M. T. Cicero*, C. D. Yonge, G. Bell, editors, 1919.

Daniel, William A., *The Education of Negro Ministers*, Geo. H. Daren, New York, N. Y., 1925.

Davenport, Frederick M., *Primitive Traits in Religious Revivals*, Macmillan, New York, N. Y., 1905.

Dowd, Jerome, *The Negro in American Life*, Century, New York, N. Y., 1926.

Doyle, Bertram Wilbur, *The Etiquette of Race Relations in the South*, University of Chicago Press, Chicago, Ill., 1937.

DuBois, W. E. B., *Black Reconstruction*, Harcourt, New York, N. Y., 1935.

—————————, *Souls of Black Folk*, McClurg, Chicago, Ill., 1903.

Durkheim, Emile, *The Elementary Forms of the Religious Life*, London, 1915.

Evans, Maurice S., *Black and White in the Southern States*, Longmans, Green, London, 1915.

Foxcroft, Thomas, *Some Seasonable Thoughts on Evangelical Preaching; Its Nature, Usefulness and Obligation*, Rogers & Fowle, Boston, 1740.

Franklin, John Hope, *From Slavery to Freedom*, Knopf, New York, N. Y., 1947.

Frazier, E. Franklin, *The Negro Family in the United States*, University of Chicago Press, Chicago, Ill., 1939.

Freud, Sigmund, *The Future of an Illusion*, translated by W. D. Robson-Scott, London, Hogarth Press and Institute of Psycho-analysis, 1928.

Gallagher, Buell G. *American Caste and the Negro College*, Columbia University Press, New York, N. Y., 1938.

Glanville, *An Essay Concerning. . . ,* Printed by A. C. for H. Groome, London, 1678.

Good, Alvin, *Sociology and Education*, Harper, New York, N. Y., 1926

Gordon, William S., *Recollections of the old Quarter*, Moose Brothers, Lynchburg, Va., 1902.

Gray, T. R., *The Confession, Trial and Execution of Nat Turner*, Petersburg, Va., 1881.

Gresley, W., *Ecclesiastes Anglicanus*, Appleton, New York, N. Y., 1843

Groves, Ernest R., *Introduction to Mental Hygiene*, Holt, New York, N. Y., 1930.

Hatcher, William E., *John Jasper*, New York, N. Y., 1908.

Hill, T. Arnold, *The Negro and Economic Reconstruction*, Bronze Booklet no. 5, Assoc. in Negro Folk Educ., Washington, D. C.

Huxley, Julian, *Science and Social Needs*, Harper, New York, N. Y., 1935.

James, William, *Psychology, Briefer Course*, Holt, New York, N. Y., 1900.

Johnson, James Weldon, *God's Trombones, Seven Negro Sermons in Verse*, Viking, New York, N. Y., 1932.

Ketcham, V. A., in Sanford and Yeager, *Business Speeches by Business Men*, McGraw-Hill, New York, N. Y., 1930.

Kingsley, Mary H., *Travels in West Africa*, Macmillan, New York, N. Y., 1897.

Krapp, George Phillip, *The English Language in America*, vol. I, Century, for Modern Language Assoc., New York, N. Y., 1935.

Lee, G. C., *The World's Orators, International*, Philadelphia, Pa., vol. 4, 1906.

Leonard, Arthur G., *The Lower Niger and Its Tribes*, Macmillan, New York, N. Y., 1906.

Loggins, Vernon, *The Negro Author*, New York, N. Y., 1931.

Macaulay, Thomas Babington, *History of England* (from last London edition), Harper, New York, N. Y., n.d., vol. I.

Mays, Benjamin E. and Nicholson, Joseph W., *The Negro's Church*, Institute of Social and Religious Research, New York, N. Y., 1933.

Murray, James A. H., ed., *A New English Dictionary*, Clarendon, Oxford, 1888.

Murray, John, *Travels of Mungo Park*, vol. I, London.

Myrdal, Gunnar, *An American Dilemma*, Harper, New York, N. Y., 1944.

Nassau, Robert H., *Fetichism in West Africa*, Duckwarth, London, 1904.

O'Gorman, Thomas, *A History of the Roman Catholic Church in the United States*, Christian Literature, New York, N. Y., 1895.

Pemberton, Ebenezer, *A Sermon Preached at the Ordination of the Reverend Mr. Walter Wilmot*, Apr. 12, 1738, Draper, Boston, 1738.

Phillips, Arthur Edward, *Effective Speaking*, Newton, Chicago, Ill., 1926.

Powdermaker, Hortense, *After Freedom*, Viking, New York, N. Y., 1939.

Quintilian, *Institutes of Oratory*, II, J. S. Watson, ed., Bell, London, 1891.

Randolph, E. A. *Life of Reverend John Jasper*, Richmond, Va., 1884.

Raper, Arthur A., *Preface to Peasantry: A Tale of Two Black Belt Counties*, University of North Carolina Press, Chapel Hill, N. C., 1936.

Redding, J. Saunders, *No Day of Triumph*, Harper, New York, N. Y., 1942.

Reid, Ira D. A., *In a Minor Key*, American Council on Education, Washington, D. C., 1940.

Reuter, Edward B., *The American Race Problem*, Crowell, New York, N. Y., 1927.

Richardson, Harry V., *Dark Glory*, Friendship Press, New York, N. Y., 1947.

Rothe, Hans, Max Reinhardt: *25 Jahre Deutsches Theater*, Piper, Munchen, Germany, 1930.

Turner, Lorenzo Dow, *Africanisms in the Gullah Dialect*, University of Chicago Press, Chicago, Ill., 1949.

Washington, Booker T., *The Story of the Negro*, I, New York, N. Y., 1909.

——————, *Up from Slavery*, Doubleday, New York, N. Y., 1924.

Weatherford, W. D., *Negro Life in the South*, Association Press, New York, N. Y., 1911.

——————, *Present Forces in Negro Progress*, Association Press, New York, 1912.

——————, *The Negro from Africa to America*, Doubleday, New York, N. Y., 1924.

——————, and Johnson, Charles S., *Race Relations*, Heath, New York, N. Y., 1934.

Wesley, Chas. W., Richard Allen, *Apostle of Freedom*, Associated Publishers, Washington, D. C., 1935.

Woodson, Carter G., *Negro Orators and their Orations*, Associated Publishers, Washington, D. C., 1925.

——————, *The African Background Outlined*, Washington, D. C., 1936.

——————, *The History of the Negro Church*, Associated Publishers, Washington, D. C., 2nd ed., 1921.

——————, *The Negro in Our History*, Washington, D. C., 1928.

Wright, Richard, *12 Million Black Voices, A Folk History of the Negro in the United States*, Viking, New York, N. Y., 1941.

PERIODICALS

Annals, of the American Pulpit, vols. 5, 15.

Bond, Horace Mann, "Self-Respect as a Factor in Racial Advancement," *Annals of the American Academy of Political and Social Science,* vol. cxxxx, Nov. 1928.

Commercial Appeal, Memphis, Tenn., Mar. 31, 1949.

De Sales, Raoul De Roussy, "The Idea of Happiness," *Saturday Review of Literature,* v. 25, no. 7, Feb. 14, 1942.

Dialect Notes. Publication of American Dialect Society. vol. 2 (parts 1-4, 1900-1904), New Haven, Conn.

Dixon, C., "Religion in the Light of Psychoanalysis," *Psychoanalytic Review,* Jan. 1921.

DuBois, W. E. B., "A Selected Bibliography of the Negro American," *Atlanta University Publications,* Atlanta University Press, Atlanta, Ga. no. 3, 1909.

——————, ed., "The Negro Church," *Atlanta University Publications,* Atlanta University Press, Atlanta, Ga., no. 8, 1903.

Frazier, E. Franklin, "The Negro Family," *Annals of the American Academy of Political and Social Science,* vol. cxxx, no. 229, 1926.

Frobenius, Leo, "Early African Culture as an Indication of Present Negro Potentialities," *Annals of the American Academy of Political and Social Science,* vol. cxxxx, no. 229, Nov. 1928.

Hance, Kenneth G., "The Elements of the Rhetorical Theory of Phillips Brooks," *Speech Monographs,* Dec. 1938, vol. 5, no. 1.

Haynes, George E., "The Church and Negro Progress," *Annals of the American Academy of Political and Social Science,* vol. cxxxx, Nov. 1928.

Herskovits, Melvin J., and Herskovits, Frances S., "An Outline of Dahomean Religious Belief," *American Anthropological Association,* no. 41, 1933.

Herskovits, Melvin J., "The Negro in the New World," *American Anthropologist,* vol. 32, Nov. 1930.

Isaacs, Edith J. R., *Theater Arts,* Aug. 1942.

Jackson *Daily News,* Jackson, Miss., "Carter says South Holds Destiny of Nation in Hands," Mar. 5, 1949.

Lofton, John M., Jr., "Denmark Vesey's Call to Arms," *Journal of Negro History,* Oct. 1948.

Luschan, Felix von, "Anthropological View of Race," Atlanta University Publications, Atlanta University Press, Atlanta Ga., 1915.

McBurney, James Howard, "The Place of the Enthymeme in Rhetorical Theory," *Speech Monographs,* Oct. 1936, vol. 3, no. 1.

"Nat Turner's Insurrection," *Atlantic Monthly,* v. 8, Aug. 1861.

New South, Feb. 1949, vol. 4, no. 2.

New York *Times,* "Psychotherapy of a Primitive Folk," Oct. 30, 1949, p. E-9.

New York *Weekly Magazine,* "Adahoonzon's Speech," vol. ii, no. 95, Apr. 26, 1796.

Park, Robert E., "The Conflict and Fusion of Cultures with Special Reference to the Negro," *Journal of Negro History,* vol. iv, no. 2, April 1919.

Rodgers, Mary, "All Is Peaceful in Their World," The Louisville (Ky.) *Courier-Journal*, Sept. 15, 1940.

Small, Albion W., "The Church and Class Conflicts," *American Journal of Sociology*, vol. 24, no. 5, Mar. 1919.

Stokes, Anson Phelps, *Thirty-five Year Report of the Phelps-Stokes Fund*, New York, N. Y., 1948.

Time Magazine, "Sickle for the Harvest," November 14, 1949, pp. 63 ff.

Todd, T. Wingate, "An Anthropologist's Study of Negro Life," *Journal of Negro History*, vol. 16, no. 1, Jan. 1931.

United States Census, *Sixteenth Census of the United States*, Department of Commerce, Washington, D. C., series P-10, no. 1., 1942.

Washington, Forrest B., "Recreational Facilities for the Negro," *Annals of the American Academy of Political and Social Science*, Nov. 1928.

Wise, C. M. "Southern American Dialect," *American Speech*, 8 (2), Columbia University Press, New York, N. Y., 1933.

THESES

Allen, Helen Bernice, *The Minister of the Gospel in Negro American Fiction*, M.A. thesis, Department of English, Fisk University, Nashville, Tenn. 1937.

Bennett, Winifred De Witt, *A Survey of American Negro Oratory*, George Washington University, Washington, D. C., Feb. 1935.

Erb, John David, *Is There a Positive Correlation Between Successful Preaching and the Use of Vivid Imagery Word Concepts?* M.A. thesis, Ohio State University, Columbus, O., 1938.

Farrison, William Edward, *The Phonology of the Illiterate Negro Dialect of Guilford County, North Carolina*, Ph.D. thesis, Ohio State University Press, Columbus, O., 1937.

Gullick, Joseph I., *A Survey of American Pulpit Eloquence*, M.A. thesis, Columbian College, George Washington University, Washington, D.C., 1933.

Hitchcock, Orville A. *A Critical Study of the Oratorical Technique of Jonathan Edwards*, Ph.D. thesis, State University of Iowa, Iowa City, Ia., Aug. 1936.

Jones, Alice Marie, *The Negro Folk Sermon, A Study in the Sociology of Folk Culture*, M.A. thesis, Fisk University, Nashville, Tenn., July 1942.

Runion, Howard L., *An Objective Study of the Speech Style of Woodrow Wilson*, Ph.D. thesis, Department of Speech, University of Michigan, Ann Arbor, Mich.

Woolridge, Nancy Bullock, *The Negro Preacher in American Fiction Before 1900.* Ph.D. thesis, Department of English, University of Chicago, Chicago, Ill., 1942.

Index

Books in the African American Life Series

Coleman Young and Detroit Politics: From Social Activist to Power Broker, by Wilbur Rich, 1988

Great Black Russian: A Novel on the Life and Times of Alexander Pushkin, by John Oliver Killens, 1989

Indignant Heart: A Black Worker's Journal, by Charles Denby, 1989 (reprint)

The Spook Who Sat by the Door, by Sam Greenlee, 1989 (reprint)

Roots of African American Drama: An Anthology of Early Plays, 1858-1938, edited by Leo Hamalian and James V. Hatch, 1990

Walls: Essays, 1985-1990, by Kenneth McClane, 1991

Voices of the Self: A Study of Language Competence, by Keith Gilyard, 1991

Say Amen, Brother! Old-Time Negro Preaching: A Study in American Frustration, by William H. Pipes, 1992 (reprint)